REA: THE TEST PREP TEACHERS RECOMMEND

2nd Edition

BOB MILLER'S
MATH FOR THE ACT®

D1400016

Bob Miller

Research & Education Association
Visit our website: www.rea.com

Planet Friendly Publishing
✔ Made in the United States
✔ Printed on Recycled Paper
   Text: 10%   Cover: 10%
Learn more: www.greenedition.org

At REA we're committed to producing books in an Earth-friendly manner and to helping our customers make greener choices.

Manufacturing books in the United States ensures compliance with strict environmental laws and eliminates the need for international freight shipping, a major contributor to global air pollution.

And printing on recycled paper helps minimize our consumption of trees, water and fossil fuels. This book was printed on paper made with **10% post-consumer waste**. According to the Environmental Paper Network's Paper Calculator, by using this innovative paper instead of conventional papers, we achieved the following environmental benefits:

Trees Saved: 6 • Air Emissions Eliminated: 1292 pounds
Water Saved: 1207 gallons • Solid Waste Eliminated: 381 pounds

Courier Corporation, the manufacturer of this book, owns the Green Edition Trademark.
For more information on our environmental practices, please visit us online at **www.rea.com/green**

Research & Education Association
61 Ethel Road West
Piscataway, New Jersey 08854
E-mail: info@rea.com

BOB MILLER'S
Math for the ACT®, 2nd Edition

Printed in the United States of America

Library of Congress Control Number 2012936640

ISBN-13: 978-0-7386-1096-2
ISBN-10: 0-7386-1096-8

REA® is a registered trademark of
Research & Education Association, Inc.

TABLE OF CONTENTS

ACKNOWLEDGMENTS

I have many people to thank.

I thank my wife, Marlene, who makes life worth living, who is truly the wind under my wings.

I thank the rest of my family: children Sheryl and Eric and their spouses Glenn and Wanda (who are also like my children); grandchildren Kira, Evan, Sean, Sarah, and Ethan; my brother Jerry; and my parents, Cele and Lee; and my in-law parents, Edith and Siebeth.

I thank Larry Kling and Michael Reynolds and Mel Friedman for making this book possible.

I thank Martin Levine for making my whole writing career possible.

I have been negligent in thanking my great math teachers of the past. I thank Mr. Douglas Heagle, Mr. Alexander Lasaka, Mr. Joseph Joerg, and Ms. Arloeen Griswold, the best math teacher I ever had, of George W. Hewlett High School; Ms. Helen Bowker of Woodmere Junior High; and Professor Pinchus Mendelssohn and Professor George Bachman of Polytechnic University. The death of Professor Bachman was an extraordinary loss to our country, which produces too few advanced degrees in math. Every year, two or three of Professor Bachman's students would receive a Ph.D. in math, and even more would receive their M.S. in math. In addition, he wrote four books and numerous papers on subjects that had never been written about or had been written so poorly that nobody could understand the material. His teachings and writings were clear and memorable.

As usual, the last three thanks go to three terrific people: a great friend, Gary Pitkofsky; another terrific friend and fellow lecturer, David Schwinger; and my cousin, Keith Robin Ellis, the sharer of our dreams.

Bob Miller

DEDICATION

To my wife, Marlene. I dedicate this book and everything else I ever do to you.
I love you very, very much.

BIOGRAPHY

I received my B.S. in the Unified Honors Program sponsored by the Ford Foundation and my M.S. in math from Polytechnic Institute of NYU. After teaching my first class, as a substitute for a full professor, I heard one student say to another upon leaving the classroom, "At least we have someone who can teach the stuff." I was hooked forever on teaching. Since then, I have taught at C.U.N.Y., Westfield State College, Rutgers, and Poly. No matter how I feel, I always feel a lot better when I teach. I always feel great when students tell me they used to hate math or couldn't do math and now they like it more and can do it better.

My main blessing is my family. I have a fantastic wife in Marlene. My kids are wonderful: daughter Sheryl, son Eric, son-in-law Glenn, and daughter-in-law Wanda. My grandchildren are terrific: Kira, Evan, Sean, Sarah, and Ethan. My hobbies are golf, bowling, bridge, crossword puzzles, and Sudoku. My ultimate goals are to write a book to help parents teach their kids math, a high school text that will advance our kids' math abilities, and a calculus text students can actually understand.

To me, teaching is always a great joy. I hope that I can give some of that joy to you. I do know this book will help you get the score you need to get into the college of your choice.

OTHER BOOKS

Bob Miller's Math for the GMAT

Bob Miller's Math for the GRE

Bob Miller's Basic Math and Pre-Algebra for the Clueless, Second Edition

Bob Miller's Algebra for the Clueless, Second Edition

Bob Miller's Geometry for the Clueless, Second Edition

Bob Miller's Math SAT for the Clueless, Second Edition

Bob Miller's Pre-Calc with Trig for the Clueless, Third Edition

Bob Miller's High School Calc for the Clueless

Bob Miller's Calc 1 for the Clueless, Second Edition

Bob Miller's Calc 2 for the Clueless, Second Edition

Bob Miller's Calc 3 for the Clueless

ABOUT RESEARCH & EDUCATION ASSOCIATION

Founded in 1959, Research & Education Association (REA) is dedicated to publishing the finest and most effective educational materials—including test preps and study guides—for students in middle school, high school, college, graduate school, and beyond. Today, REA's wide-ranging catalog is a leading resource for teachers, students, and professionals.

REA ACKNOWLEDGMENTS

In addition to our author, we would like to thank Larry B. Kling, Vice President, Editorial, for his overall direction; Pam Weston, Publisher, for setting the quality standards for production integrity and managing the publication to completion; Michael Reynolds, Managing Editor, for project management; Mel Friedman, Lead Mathematics Editor, for editorial contributions; Christine Saul, Senior Graphic Artist, for designing our cover; and Aquent Publishing Services, for typesetting this edition. Cover photo by Eric L. Miller.

ABOUT THIS BOOK

Congratulations!!!! You are about to enter the second part of your education, and for you, the ACT is the first step toward college.

I've written this book as if you were in front of me and I was teaching you personally. I teach some of the areas in greater detail than others because I have found many students have problems with these topics. They include factoring, algebraic fractions, trig, and, yes, percentage problems. Chapter 17 presents four sample practice tests, each of which contains 60 questions—the same number of questions you'll see on the actual ACT Math test. Carefully check your answers against my answer explanations so you can see your skills improve.

If you want any topics explained more fully than this book presents, you might want to check one of my other books. If you want any questions explained or something added to the book, please send your question to REA along with your e-mail address, and I'll respond to you. E-mail me at info@rea.com.

Now, enjoy the book and learn!!

CHAPTER 1: *Basic Basics*

"All math begins with whole numbers. Master them and you will begin to speak the language of math."

Our great adventure begins with our basic terms. It is very important to understand what a question asks as well as how to answer it. The word *numbers* has many meanings, as we start to see here.

NUMBERS

Whole numbers: 0, 1, 2, 3, 4, . . .

Integers: 0, ±1, ±2, ±3, ±4, . . . , where ±3 stands for both +3 and −3.

Positive integers are integers that are greater than 0. In symbols, $x > 0$, x an integer.

Negative integers are integers that are less than 0. In symbols, $x < 0$, x an integer.

Even integers: 0, ±2, ±4, ±6, . . .

Odd integers: ±1, ±3, ±5, ±7, . . .

Inequalities

For any numbers represented by *a, b, c,* or *d* on the number line:

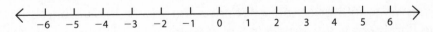

We say $c > d$ (*c* is greater than *d*) if *c* is to the right of *d* on the number line.

We say $d < c$ (*d* is less than *c*) if *d* is to the left of *c* on the number line.

$c > d$ is equivalent to $d < c$.

$a \leq b$ means $a < b$ or $a = b$; likewise, $a \geq b$ means $a > b$ or $a = b$.

Example 1: $4 \leq 7$ is true because $4 < 7$; $9 \leq 9$ is true because $9 = 9$; but $7 \leq 2$ is false because $7 > 2$.

Example 2:   Find all integers between -4 and 5.

Solution: $\{-3, -2, -1, 0, 1, 2, 3, 4\}$.

Notice that the word *between* does *not* include the endpoints.

Example 3:   Graph all the multiples of five between 20 and 40 inclusive.

Solution:

Notice that *inclusive* means to include the endpoints.

Odd and Even Numbers

Here are some facts about odd and even integers that you should know.

- The sum of two even integers is even.

- The sum of two odd integers is even.

- The sum of an even integer and an odd integer is odd.

- The product of two even integers is even.

- The product of two odd integers is odd.

- The product of an even integer and an odd integer is even.

- If n is even, n^2 is even. If n^2 is even and n is an integer, then n is even.

- If n is odd, n^2 is odd. If n^2 is odd and n is an integer, then n is odd.

OPERATIONS ON NUMBERS

Product is the answer in multiplication, **quotient** is the answer in division, **sum** is the answer in addition, and **difference** is the answer in subtraction.

Because $3 \times 4 = 12$, 3 and 4 are said to be **factors** or **divisors** of 12, and 12 is both a **multiple** of 3 and a **multiple** of 4.

A **prime** is a positive integer with exactly two distinct factors, itself and 1. The number 1 is not a prime because only $1 \times 1 = 1$. It might be a good idea to memorize the first eight primes:

2, 3, 5, 7, 11, 13, 17, and 19

The number 4 has more than two factors: 1, 2, and 4. Numbers with more than two factors are called **composites**. The number 28 is a **perfect** number because if we add the factors less than 28, they add to 28.

Example 4:   Write all the factors of 28.

Solution: 1, 2, 4, 7, 14, and 28.

Example 5:   Write 28 as the product of prime factors.

Solution: $28 = 2 \times 2 \times 7$.

Example 6:   Find all the primes between 70 and 80.

Solution: 71, 73, 79. How do we find this easily? First, because 2 is the only even prime, we have to check only the odd numbers. Next, we have to know the divisibility rules:

- A number is divisible by 2 if it ends in an even number. We don't need this here because then it can't be prime.

- A number is divisible by 3 (or 9) if the sum of the digits is divisible by 3 (or 9). For example, 456 is divisible by 3 because the sum of the digits is 15, which is divisible by 3 (it's not divisible by 9, but that's okay).

- A number is divisible by 4 if the number named by the last two digits is divisible by 4. For example, 3936 is divisible by 4 because 36 is divisible by 4.

- A number is divisible by 5 if the last digit is 0 or 5.

- The rule for 6 is a combination of the rules for 2 and 3.

- It is easier to divide by 7 than to learn the rule for 7.

- A number is divisible by 8 if the number named by the last *three* digits are divisible by 8.

- A number is divisible by 10 if it ends in a zero, as you know.

- A number is divisible by 11 if the difference between the sum of the even-place digits (2nd, 4th, 6th, etc.) and the sum of the odd-place digits (1st, 3rd, 5th, etc.) is a multiple of 11. For example, for the number 928,193,926: the sum of the odd digits (9, 8, 9, 9, and 6) is 41; the sum of the even digits (2, 1, 3, 2) is 8; and $41 - 8$ is 33, which is divisible by 11. So 928,193,926 is divisible by 11.

That was a long digression!!!!! Let's get back to example 6.

We have to check only 71, 73, 75, 77, and 79. The number 75 is not a prime because it ends in a 5. The number 77 is not a prime because it is divisible by 7. To see if the other three are prime, for any number less than 100 you have to divide by the primes 2, 3, 5, and 7 only. You will quickly find they are primes.

Rules for Operations on Numbers

 ( ) are called parentheses (singular: parenthesis); [ ] are called brackets; { } are called braces.

Rules for adding signed numbers

1.   If all the signs are the same, add the numbers and use that sign.

2.   If two signs are different, subtract them, and use the sign of the larger numeral.

> **Example 7:**   **a.** $3 + 7 + 2 + 4 = +16$ **c.** $5 - 9 + 11 - 14 = 16 - 23 = -7$
>
> **b.** $-3 - 5 - 7 - 9 = -24$ **d.** $2 - 6 + 11 - 1 = 13 - 7 = +6$

Rules for multiplying and dividing signed numbers
Look at the minus signs only.

1.   Odd number of minus signs—the answer is minus.

2.   Even number of minus signs—the answer is plus.

> **Example 8:** $\dfrac{(-4)(-2)(-6)}{(-2)(+3)(-1)} =$
>
> **Solution:**   Five minus signs, so the answer is minus, -8.

Rule for subtracting signed numbers
The sign $(-)$ means subtract. Change the problem to an addition problem.

> **Example 9:**   **a.** $(-6) - (-4) = (-6) + (+4) = -2$
>
> **b.** $(-6) - (+2) = (-6) + (-2) = -8$, because it is now an adding problem.

Order of Operations

In doing a problem such as $4 + 5 \times 6$, the **order of operations** tells us whether to multiply or add first:

1.   If given letters, substitute in parentheses the value of each letter.

2.   Do operations in parentheses, inside ones first, and then the tops and bottoms of fractions.

3. Do exponents next. (Chapter 3 discusses exponents in more detail.)
4. Do multiplications and divisions, left to right, as they occur.
5. The last step is adding and subtracting. Left to right is usually the safest way.

Example 10: $4 + 5 \times 6 =$

Solution: $4 + 30 = 34$

Example 11: $(4 + 5)6 =$

Solution: $(9)(6) = 54$

Example 12: $1000 \div 2 \times 4 =$

Solution: $(500)(4) = 2000$

Example 13: $1000 \div (2 \times 4) =$

Solution: $1000 \div 8 = 125$

Example 14: $4[3 + 2(5 - 1)] =$

Solution: $4[3 + 2(4)] = 4[3 + 8] = 4(11) = 44$

Example 15: $\dfrac{3^4 - 1^{10}}{4 - 10 \times 2} =$

Solution: $\dfrac{81 - 1}{4 - 20} = \dfrac{80}{-16} = -5$

Example 16: If $x = -3$ and $y = -4$, find the value of:

    a. $7 - 5x - x^2$

    b. $xy^2 - (xy)^2$

Solutions: **a.** $7 - 5x - x^2 = 7 - 5(-3) - (-3)^2 = 7 + 15 - 9 = 13$

    b. $xy^2 - (xy)^2 = (-3)(-4)^2 - ((-3)(-4))^2 = (-3)(16) - (12)^2$

                $= -48 - 144 = -192$

Before we get to the exercises, let's talk about ways to describe a group of numbers (data).

DESCRIBING DATA

Four of the measures that describe data are used on the ACT. The first three are measures of central tendency; the fourth, the range, measures the span of the data.

Mean: Add up the numbers and divide by how many numbers you have added up.

Median: Middle number. Put the numbers in numeric order and see which one is in the middle. If there are two "middle" numbers, take the average of them. This happens with an even number of data points.

Mode: Most common. Which number(s) appears the most times? A set with two modes is called bimodal. There can actually be any number of modes, including everything is a mode.

Range: Highest number minus the lowest number.

Example 17: Find the mean, median, mode, and range for 5, 6, 9, 11, 12, 12, and 14.

Solutions: Mean: $\dfrac{5 + 6 + 9 + 11 + 12 + 12 + 14}{7} = \dfrac{69}{7} = 9\dfrac{6}{7}$

Median: 11

Mode: 12

Range: $14 - 5 = 9$

Example 18: Find the mean, median, mode, and range for 4, 4, 7, 10, 20, 20.

Solutions: Mean: $\dfrac{4 + 4 + 7 + 10 + 20 + 20}{6} = \dfrac{65}{6} = 10\dfrac{5}{6}$

Median: For an even number of points, it is the mean of the middle two:

$\dfrac{7 + 10}{2} = 8.5$

Mode: There are two: 4 and 20 (blackbirds?)

Range: $20 - 4 = 16$

Example 19:   Jim received 83 and 92 on two tests. What grade must the third test be in order to have an average (mean) of 90?

Solution: There are two solution methods.

Method 1: To get a 90 average on three tests, Jim needs
$3(90) = 270$ points. So far, he has $83 + 92 = 175$ points. So Jim needs
$270 - 175 = 95$ points on the third test.

Method 2 (my favorite): 83 is -7 from 90. 92 is $+2$ from 90.
$-7 + 2 = -5$ from the desired 90 average. Jim needs
$90 + 5 = 95$ points on the third test. (Jim needs to "make up" the 5-point deficit, so add it to the average of 90.)

The second method is my choice, but it is always your choice which method you can do easier and faster.

Ⓠ   **Finally, after a long introduction, we get to some exercises.**

Exercise 1:   If $x = -5$, the value of $-3 - 4x - x^2$ is

$-3 - 4(-5) - (-5^2)$

$-3 + 20 - 25$

-8

   A. -48 D. 13

   B. -8 E. 4

   C. 2

Exercise 2: $-0(2) - \dfrac{0}{2} - 2 =$

$-0 - 0 - 2$

   A. 0   D. -6

   B. -2 E. Undefined

   C. -4

Exercise 3:   The scores on three tests were 90, 91, and 98. What does the score on the fourth test have to be in order to get exactly a 95 average (mean)?

   A. 97   D. 100

   B. 98   E. Not possible

   C. 99

$$\frac{90 + 91 + 98 + x}{4} = 95$$

$$\begin{array}{r} 90 \\ 91 \\ 98 \\ \hline 279 \end{array}$$

$$\begin{array}{r} 279 + x \\ -279 \\ \hline \end{array} = \begin{array}{r} 380 \\ -279 \\ \hline \end{array}$$

$$x = 101$$

Exercise 4: On a true-false test, 20 students scored 90, and 30 students scored 100. The sum of the mean, median, and mode is

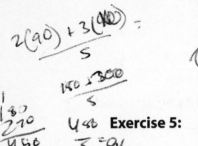

A. 300

B. 296

C. 295

D. 294

E. 275

$$\frac{20(90) + 30(100)}{50}$$

$$\frac{1800 + 3000}{50} \quad \frac{3800}{50}$$

Exercise 5: On a test, m students received a grade of x, n students received a grade of y, and p students received a grade of z. The average (mean) grade is:

A. $\dfrac{mxnypz}{xyz}$

B. $\dfrac{mx + ny + pz}{x + y + z}$

C. $\dfrac{mx + ny + pz}{xyz}$

D. $\dfrac{mx + ny + pz}{m + n + p}$

E. $mnp + \dfrac{xyz}{x + y + z}$

Exercise 6: The largest positive integer in the following list that divides evenly into 2,000,000,000,000,003 is

A. 33

B. 11

C. 10

D. 3

E. 1

Exercise 7: If m and n are odd integers, which of the following is odd?

A. $mn + 3$

B. $m^2 + (n + 2)^2$

C. $mn + m + n$

D. $(m + 1)(n - 2)$

E. $m^4 + m^3 + m^2 + m$

Exercise 8: If $m + 3$ is a multiple of 4, which of these is also a multiple of 4?

A. $m - 3$

B. m

C. $m + 4$

D. $m + 9$

E. $m + 11$

Exercise 9: If p and q are primes, which one of the following *can't* be a prime?

A. pq

B. $p + q$

C. $pq + 2$

D. $2pq + 1$

E. $p^2 + q^2$

Exercise 10: The sum of the first n positive integers is p. In terms of n and p, what is the sum of the next n positive integers?

A. np

B. $n + p$

C. $n^2 + p$

D. $n + p^2$

E. $2n + 2p$

Exercise 11: Let p be prime, with $20p$ divisible by 6; p could be

A. 3

B. 4

C. 5

D. 6

E. 7

For Exercises 12–14, use the following numbers: 8, 10, 10, 16, 16, 18 .

Exercise 12: The mean is

A. 8

B. 10

C. 13

D. 16

E. There are two of them.

Exercise 13: The median is

A. 8

B. 10

C. 13

D. 16

E. There are two of them.

Exercise 14: The mode is

A. 8

B. 10

C. 13

D. 16

E. There are two of them.

Sometimes statistics are given in frequency distribution tables, such as this one showing the grades Sandy received on 10 English quizzes.

Sandy's Quiz Scores

Grade	Number
100	4
98	3
95	2
86	1
Total	10

This chart is for Exercises 15–17.

Exercise 15: The mean is

A. 96   D. 99

B. 97   E. 100

C. 98

Exercise 16: The median is

A. 96   D. 99

B. 97   E. 100

C. 98

Exercise 17: The mode is

A. 96   D. 99

B. 97   E. 100

C. 98

 Let's look at the answers.

Answer 1:   B: $-3 - 4(-5) - (-5)^2 = -3 + 20 - 25 = -8$.

Answer 2:   B: $0 - 0 - 2 = -2$.

Answer 3:   E: $95(4) = 380$ points; $90 + 91 + 98 = 279$ points. The fourth test would have to be $380 - 279 = 101$.

Answer 4:   B: The median is 100; the mode is 100; for the mean, we can use 2 and 3 instead of 20 and 30 because the ratio is the same: $\dfrac{2(90) + 3(100)}{5} = 96$.

Answer 5:   D: $Mean = \dfrac{\text{total value of items}}{\text{total number of items}} = \dfrac{mx + ny + pz}{m + n + p}$.

Answer 6:   E: The number is not divisible by 11 because $3 - 2 = 1$, which is not a multiple of 11. It is not divisible by 3 because $3 + 2 = 5$ is not divisible by 3. Because is it not divisible by 11 or 3, it is not divisible by 33. Finally, it is not divisible by 10 because it does not end in a 0. So the answer is E because all numbers are divisible by 1.

Answer 7:   C: Only C is the sum of three odd integers. All of the other answer choices are even.

Answer 8:   E: If $m + 3$ is a multiple of 4, then $m + 3 + 8$ is a multiple of 4 because 8 is a multiple of 4.

Answer 9:   A: By substituting proper primes, all the others might be prime.

Answer 10:   C: Say $n = 5$; $p = 1 + 2 + 3 + 4 + 5$. The next five are $(1 + 5) + (2 + 5) + (3 + 5) + (4 + 5) + (5 + 5) = p + n^2$.

Answer 11:   A: 3 and 6 will work, but only 3 is a prime.

Answer 12:   C: $\dfrac{8 + 10 + 10 + 16 + 16 + 18}{6} = 13$.

Answer 13:   C: There are an even number of numbers, so we have to take the average of the middle two: $\dfrac{10 + 16}{2} = 13$.

Answer 14:   E: It's bimodal; the modes are 10 and 16, each appearing twice.

Answer 15:   B: The mean is the longest measure to compute: $\dfrac{4 \times 100 + 3 \times 98 + 2 \times 95 + 86}{10} = 97$.

Answer 16:   C: The median is determined by putting all of the numbers in order, so we have 100, 100, 100, 100, 98, 98, 98, 95, 95, 86. The middle terms are 98 and 98, so the median is 98.

Answer 17:   E: The mode is 100 because that is the most common score; there are four of them.

CHAPTER 2: *We Must Look at Arithmetic*

"*One must master the parts as well as the whole to fully understand.*"

Although the ACT does allow calculators, it is necessary to be able to do some of the work without the calculator, especially fractions. Let's start with decimals.

DECIMALS

Rule 1: When adding or subtracting, line up the decimal points.

Example 1: Add: 3.14 + 234.7 + 86

Solution:
```
     3.14
   234.7
 +  86.
   ------
   323.84
```

Example 2: Subtract: 56.7 − 8.82

Solution:
```
   56.70
 −  8.82
   ------
   47.88
```

Rule 2: In multiplying numbers, count the number of decimal places and add them. In the product, this will be the number of decimal places for the decimal point.

Example 3: Multiply 45.67 by .987.

Solution: The answer will be 45.07629. You will need to know the answer has five decimal places.

Example 4:   Multiply 2.8 by .6:

Solution: The answer is 1.68. The ACT will expect you to do this problem. Let's try another.

Example 5:   What is the value of $2b^2 - 2.4b - 1.7$ if $b = .7$?

Solution: The standard way to do this type of problem is to directly substitute.
$2(.7)^2 - 2.4(.7) - 1.7 = 2(.49) - 1.68 - 1.7 = .98 - 1.68 - 1.7 = -2.40$.

You will be given answers from which to choose, so approximations may work just as well and are quicker. $(.7)(.7) = .49$; times 2 is .98, or approximately 1. -2.4 times $.7 = 1.68$ or approximately 1.7; $1 - 1.7 = -.7$; added to -1.7 is -2.4. In this case, we get the same numerical value. If we didn't, our approximate answer would still probably be closer to the correct answer than to the other choices.

In the real world, and on this test, a good skill to save time is the ability to make reasonable approximations. This book will point out problems that can be approximated.

Rule 3: When you divide, move the decimal point in the divisor and the dividend the same number of places.

Example 6:   Divide 23.1 by .004.

Solution: In our heads, we write the problem as $\dfrac{23.1}{.004}$. We multiply the numerator and denominator by 1000 to move the decimal points the same number of places. We get $\dfrac{23.1}{.004} = \dfrac{23.1 \times 1000}{.004 \times 1000} = \dfrac{23100}{4} = 5775$. Note that when we multiply by 1, the fraction doesn't change, so for $\dfrac{1000}{1000} = 1$, the fraction is the same.

Rule 4: When reading a number with a decimal, read the whole part, only say the word *and* when you reach the decimal point, then read the part after the decimal point as if it were a whole number, and say the last decimal place. Whew!

Example 7:

Number	Read
4.3	Four and three tenths
2,006.73	Two-thousand six and seventy-three hundredths
1,000,017.009	One million seventeen and nine thousandths

Let's do some exercises.

Exercise 1:   Which is smallest?

A. .04   D. .04444

B. .0401   E. .041

C. .04001

Exercise 2: $\dfrac{7}{100} + \dfrac{8}{10,000} + \dfrac{9}{1,000,000} =$

A. 789   D. .070809

B. .0789   E. 078009

C. .07089

 Let's look at the answers.

Answer 1:   A: All have the same tenths (0) and hundredths (4). The rest of the places of A are zero.

Answer 2:   D: Hundredths is the second decimal place, ten-thousandths in the fourth, and millionths is the sixth place.

Now, let's go over fractions.

FRACTIONS

The top of a fraction is called the **numerator**; the bottom is the **denominator**.

Rule 1: If the bottoms of two fractions are the same, the bigger the top, the bigger the fraction.

Example 8:   Suppose I am a smart first grader. Can you explain to me which is bigger, $\dfrac{3}{5}$ or $\dfrac{4}{5}$?

Solution: Suppose we have a pizza pie. Then $\frac{3}{5}$ means we divide a pie into 5 equal parts, and I get 3. And $\frac{4}{5}$ means I get 4 pieces out of 5. So $\frac{3}{5} < \frac{4}{5}$.

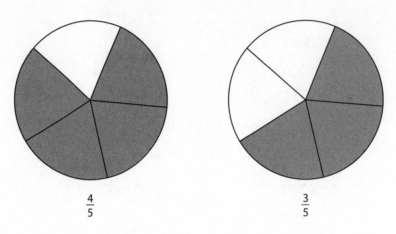

$\frac{4}{5}$ $\frac{3}{5}$

Rule 2: If the tops of two fractions are the same, the bigger the bottom, the smaller the fraction.

Example 9:   Which fraction, $\frac{3}{5}$ or $\frac{3}{4}$, is bigger?

Solution: Use another pizza pie example. In comparing $\frac{3}{5}$ and $\frac{3}{4}$, we get the same number of pieces (3). However, if the pie is divided into 4, the pieces are bigger, so $\frac{3}{5} < \frac{3}{4}$.

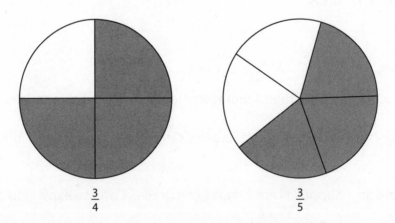

$\frac{3}{4}$ $\frac{3}{5}$

Rule 3: If the tops and bottoms are different, find the least common denominator (LCD) and compare the tops.

Before we get into this section, the teacher in me (and maybe the purist in you) must tell you we really are talking about rational numbers, not fractions. There are two definitions.

Definition 1: A **rational** number is any integer divided by an integer, with the denominator not equaling zero.

Definition 2: A **rational** number is any repeating or terminating decimal.

 Technically, $\dfrac{\pi}{6}$ is a fraction but not a rational number. We will use the term fraction *here instead of* rational number. *If it is negative, we will say "negative fraction."*

Note the following facts about fractions:

- $3 < 4$, but $-3 > -4$. Similarly, $\dfrac{3}{5} < \dfrac{4}{5}$, but $-\dfrac{3}{5} > -\dfrac{4}{5}$. We will do more of this later.

- A fraction (positive) is bigger than 1 if the numerator is bigger than the denominator.

- A fraction is less than $\dfrac{1}{2}$ if the denominator is more than twice the numerator.

- To double a fraction, either multiply the numerator by two or divide the denominator by 2.

- Adding the same positive number to the numerator and denominator makes the fraction closer to one.

- Two fractions are **equivalent** if they can be reduced to the same fraction. $\dfrac{6}{9}$ and $\dfrac{10}{15}$ are equivalent because they both reduce to $\dfrac{2}{3}$.

Ⓠ **Let's do some more exercises.**

Exercise 3:   Which fraction is largest?

A. $\dfrac{7}{4}$ D. $\dfrac{12}{5}$

B. $\dfrac{11}{8}$ E. $\dfrac{3}{100}$

C. $\dfrac{3}{2}$

Exercise 4:   Which fraction is smallest?

A. $\dfrac{3}{5}$ D. $\dfrac{9}{16}$

B. $\dfrac{5}{11}$ E. $\dfrac{100}{199}$

C. $\dfrac{7}{13}$

Exercise 5:   Which fraction is largest?

A. $\dfrac{1}{3}$ D. $\dfrac{3}{.1}$

B. $\dfrac{1}{.3}$ E. $\dfrac{3}{(.1)^2}$

C. $\dfrac{1}{(.3)^2}$

Exercise 6:   If $100 \le x \le 10{,}000$ and $.0001 \le y \le .01$, the smallest possible value of $\dfrac{x}{y}$ is

A. 10,000   D. 10,000,000

B. 100,000   E. 1,000,000,000

C. 1,000,000

Exercise 7:   Suppose we have $\dfrac{x+y}{x-y}$, where $8 \le x \le 10$ and $2 \le y \le 4$. The maximum possible value for this fraction is

A. $\dfrac{3}{2}$ D. 3

B. $\dfrac{5}{3}$ E. 6

C. $\dfrac{7}{3}$

 Let's look at the answers.

Answer 3:   D: It is the only fraction for which the top is more than double the bottom, so it is the only fraction with a value greater than 2.

Answer 4:   B: It is the only fraction less than one-half; the bottom is more than double the top.

Answer 5:   E: Answer choice A is less than 1. Comparing the other answer choices, C is bigger than B, and E is bigger than D. Because E has a bigger top and smaller bottom than C, it is larger. We will explore this in greater detail in the next chapter.

Answer 6:   A: To make a fraction as small as possible, we need a fraction with the smallest top ($x = 100$) and the biggest bottom ($y = .01$), or $\dfrac{100}{.01} = 10{,}000$.

Answer 7:   **D:** This one is not so simple. In this case, the extreme values, minimum (min) and maximum (max), occur at the "ends." We must try $x = 8$ and 10, $y = 2$ and 4, and all combinations of these numbers. In this case, the max occurs when $x = 8$ and $y = 4$.

Adding and Subtracting Fractions

If the denominators are the same, add or subtract the tops, keep the bottom the same, and reduce if necessary.

$$\frac{7}{43} + \frac{11}{43} - \frac{2}{43} = \frac{16}{43}$$

$$\frac{2}{9} + \frac{4}{9} = \frac{6}{9} = \frac{2}{3}$$

$$\frac{a}{m} + \frac{b}{m} - \frac{c}{m} = \frac{a + b - c}{m}$$

There is much more to talk about if the denominators are unlike.

The quickest way to add (or subtract) fractions with different denominators, especially if they contain letters or the denominators are small (but different), is to multiply the top and bottom of each fraction by the least common multiple, LCM. This consists of three words: multiple, common, and least.

Example 10:   What is the LCM of 6 and 8?

Solution: **Multiples** of 6 are 6, 12, 18, 24, 30, 36, 42, 48, 54, 60, 66, 72, 78, . . .

Multiples of 8 are 8, 16, 24, 32, 40, 48, 56, 64, 72, 80, . . .

Common multiples of 6 and 8 are 24, 48, 72, 96, 120, . . .

The **least common multiple** of 6 and 8 is 24.

When adding or subtracting fractions, multiply the top and bottom of each fraction by the LCM divided by the denominator of that fraction:

$$\frac{a}{b} - \frac{x}{y} = \left(\frac{a}{b} \times \frac{y}{y}\right) - \left(\frac{x}{y} \times \frac{b}{b}\right) = \frac{ay}{by} - \frac{bx}{by} = \frac{ay - bx}{by}$$

$$\frac{7}{20} - \frac{3}{11} = \left(\frac{7}{20} \times \frac{11}{11}\right) - \left(\frac{3}{11} \times \frac{20}{20}\right) = \frac{7(11) - 3(20)}{20(11)} = \frac{17}{220}$$

On the ACT, you must be able to perform these calculations quickly.

Example 11: Find the sums:

Problem	Solution
a. $\dfrac{3}{8} + \dfrac{5}{6} =$	$\dfrac{9}{24} + \dfrac{20}{24} = \dfrac{29}{24}$
b. $\dfrac{3}{4} + \dfrac{5}{6} =$	$\dfrac{3}{4} + \dfrac{5}{6} = \dfrac{9}{12} + \dfrac{10}{12} = \dfrac{19}{12}$
c. $4\dfrac{3}{8} + 5\dfrac{5}{6} =$	$4\dfrac{9}{24} + 5\dfrac{20}{24} = 9\dfrac{29}{24} = 9 + 1\dfrac{5}{24} = 10\dfrac{5}{24}$

Doing this problem on the ACT can take a long time by calculator. It is to your advantage to be able to do problems like this with paper and pencil.

Multiplication of Fractions

To multiply fractions, multiply the numerators and multiply the denominators, reducing as you go. With multiplication, it is *not* necessary to have the same denominators.

$$\frac{3}{7} \times \frac{4}{11} = \frac{12}{77}$$

$$\frac{a}{b} \times \frac{c}{d} = \frac{a \times c}{b \times d}$$

Division of Fractions

To divide fractions, invert the second fraction and multiply, reducing if necessary. To **invert** a fraction means to turn it upside down. The new fraction is called the **reciprocal** of the original fraction. So the reciprocal of $\dfrac{2}{3}$ is $\dfrac{3}{2}$; the reciprocal of -5 is $-\dfrac{1}{5}$; and the reciprocal of a is $\dfrac{1}{a}$ if $a \neq 0$.

Example 12: Do the following calculations:

Problem	Solution
a. $\dfrac{3}{4} \div \dfrac{11}{5} =$	$\dfrac{3}{4} \times \dfrac{5}{11} = \dfrac{15}{44}$
b. $\dfrac{m}{n} \div \dfrac{p}{q} =$	$\dfrac{m}{n} \times \dfrac{q}{p} = \dfrac{m \times q}{n \times p}$

c. $\dfrac{1}{4} \div 5 =$ $\qquad$ $\dfrac{1}{4} \times \dfrac{1}{5} = \dfrac{1}{20}$

d. $3\dfrac{1}{5} \times 1\dfrac{1}{6} =$ $\qquad$ $\dfrac{16}{5} \times \dfrac{7}{6} = \dfrac{8}{5} \times \dfrac{7}{3} = \dfrac{56}{15}$ or $3\dfrac{11}{15}$

Let's do a few problems. Try to do them without paper and pencil.

Example 13: Problem $\qquad\qquad\qquad$ Solution

a. $\dfrac{7}{9} - \dfrac{3}{22} =$ $\qquad$ $\dfrac{127}{198}$

b. $\dfrac{3}{4} + \dfrac{5}{6} - \dfrac{1}{8} =$ $\qquad$ $\dfrac{35}{24}$, or $1\dfrac{11}{24}$

c. $\dfrac{3}{10} + \dfrac{2}{15} - \dfrac{4}{5} =$ $\qquad$ $\dfrac{-11}{30}$

d. $\dfrac{1}{4} + \dfrac{1}{8} + \dfrac{7}{16} =$ $\qquad$ $\dfrac{13}{16}$

e. $2 + \dfrac{2}{3} + \dfrac{2}{9} + \dfrac{2}{27} =$ $\qquad$ $2\dfrac{26}{27}$, or $\dfrac{80}{27}$

f. $\dfrac{5}{24} - \dfrac{7}{18} =$ $\qquad$ $-\dfrac{13}{72}$

g. $\dfrac{10}{99} - \dfrac{9}{100} =$ $\qquad$ $\dfrac{109}{9900}$

h. $\dfrac{7}{9} \times \dfrac{5}{3} =$ $\qquad$ $\dfrac{35}{27}$, or $1\dfrac{8}{27}$

i. $\dfrac{11}{12} \div \dfrac{9}{11} =$ $\qquad$ $\dfrac{121}{108}$, or $1\dfrac{13}{108}$

j. $\dfrac{5}{9} \times \dfrac{6}{7} =$ $\qquad$ $\dfrac{10}{21}$

k. $\dfrac{12}{13} \div \dfrac{8}{39} =$ $\qquad$ $\dfrac{9}{2}$, or $4\dfrac{1}{2}$

l. $\dfrac{10}{12} \div \dfrac{15}{40} =$ $\qquad$ $\dfrac{20}{9}$, or $2\dfrac{2}{9}$

m. $\dfrac{2}{3} \div 12 =$ $\dfrac{1}{18}$

n. $\dfrac{2}{3} \times \dfrac{3}{4} \times \dfrac{4}{5} \times \dfrac{5}{6} \times \dfrac{6}{7} =$ $\dfrac{2}{7}$

o. $\dfrac{5}{8} \times \dfrac{7}{6} \div \dfrac{35}{24} =$ $\dfrac{1}{2}$

p. $3\dfrac{2}{3} + 4\dfrac{3}{4} =$ $8\dfrac{5}{12}$

q. $5\dfrac{1}{6} - 3\dfrac{5}{6} =$ $1\dfrac{1}{3}$

r. $7\dfrac{3}{7} - 2\dfrac{1}{2} =$ $4\dfrac{13}{14}$

s. $3\dfrac{4}{5} \times \dfrac{3}{38} =$ $\dfrac{3}{10}$

t. $4\dfrac{1}{5} \div 8\dfrac{2}{5} =$ $\dfrac{1}{2}$

Q **Let's do some more exercises.**

Exercise 8: What number, when multiplied by $\dfrac{3}{4}$, gives $\dfrac{7}{8}$?

A. $\dfrac{21}{32}$ D. $\dfrac{8}{7}$

B. $\dfrac{6}{5}$ E. $\dfrac{4}{3}$

C. $\dfrac{7}{6}$

Exercise 9: The average (mean) of $\dfrac{1}{4}$ and $\dfrac{1}{8}$ is

A. $\dfrac{1}{12}$ D. $\dfrac{5}{32}$

B. $\dfrac{1}{6}$ E. $\dfrac{7}{24}$

C. $\dfrac{3}{16}$

Let's look at the answers.

Answer 8: **C:** We need to solve $\frac{3}{4}x = \frac{7}{8}$. Then $x = \frac{7}{8} \times \frac{4}{3} = \frac{7}{6}$. I hate to keep emphasizing this, but you need to be able to do this is your head. The ACT seems to like this kind of question.

Answer 9: **C:** $\frac{\left(\frac{1}{4} + \frac{1}{8}\right)}{2} = \frac{\left(\frac{3}{8}\right)}{2} = \frac{3}{16}$.

Changing from Decimals to Fractions and Back

To change from a decimal to a fraction, we read it and write it.

Example 14: Change 4.37 to a fraction.

Solution: We read it as 4 and 37 hundredths: $4\frac{37}{100} = \frac{437}{100}$, if necessary. That's it.

Example 15: Change to decimals:

   a. $\frac{7}{4}$ b. $\frac{1}{6}$

Solution: For the fractions on the ACT, the decimal will either terminate or repeat.

   a. Divide 4 into 7.0000: $7.0000 \div 4 = 1.75$

   b. Divide 6 into 1.0000: $1.0000 \div 6 = .1666\ldots = .1\overline{6}$

The bar over the 6 means it repeats forever; for example, $.3454545\ldots = .3\overline{45}$. The bar over the 45 means 45 repeats forever, but not the 3.

PERCENTAGES

% means hundredths: $1\% = \frac{1}{100} = .01$.

Follow these rules to change between percentages and decimals and fractions:

Rule 1: To change a percentage to a decimal, move the decimal point two places to the left and drop the % sign.

Rule 2: To change a decimal to a percentage, move the decimal point two places to the right and add a % sign.

Rule 3: To change from a percentage to a fraction, divide by 100% and simplify, or change the % sign to $\frac{1}{100}$ and multiply.

Rule 4: To change a fraction to a percentage, first change to a decimal, and then to a percentage.

Example 16: Change 12%, 4%, and .7% to decimals.

Solutions: 12% = 12.% = .12; 4% = 4.% = .04; .7% = .007.

Example 17: Change .734, .2, and 34 to percentages.

Solutions: .734 = 73.4%; .2= 20%; 34 = 34. = 3400%.

Example 18: Change 42% to a fraction.

Solution: $42\% = .42 = \dfrac{42}{100} = \dfrac{21}{50}$, or $42\% = 42 \times \dfrac{1}{100} = \dfrac{42}{100} = \dfrac{21}{50}$

Example 19: Change $\dfrac{7}{4}$ to a percentage.

Solution: $\dfrac{7}{4} = 1.75 = 175\%$

Two hundred years ago, when I was in elementary school, we had to learn the following decimal, fraction, and percentage equivalents. Although the ACT allows calculators (remember, you are responsible for knowing which calculators are permitted), if you know this chart you will do better on this test. It is a timed test, and knowing this chart will save time. In addition, if you ever do any shopping, you'll know how much you will save even if the person doing the selling probably doesn't know. Also if you want to go to graduate school (I hope you all do), most of those aptitude tests for getting into graduate school do not allow calculators. By the time you are ready, it is possible that none of the graduate tests will allow calculators.

Fraction	Decimal	Percentage	Fraction	Decimal	Percentage
$\dfrac{1}{2}$	.5	50%	$\dfrac{1}{8}$	.125	$12\dfrac{1}{2}\%$
$\dfrac{1}{4}$	.25	25%	$\dfrac{3}{8}$	.375	$37\dfrac{1}{2}\%$
$\dfrac{3}{4}$	.75	75%	$\dfrac{5}{8}$	.625	$62\dfrac{1}{2}\%$
$\dfrac{1}{5}$	.2	20%	$\dfrac{7}{8}$	.875	$87\dfrac{1}{2}\%$
$\dfrac{2}{5}$	.4	40%	$\dfrac{1}{16}$	.0625	$6\dfrac{1}{4}\%$
$\dfrac{3}{5}$	.6	60%	$\dfrac{3}{16}$	.1875	$18\dfrac{3}{4}\%$
$\dfrac{4}{5}$	.8	80%	$\dfrac{5}{16}$	.3125	$31\dfrac{1}{4}\%$

(continued)

Fraction	Decimal	Percentage	Fraction	Decimal	Percentage
$\frac{1}{6}$	$.1\overline{6}$	$16\frac{2}{3}\%$	$\frac{7}{16}$	$.4375$	$43\frac{3}{4}\%$
$\frac{1}{3}$	$.\overline{3}$	$33\frac{1}{3}\%$	$\frac{9}{16}$	$.5625$	$56\frac{1}{4}\%$
$\frac{2}{3}$	$.\overline{6}$	$66\frac{2}{3}\%$	$\frac{11}{16}$	$.6875$	$68\frac{3}{4}\%$
$\frac{5}{6}$	$.8\overline{3}$	$83\frac{1}{3}\%$	$\frac{13}{16}$	$.8125$	$81\frac{1}{4}\%$
			$\frac{15}{16}$	$.9375$	$93\frac{3}{4}\%$

If you can't memorize all of these with denominator 16, memorize at least $\frac{1}{16}$ and $\frac{15}{16}$.

If you are good at doing percentage problems, skip this next section. Otherwise, here's a really easy way to do percentage problems. Make the following pyramid:

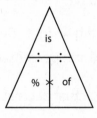

Example 20: What is 12% of 1.3?

Solution:

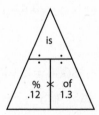

Put .12 in the % box (always change to a decimal in this box) and 1.3 in the "of" box. It tells us to multiply .12 × 1.3 = .156. That's all there is to it.

Example 21: 8% of what is 32?

Solution:

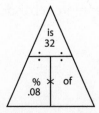

.08 goes in the % box. 32 goes in the "is" box. 32 ÷ .08 = 400.

Example 22:   9 is what % of 8?

Solution:

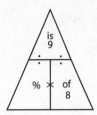

9 goes in the "is" box. 8 goes in the "of" box. 9 ÷ 8 × 100% = 112.5%.

The goal is to be able to do percentage problems without writing the pyramid.

Example 23:   In ten years, the population increases from 20,000 to 23,000. Find the actual increase and the percentage increase.

Solution: The actual increase is 23,000 − 20,000 = 3,000. The percentage increase is $\dfrac{3000}{20{,}000} \times 100\%$ = 15% increase.

Example 24:   The cost of producing widgets decreased from 60 cents to 50 cents. Find the actual decrease and percentage decrease.

Solution: 60 − 50 = 10 cent actual decrease; $\dfrac{10}{60} = 16\dfrac{2}{3}\%$ decrease.

Note   *Percentage increases and decreases are figured on the original amount.*

Example 25:   The cost of a $2000 large-screen TV set is decreased by 30%. If there is a 7% sales tax, how much does it cost?

Solution: $2000 × .30 = $600 discount. $2000 − $600 = $1400 cost. $1400 × .07 is $98. The total price is $1400 + $98 = $1498.

Note   *If we took 70% (or 100% − 30%) of $2000, we would immediately get the cost.*

There is an interesting story about why women wear miniskirts in London, England. It seems that the sales tax is $12\dfrac{1}{2}\%$ on clothes! But children's clothes are tax exempt. A girl's dress is any dress where the skirt is less than 24 inches, so that is why women in London wear miniskirts!

Q **Let's do some exercises.**

Exercise 10: The product of 2 and $\dfrac{1}{89}$ is:

    A. $2\dfrac{1}{89}$ D. $\dfrac{2}{89}$

    B. $1\dfrac{88}{89}$ E. $\dfrac{1}{172}$

    C. 172

Exercise 11: $\dfrac{1}{50}$ of 2% of .02 is

    A. .08   D. .000008

    B. .008   E. .00000008

    C. .0008

Exercise 12: 30% of 20% of a number is the same as 40% of what percentage of the same number?

    A. 10   D. 18

    B. $12\dfrac{1}{2}$ E. Can't be determined without the number

    C. 15

Exercise 13: A fraction between $\dfrac{3}{43}$ and $\dfrac{4}{43}$ is

    A. $\dfrac{1}{9}$ D. $\dfrac{7}{86}$

    B. $\dfrac{3}{28}$ E. $\dfrac{9}{1849}$

    C. $\dfrac{5}{47}$

Exercise 14: The reciprocal of $2 - \dfrac{3}{4}$ is

    A. $\dfrac{1}{2} - \dfrac{4}{3}$ D. $\dfrac{5}{4}$

    B. $-\dfrac{5}{4}$ E. $\dfrac{4}{5}$

    C. $-\dfrac{4}{5}$

Exercise 15: A price increase of 20% followed by a decrease of 20% means the price is

A. Up 4%   D. Down 2%

B. Up 2%   E. Down 4%

C. The original price

Exercise 16: A price decreases 20% followed by a 20% increase. The final price is

A. Up 4%   D. Down 2%

B. Up 2%   E. Down 4%

C. The original price

Exercise 17: A 50% discount followed by another 50% discount gives a discount of

A. 25%   D. 90%

B. 50%   E. 100%

C. 75%

Exercise 18: $83\frac{1}{3}\%$ of $37\frac{1}{2}\%$ is

A. $\dfrac{1}{2}$ D. $\dfrac{5}{16}$

B. $\dfrac{2}{5}$ E. $\dfrac{3}{32}$

C. $\dfrac{1}{4}$

Exercise 19: Which is equivalent to .0625?

A. $\dfrac{3}{8}$ D. $\dfrac{1}{18}$

B. $\dfrac{1}{8}$ E. $\dfrac{1}{80}$

C. $\dfrac{1}{16}$

Exercise 20: If the fractions $\dfrac{19}{24}, \dfrac{1}{2}, \dfrac{3}{8}, \dfrac{3}{4}$, and $\dfrac{9}{16}$ were ordered least to greatest, the middle number would be

A. $\dfrac{19}{24}$ D. $\dfrac{3}{4}$

B. $\dfrac{1}{2}$ E. $\dfrac{9}{16}$

C. $\dfrac{3}{8}$

Exercise 21: $\dfrac{31}{125} =$

A. 0.320   D. 0.252

B. 0.310   E. 0.248

C. 0.288

 Let's look at the answers.

Answer 10: D: $\dfrac{2}{1} \times \dfrac{1}{89} = \dfrac{2}{89}$.

Answer 11: D: $.02 \times .02 \times .02 = .000008$.

Answer 12: C: We can forget the number and forget the percentages. $(30)(20) = (40)(?)$. $? = 15$.

Answer 13: D: $\dfrac{3}{43} = \dfrac{6}{86}$; $\dfrac{4}{43} = \dfrac{8}{86}$; between is $\dfrac{7}{86}$. As another example like this one, to get nine numbers between $\dfrac{3}{43}$ and $\dfrac{4}{43}$, multiply both fractions, top and bottom, by 10 (one more than nine), and the fractions in between would be $\dfrac{31}{430}, \dfrac{32}{430}, \dfrac{33}{430}$, etc.

Answer 14: E: $2 - \dfrac{3}{4} = \dfrac{5}{4}$. Its reciprocal is $\dfrac{4}{5}$.

Answer 15:   **E:** Let $100 be the original price. A 20% increase means a $20 increase. Then a 20% decrease is ($120) $\times$ (.20) = $24.

$120 − $24 = $96, or a $4 decrease from the original price. $\dfrac{\$4}{\$100}$ is a 4% decrease.

Answer 16:   **E:** Suppose we have $100. Increased by 20%, we have $120. But another 20% less (now on a larger amount) is $24 less. We are at $96, down 4% from the original price. Suppose we take 20% off first. We are at $80. Now 20% up (on a smaller amount) is $16. We are again at $96 or again down 4% from the original price.

Answer 17:   **C:** $100 discounted 50% is $50. 50% of $50 is $25, for a 75% discount. This is why after December, a 50% discount followed by 20% is 60%, but sounds like 70% off.

Answer 18:   **D:** If you memorized the fraction table, you would recognize this problem as the same as $\left(\dfrac{5}{6}\right)\left(\dfrac{3}{8}\right) = \dfrac{5}{16}$.

Answer 19:   **C:** It is easy if you've memorized the fraction table.

Answer 20:   **E:** If we changed each number to a fraction with a denominator of 48 (the LCM), we would get $\dfrac{19}{24} = \dfrac{38}{48}, \dfrac{1}{2} = \dfrac{24}{48}, \dfrac{3}{8} = \dfrac{18}{48}, \dfrac{3}{4} = \dfrac{36}{48}$, and $\dfrac{9}{16} = \dfrac{27}{48}$, and it is easy to see that $\dfrac{27}{48} = \dfrac{9}{16}$ is the middle number.

Answer 21:   **E:** There are two ways to do this problem. If you recognize that $\dfrac{31}{125} < \dfrac{1}{4} (= .25)$ because the bottom is more than 4 times the top, you see that answer choice E is the only one less than $\dfrac{1}{4}$. Another way to answer this question is to multiply the top and bottom of $\dfrac{31}{125}$ by 8, and get $\dfrac{248}{1000} = .248$, which is answer choice E.

Enough! Let's do some algebra now. We will see these topics throughout the book.

CHAPTER 3: *Exponents, the Powers That Be*

"The power of exponents will bring you strength and knowledge."

Exponents are a very popular topic on the ACT. They are a good test of knowledge and thinking, are short to write, and it is relatively easy to make up new problems. Let's review some basic rules of exponents.

Rule	**Examples**
1. $x^m x^n = x^{m+n}$	$x^6 x^4 x = x^{11}$ and $(x^6 y^7)(x^4 y^{10}) = x^{10} y^{17}$
2. $\dfrac{x^m}{x^n} = x^{m-n}$ or $\dfrac{1}{x^{n-m}}$	$\dfrac{x^8}{x^6} = x^2$, $\dfrac{x^3}{x^7} = \dfrac{1}{x^4}$, and $\dfrac{x^4 y^5 z^9}{x^9 y^2 z^9} = \dfrac{y^3}{x^5}$
3. $(x^m)^n = x^{mn}$	$(x^5)^7 = x^{35}$
4. $(xy)^n = x^n y^n$	$(xy)^3 = x^3 y^3$ and $(x^7 y^3)^{10} = x^{70} y^{30}$
5. $\left(\dfrac{x}{y}\right)^n = \dfrac{x^n}{y^n}$	$\left(\dfrac{x}{y}\right)^6 = \dfrac{x^6}{y^6}$ and $\left(\dfrac{y^4}{z^5}\right)^3 = \dfrac{y^{12}}{z^{15}}$
6. $x^{-n} = \dfrac{1}{x^n}$ and $\dfrac{1}{x^{-m}} = x^m$	$2^{-3} = \dfrac{1}{2^3} = \dfrac{1}{8}$, $\dfrac{1}{4^{-3}} = 4^3 = 64$, $\dfrac{x^{-4} y^{-5} z^6}{x^{-6} y^4 z^{-1}} = \dfrac{x^6 z^6 z^1}{x^4 y^5 y^4} = \dfrac{x^2 z^7}{y^9}$, and $\left(\dfrac{x^3}{y^{-4}}\right)^{-2} = \left(\dfrac{y^{-4}}{x^3}\right)^2 = \dfrac{y^{-8}}{x^6} = \dfrac{1}{x^6 y^8}$
7. $x^0 = 1$, $x \neq 0$; 0^0 is indeterminate	$(7ab)^0 = 1$ and $7x^0 = 7(1) = 7$

8. $x^{\frac{p}{r}} = x^{\frac{power}{root}}$

Even though either order of computing the power and root gives the same answer, we usually do the root first. $25^{\frac{3}{2}} = \left(\sqrt{25}\right)^3 = 125$; $4^{-\frac{3}{2}} = \dfrac{1}{4^{\frac{3}{2}}} = \dfrac{1}{\left(\sqrt{4}\right)^3} = \dfrac{1}{8}$

Although calculators are allowed on this test, knowing as many of these equivalents as possible will save time—time you will need to do the last questions in the math section.

$2^2 = 4$	$2^3 = 8$	$2^4 = 16$	$2^5 = 32$	$2^6 = 64$	$2^7 = 128$
$2^8 = 256$	$2^9 = 512$	$2^{10} = 1024$	$3^2 = 9$	$3^3 = 27$	$3^4 = 81$
$3^5 = 243$	$3^6 = 729$	$4^2 = 16$	$4^3 = 64$	$4^4 = 256$	$5^2 = 25$
$5^3 = 125$	$6^2 = 36$	$6^3 = 216$	$7^2 = 49$	$8^2 = 64$	$9^2 = 81$
$10^2 = 100$	$11^2 = 121$	$12^2 = 144$	$13^2 = 169$	$14^2 = 196$	$15^2 = 225$
$16^2 = 256$	$17^2 = 289$	$18^2 = 324$	$19^2 = 361$	$20^2 = 400$	$21^2 = 441$
$22^2 = 484$	$23^2 = 529$	$24^2 = 576$	$25^2 = 625$	$26^2 = 676$	$27^2 = 729$
$28^2 = 784$	$29^2 = 841$	$30^2 = 900$	$31^2 = 961$	$32^2 = 1024$	

Over the years, I have asked my students to memorize these powers for a number of reasons. In math, these powers occur often. They occur when we use the Pythagorean theorem (mostly the squares). They are used going backward to find roots (next chapter). Also, they show number patterns of the squares (look at the last digits of each of the squares). All of these topics are on the ACT.

Even though the ACT does not ask comparison-type questions, it is necessary to be able to compare x and x^2. Similar results hold for x^3, x^4, and so on.

If $x > 1$, then $x^2 > x$, because $4^2 > 4$.

If $x = 1$, then $x^2 = x$, because $1^2 = 1$.

If $0 < x < 1$, then $x > x^2$, because $\dfrac{1}{2} > \left(\dfrac{1}{2}\right)^2 = \dfrac{1}{4}$!!

If $x = 0$, then $x = x^2$, because $0 = 0^2$.

If $x < 0$, then $x^2 > x$, because the square of a negative is a positive.

Also recall that if $0 < x < 1$, then $\dfrac{1}{x} > 1$, and if $x > 1$, then $0 < \dfrac{1}{x} < 1$.

Also if $-1 < x < 0$, then $\dfrac{1}{x} < -1$, and if $x < -1$, then $-1 < \dfrac{1}{x} < 0$.

Here are some exponential problems to practice, including some with negative exponents.

Example 1:   Simplify the following:

Problem	Solution
a. $(-3a^4bc^6)(-5ab^7c^{10})(-100a^{100}b^{200}c^{2000}) =$	$-1500a^{105}b^{208}c^{2016}$
b. $(10ab^4c^7)^3 =$	$1000a^3b^{12}c^{21}$
c. $(4x^6)^2(10x)^3 =$	$16{,}000x^{15}$
d. $((2b^4)^3)^2 =$	$64b^{24}$
e. $(-b^6)^{101} =$	$-b^{606}$
f. $(-ab^8)^{202} =$	$a^{202}b^{1616}$
g. $\dfrac{24e^9f^7g^5}{72e^9f^{11}g^7} =$	$\dfrac{1}{3f^4g^2}$
h. $\dfrac{\left(x^4\right)^3}{x^4} =$	x^8
i. $\left(\dfrac{m^3n^4}{m^7n}\right)^5 =$	$\dfrac{n^{15}}{m^{20}}$
j. $\left(\dfrac{\left(p^4\right)^3}{\left(p^6\right)^5}\right)^{10} =$	$\dfrac{1}{p^{180}}$
k. $(-10a^{-4}b^5c^{-2})(4a^{-7}b^{-1}) =$	$\dfrac{-40b^4}{a^{11}c^2}$
l. $(3ab^{-3}c^4)^{-3} =$	$\dfrac{b^9}{27a^3c^{12}}$

m. $(3x^4)^{-4}\left(\left(\dfrac{1}{9x^8}\right)^{-1}\right)^2 =$ 1

n. $(2x^{-4})^2(3x^{-3})^{-2} =$ $\dfrac{4}{9x^2}$

o. $\left(\dfrac{(2y^3)^{-2}}{(4x^{-5})}\right)^{-2} =$ $\dfrac{256y^{12}}{x^{10}}$

Q **Now, let's try some exercises.**

Exercise 1: $0 < x < 1$: Arrange in order of smallest to largest: x, x^2, x^3.

A. $x < x^2 < x^3$ D. $x^3 < x^2 < x$

B. $x < x^3 < x^2$ E. $x^3 < x < x^2$

C. $x^2 < x < x^3$

Exercise 2: $-1 < x < 0$: Arrange in order of largest to smallest: x^2, x^3, x^4.

A. $x^4 > x^3 > x^2$ D. $x^2 > x^3 > x^4$

B. $x^4 > x^2 > x^3$ E. $x^2 > x^4 > x^3$

C. $x^3 > x^4 > x^2$

Exercise 3: $0 < x < 1$.

I: $x > \dfrac{1}{x^2}$

II: $\dfrac{1}{x^2} > \dfrac{1}{x^4}$

III: $x - 1 > \dfrac{1}{x - 1}$

Which statement(s) are always true?

A. None   D. III only

B. I only   E. All

C. II only

Exercise 4: $(5ab^3)^3 =$

A. $15ab^6$ D. $125a^3b^6$

B. $75ab^6$ E. $125a^3b^9$

C. $125ab^9$

Exercise 5: $\dfrac{\left(2x^5\right)^3\left(3x^{10}\right)^2}{6x^{15}} =$

A. 1

B. x^{20}

C. $2x^{20}$

D. $12x^{20}$

E. $12x^{210}$

Exercise 6: $\left(\dfrac{12x^6}{24x^9}\right)^3 =$

A. $1728x^{27}$

B. $\dfrac{1}{1728x^{27}}$

C. $\dfrac{1}{6x^9}$

D. $\dfrac{1}{8x^9}$

E. $\dfrac{1}{8x^{27}}$

Exercise 7: $\dfrac{\left(4x^4\right)^3}{\left(8x^6\right)^2} =$

A. $\dfrac{1}{2}$

B. 1

C. $\dfrac{1}{2}x^{28}$

D. x^{28}

E. $\dfrac{1}{2x}$

Exercise 8: $-1 \leq x \leq 5$. Where is x^2 located?

A. $-1 \leq x^2 \leq 5$

B. $0 \leq x^2 \leq 25$

C. $1 \leq x^2 \leq 5$

D. $1 \leq x^2 \leq 10$

E. $1 \leq x^2 \leq 25$

Exercise 9: $2^m + 2^m =$

A. 2^{m+1}

B. 2^{m+2}

C. 2^{m+4}

D. 2^{m^2}

E. 4^m

Exercise 10: $\dfrac{m^{-5}n^6p^{-2}}{m^{-3}n^9p^0} =$

    A. $m^2n^3p^2$ **D.** $\dfrac{1}{m^2n^3p^2}$

    B. $\dfrac{1}{m^2n^3}$ **E.** None of these

    C. $\dfrac{m^2}{n^3p^2}$

Exercise 11: If $8^{2n+1} = 2^{n+18}$; $n =$

    A. 3   **D.** 13

    B. 7   **E.** 17

    C. 10

Exercise 12: $p = 4^n$; $4p =$

    A. 4^{n+1} **D.** 16^p

    B. 4^{n+2} **E.** 64^p

    C. 3^{n+4}

Exercise 13: $y^3 = 64$; $y^{-2} =$

    A. -4 **D.** $\dfrac{1}{16}$

    B. $-\dfrac{1}{8}$ **E.** $-\dfrac{1}{16}$

    C. $\dfrac{1}{8}$

Exercise 14: Suppose $x^2 = y^2$.

    I: $x = y$.

    II: $x = -y$.

    III: $x^2 = xy$.

    Which statements are always true?

    A. None   **D.** III only

    B. I only   **E.** All statements are true

    C. II only

Exercise 15: $3^{-2} =$

A. $\dfrac{1}{3}$

B. $\dfrac{1}{6}$

C. $\dfrac{1}{9}$

D. $-\dfrac{1}{9}$

E. $-\dfrac{1}{6}$

Exercise 16: $x^{\frac{3}{4}} = 8; x =$

A. $\dfrac{32}{3}$

B. 16

C. 64

D. 256

E. 1024

Exercise 17: n is an integer, and $(-2)^{6n} = 8^{n+4}; n =$

A. 2

B. 3

C. 4

D. 6

E. 8

 Let's look at the answers.

Answer 1: D: If $0 < x < 1$, the higher the power, the smaller the number.

Answer 2: E: Take, for example, $x = -\dfrac{1}{2}$. $\left(-\dfrac{1}{2}\right)^2 = \dfrac{1}{4}; \left(-\dfrac{1}{2}\right)^3 = -\dfrac{1}{8};$ $\left(-\dfrac{1}{2}\right)^4 = \dfrac{1}{16}$. Be careful! This exercise asks for largest to smallest. Notice that x^3 has to be the smallest because it is the only negative number, so the answer choices are reduced to two, B and E.

Answer 3: D: Statement I is false: $0 < x < 1$, so $\dfrac{1}{x} > 1$ and $\dfrac{1}{x^2} > 1$ also. Statement II is false: $x^2 > x^4$, so $\dfrac{1}{x^2} < \dfrac{1}{x^4}$. Statement III is true: $0 < x < 1$; so $-1 < x - 1 < 0$; this means $\dfrac{1}{x-1} < -1$

Answer 4: E: $5^3 a^3 (b^3)^3 = 125 a^3 b^9$.

Answer 5:   D: $\left(\dfrac{8 \times 9}{6}\right) x^{15 + 20 - 15} = 12x^{20}$.

Answer 6:   D: $\left(\dfrac{1}{2x^3}\right)^3 = \dfrac{1}{8x^9}$.

Answer 7:   B: The numerator and denominator of the fraction each equal $64x^{12}$.

Answer 8:   B: This is very tricky. Because 0 is between -1 and 5 and $0^2 = 0$.

Answer 9:   A: This is one of the few truly hard problems because it is an addition problem:

$$2^m + 2^m = 1 \times 2^m + 1 \times 2^m = 2 \times 2^m = 2^1 \times 2^m = 2^{m+1}.$$

Similarly, $3^m + 3^m + 3^m = 3^{m+1}$ and four 4^m terms added equal 4^{m+1}.

Answer 10:   D: $\dfrac{m^{-5}n^6p^{-2}}{m^{-3}n^9p^0} = \dfrac{m^3n^6}{m^5n^9p^2} = \dfrac{1}{m^2n^3p^2}$.

Answer 11:   A: $8^{2n+1} = (2^3)^{2n+1} = 2^{n+18}$. If the bases are equal, the exponents must be equal. $3(2n+1) = n + 18$; so $n = 3$.

Answer 12:   A: $p = 4^n$; $4p = 4(4^n) = 4^1 4^n = 4^{n+1}$.

Answer 13:   D: $y^3 = 64$; $y = 4$; $y^{-2} = \left(\dfrac{1}{4}\right)^2 = \dfrac{1}{16}$.

Answer 14:   A: None! Because $x = y$ or $x = -y$, all of the statements are true sometimes, but none is always true.

Answer 15:   C: $3^{-2} = \left(\dfrac{1}{3}\right)^2 = \dfrac{1}{9}$.

Answer 16:   B: $x^{\frac{3}{4}} = 8$; $x = \left(x^{\frac{3}{4}}\right)^{\frac{4}{3}} = 8^{\frac{4}{3}} = \left(\sqrt[3]{8}\right)^4 = 2^4 = 16$

Answer 17:   C: We can ignore the minus sign, because both sides must be positive. $2^{6n} = 8^{n+4} = 2^{3(n+4)}$. So $6n = 3n + 12$, and $n = 4$.

This chapter seems the only good place to introduce the topic of **scientific notation**. On your calculator, if you see 3.176 and to the right of it you see 27, the number is written in scientific notation. It means 3.176×10^{27}.

A number in scientific notation is of the form $n \times 10^m$, where n is at least 1 but less than 10.

Example 2:   Write 567000 in scientific notation.

Solution: Put the decimal place after the first digit 5.67; then count the number of places to the right (of 5) to the end of the original number. This is the power of 10, or *m*, and the answer is 5.67×10^5. It is a positive exponent because we are counting to the right and because the original number is larger than 10.

Example 3:   Write 0.000000097 in scientific notation.

Solution: Again, put the decimal after the first digit, 9.7; then count the number of places from the decimal point after the 9 left to where it was in the original number. It is 8 places; the exponent of 10 is negative here because it is to the left and the entire number is less than 1. The answer is $0.000000097 = 9.7 \times 10^{-8}$.

Example 4:   Compute the following in scientific notation: $\dfrac{60000 \times .008}{.00002 \times 200000000}$

Solution: Write all the numbers in scientific notation : $\dfrac{6 \times 10^4 \times 8 \times 10^{-3}}{2 \times 10^{-5} \times 2 \times 10^8}$.

Separate the number parts from the powers of ten. Bring negative exponents in the top to the bottom and the bottom to the top, making all of them positive. Then do the math.

$$\frac{6 \times 8}{2 \times 2} \times \frac{10^4 \times 10^5}{10^3 \times 10^8} = 12 \times \frac{10^9}{10^{11}} = 12 \times 10^{-2} = 1.2 \times 10^1 \times 10^{-2} = 1.2 \times 10^{-1}$$

On the ACT, the problems are shorter! Now let's go to a radical chapter.

CHAPTER 4: *Radical Radicals*

"We must go to the root of the problem to be enlightened."

The square root symbol ($\sqrt{}$) is probably the one symbol most people actually like, even for people who don't like math. How else can you explain the square root symbol on a business calculator? I have yet to find a use for it. Here are some basic facts about square roots that you should know.

1. You should know the following square roots:

   $\sqrt{0} = 0$ $\sqrt{1} = 1$ $\sqrt{4} = 2$ $\sqrt{9} = 3$ $\sqrt{16} = 4$ $\sqrt{25} = 5$

   $\sqrt{36} = 6$ $\sqrt{49} = 7$ $\sqrt{64} = 8$ $\sqrt{81} = 9$ $\sqrt{100} = 10$

   The numbers under the radicals (square root signs) are called perfect squares because their square roots are whole numbers.

2. $\sqrt{2} \approx 1.4$ (actually it is 1.414 . . .), and $\sqrt{3} \approx 1.73$ (actually it is 1.732 . . . , the year George Washington was born).

3. $\sqrt{\dfrac{a}{b}} = \dfrac{\sqrt{a}}{\sqrt{b}}$, so $\sqrt{\dfrac{25}{9}} = \dfrac{5}{3}$ $\sqrt{\dfrac{7}{36}} = \dfrac{\sqrt{7}}{6}$ $\sqrt{\dfrac{45}{20}} = \sqrt{\dfrac{9}{4}} = \dfrac{3}{2}.$

4. A method of simplification involves finding all the prime factors:

   $\sqrt{200} = \sqrt{(2)(2)(2)(5)(5)} = (2)(5)\sqrt{2} = 10\sqrt{2}$. We can also simplify by using $\sqrt{200} = \sqrt{100 \times 2} = 10\sqrt{2}$. With paper and pencil, the first method has always been better for my students. Without paper and pencil on the ACT, you have to decide which method works best for you.

5. Adding and subtracting radicals involves combining like radicals:

   $4\sqrt{7} + 5\sqrt{11} + 6\sqrt{7} - 9\sqrt{11} = 10\sqrt{7} - 4\sqrt{11}$

6. Multiplication of radicals follows this rule: $a\sqrt{b} \times c\sqrt{d} = ac\sqrt{bd}$.

   Therefore, $3\sqrt{13} \times 10\sqrt{7} = 30\sqrt{91}$, and

   $10\sqrt{8} \times 3\sqrt{10} = 10 \times 3\sqrt{2 \times 2 \times 2 \times 2 \times 5} = 10 \times 3 \times 2 \times 2 \times \sqrt{5} = 120\sqrt{5}.$

7. If a single radical appears in the denominator of a fraction, rationalize the denominator (change it to a nonradical) by multiplying both numerator and denominator by the radical:

$$\frac{20}{7\sqrt{5}} = \frac{20}{7\sqrt{5}} \times \frac{\sqrt{5}}{\sqrt{5}} = \frac{20\sqrt{5}}{35} = \frac{4\sqrt{5}}{7} \text{ and } \frac{7}{\sqrt{45}} = \frac{7}{3\sqrt{5}} \times \frac{\sqrt{5}}{\sqrt{5}} = \frac{7\sqrt{5}}{15}$$

8. If the denominator has two terms, one or both of the terms having a square root, multiply the numerator and denominator by its **conjugate**, the same term with a different sign between.

$$\frac{3}{7 + \sqrt{5}} = \frac{3}{7 + \sqrt{5}} \times \frac{7 - \sqrt{5}}{7 - \sqrt{5}} = \frac{21 - 3\sqrt{5}}{49 - 5} = \frac{21 - 3\sqrt{5}}{44}$$

$$\frac{\sqrt{a} + \sqrt{b}}{\sqrt{a} - \sqrt{b}} = \frac{\sqrt{a} + \sqrt{b}}{\sqrt{a} - \sqrt{b}} \times \frac{\sqrt{a} + \sqrt{b}}{\sqrt{a} + \sqrt{b}} = \frac{a + 2\sqrt{ab} + b}{a - b}$$

9. If $c, d > 0$, $\sqrt{c} + \sqrt{d} > \sqrt{c + d}$. Why? If we square the right side, we get $c + d$. If we square the left side, we get $c + d +$ the middle term $(2\sqrt{cd})$.

10. You should know the following cube roots:

$$\sqrt[3]{1} = 1 \qquad \sqrt[3]{8} = 2 \qquad \sqrt[3]{27} = 3 \qquad \sqrt[3]{64} = 4 \qquad \sqrt[3]{125} = 5$$

$$\sqrt[3]{-1} = -1 \qquad \sqrt[3]{-8} = -2 \qquad \sqrt[3]{-27} = -3 \qquad \sqrt[3]{-64} = -4 \qquad \sqrt[3]{-125} = -5$$

11. The square root varies according to the value of the radicand:

If $a > 1$, $a > \sqrt{a}$. For example, $9 > \sqrt{9}$.

If $a = 1$, $a = \sqrt{a}$ because the square root of 1 is 1.

If $0 < a < 1$, $a < \sqrt{a}$. When we take the square root of a positive number, it becomes closer to 1, so $\sqrt{\frac{1}{4}} = \frac{1}{2} > \frac{1}{4}$.

If $a = 0$, $a = \sqrt{a}$ because the square root of 0 is 0.

If $a > 0$ and $\sqrt{a} < 1$, then $\frac{1}{\sqrt{a}} > 1$. Also, if $\sqrt{a} > 1$, then $\frac{1}{a} < 1$.

12. The square root or any even root of a negative number is imaginary (undefined).

13. The cube root or any odd root of a positive is a positive, of a negative is a negative, and any root of 0 is 0. All are always defined.

Note $\sqrt{9} = 3$, $-\sqrt{9} = -3$, *but* $\sqrt{-9}$ *is imaginary. The equation* $x^2 = 9$ *has two solutions,* $\pm\sqrt{9}$, *or* ±3, *which stands for both* $+3$ *and* -3.

In Chapter 16 we'll do imaginary numbers.

Q **Let's try some exercises.**

Exercise 1: $\left(\sqrt{12} + \sqrt{27}\right)^2 =$

    A. 15   **D.** 225

    B. 39   **E.** 675

    C. 75

Exercise 2: Suppose $0 < a < 1$.

    I: $a^2 > \sqrt{a}$

    II: $\sqrt{a} > \sqrt{a^3}$

    III: $\sqrt{a} > \dfrac{1}{\sqrt{a^7}}$

    A. I is correct   **D.** I and III are correct

    B. II is correct   **E.** II and III are correct

    C. III is correct

Exercise 3: $c = \left(\dfrac{1}{17}\right)^2 - \sqrt{\dfrac{1}{17}}$. Which answer choice is true for c?

    A. $c < -2$ **D.** $0 < c < 1$

    B. $-2 < c < -1$ **E.** $1 < c < 2$

    C. $-1 < c < 0$

Exercise 4: $0 < m < 1$. Arrange in order, smallest to largest, $a = \dfrac{1}{m}$, $b = \dfrac{1}{m^2}$,

    $c = \dfrac{1}{\sqrt{m}}$.

    A. $a < b < c$ **D.** $b < a < c$

    B. $a < c < b$ **E.** $c < a < b$

    C. $b < c < a$

Exercise 5:   If $\sqrt[3]{-87} = x$:

A. $-10 < x < -9$ D. $-4 < x < -3$

B. $-9 < x < -8$ E. x is undefined

C. $-5 < x < -4$

Exercise 6:   Simplified, $\dfrac{\sqrt{m}}{\sqrt{m} - \sqrt{n}} =$

A. $\dfrac{m - \sqrt{n}}{m - n}$ D. $\dfrac{m - \sqrt{mn}}{m + n}$

B. $\dfrac{m + \sqrt{n}}{m + n}$ E. 1

C. $\dfrac{m + \sqrt{mn}}{m - n}$

(A) Let's look at the answers.

Answer 1:   C: $\sqrt{12} = \sqrt{2 \times 2 \times 3} = 2\sqrt{3}$ and $\sqrt{27} = \sqrt{3 \times 3 \times 3} = 3\sqrt{3}$. Adding, we get $5\sqrt{3}$. Squaring, we get $25\sqrt{9} = 25 \times 3 = 75$.

Answer 2:   B: Let's look at the statements one by one.

Statement I: If we square a number between 0 and 1, we make it closer to 0. If we take the square root of the same number, we make it closer to 1. Statement I is wrong.

Statement II: From the previous chapter, if $0 < a < 1, a > a^3$. So are its square roots. So statement II is true.

Statement III: $\sqrt{a} < 1 . a^7 < 1$. So $\sqrt{a^7} < 1$. Then $\dfrac{1}{\sqrt{a^7}} > 1$. Statement III is false.

Answer 3:   C: $\dfrac{1}{17}$ squared is less than $\dfrac{1}{17}$, the square root is more than $\dfrac{1}{17}$, and both numbers are between 0 and 1. When we subtract a larger from a smaller number, the sign is negative, and here the numbers are fractions, so $-1 < c < 0$.

Answer 4:   **E:** If we take $m = \dfrac{1}{4}$, we see that $\sqrt{m} > m > m^2$. That makes $\dfrac{1}{\sqrt{m}} < \dfrac{1}{m} < \dfrac{1}{m^2}$, or $c < a < b$.

Answer 5:   **C:** Because $\sqrt[3]{-125} = -5$ and $\sqrt[3]{-64} = -4$, and because -87 is between -125 and -64, the cube root of -87 must be between -5 and -4.

Answer 6:   **C:** $\dfrac{\sqrt{m}}{\sqrt{m} - \sqrt{n}} \times \dfrac{\sqrt{m} + \sqrt{n}}{\sqrt{m} + \sqrt{n}} = \dfrac{m + \sqrt{mn}}{m - n}$. Note that answer choice E couldn't be correct because if the fraction was not equal to 1 before simplification, it couldn't be equal to 1 after simplification.

We'll see more root problems in the later chapters and in the review.

"Along our journey, we must learn to do. It will help us become truly happy."

Algebraic manipulative skills such as those in this chapter are areas that high school courses have tended to de-emphasize since 1985. It is necessary to show you how to do these problems and give you extra problems to practice. Of course, included will be the kind of questions the ACT asks.

COMBINING LIKE TERMS

Like terms are terms with the same letter combination (or no letter). The same letter must also have the same exponents.

Example 1: Are the following terms like or unlike?

a. $4x$ and $-5x$

b. $4x$ and $4x^2$

c. xy^2 and x^2y

Solutions: a. $4x$ and $-5x$ are like terms even though their numerical coefficients are different.

b. $4x$ and $4x^2$ are unlike terms

c. xy^2 and x^2y are unlike; $xy^2 = xyy$ and $x^2y = xxy$.

Combining like terms means adding or subtracting their numerical coefficients; exponents are unchanged. Unlike terms cannot be combined.

Example 2:   Simplify:

Problem	Solution
a. $3m + 4m + m =$	$8m$
b. $8m + 2n + 7m - 7n =$	$15m - 5n$
c. $3x^2 + 4x - 5 - 7x^2 - 4x + 8 =$	$-4x^2 + 3$

DISTRIBUTIVE LAW

The **distributive law** states:

$$a(x + y) = ax + ay$$

Example 3:   Perform the indicated operations:

Problem	Solution
a. $4(3x - 7) =$	$12x - 28$
b. $5(2a - 5b + 3c) =$	$10a - 25b + 15c$
c. $3x^4(7x^3 - 4x - 1) =$	$21x^7 - 12x^5 - 3x^4$
d. $4(3x - 7) - 5(4x - 2) =$	$12x - 28 - 20x + 10 = -8x - 18$

BINOMIAL PRODUCTS

A **binomial** is a two-term expression, such as $x + 2$. We use the **FOIL method** to multiply a binomial by a binomial. FOIL is an acronym for First, Outer, Inner, Last. This means to multiply the first two terms, then the outer terms, then the inner terms, and finally the last two terms.

Example 4:   Multiply $(x + 4)(x + 6)$

Solution:

Multiplying, we get $x^2 + 6x + 4x + 24 = x^2 + 10x + 24$.

You should know the following common binomial products:

$$(a + b)(a - b) = a^2 - b^2$$

$$(a - b)(a - b) = a^2 - 2ab + b^2$$

$$(a + b)(a + b) = a^2 + 2ab + b^2$$

Note   *For a perfect square $(a + b)^2$, the first term of the resulting trinomial is the first term squared (a^2), and the third term of the resulting trinomial is the last term squared (b^2). The middle term is twice the product of the two terms of the binomial (2ab), so*

$$(a + b)^2 = a^2 + 2ab + b^2$$

Example 5:   Perform the indicated multiplications:

Problem	Solution
a. $(x + 7)(x + 4) =$	$x^2 + 4x + 7x + 28 = x^2 + 11x + 28$
b. $(x - 5)(x - 2) =$	$x^2 - 7x + 10$
c. $(x + 6)(x - 3) =$	$x^2 + 3x - 18$
d. $(x + 6)(x - 8) =$	$x^2 - 2x - 48$
e. $(x + 5)(x - 5) =$	$x^2 - 5x + 5x - 25 = x^2 - 25$
f. $(x + 5)^2 =$	$(x + 5)(x + 5) = x^2 + 10x + 25$
g. $(x - 10)^2 =$	$x^2 - 20x + 100$
h. $(2x + 5)(3x - 10) =$	$6x^2 - 5x - 50$
i. $3(x + 4)(x + 5) =$	$3(x^2 + 9x + 20) = 3x^2 + 27x + 60$
j. $7(4x + 3)(4x - 3) =$	$7(16x^2 - 9) = 112x^2 - 63$
k. $(a + 4)(a + 7)$	$a^2 + 11a + 28$
l. $(b + 5)(b + 6)$	$b^2 + 11b + 30$
m. $(c + 1)(c + 9)$	$c^2 + 10c + 9$

n. $(d + 4)(d + 8)$ $\qquad\qquad$ $d^2 + 12d + 32$

o. $(e + 11)(e + 10)$ $\qquad\quad$ $e^2 + 21e + 110$

p. $(f - 6)(f - 2)$ $\qquad\qquad$ $f^2 - 8f + 12$

q. $(g - 10)(g - 20)$ $\qquad\quad$ $g^2 - 30g + 200$

r. $(h - 4)(h - 3)$ $\qquad\qquad$ $h^2 - 7h + 12$

s. $(i - 1)(i - 7)$ $\qquad\qquad$ $i^2 - 8i + 7$

t. $(j - 3)(j - 5)$ $\qquad\qquad$ $j^2 - 8j + 15$

Example 6: Perform the indicated multiplications:

<u>Problem</u> $\qquad\qquad\qquad\qquad$ <u>Solution</u>

a. $(k + 5)(k - 2)$ $\qquad\qquad$ $k^2 + 3k - 10$

b. $(m + 5)(m - 8)$ $\qquad\quad$ $m^2 - 3m - 40$

c. $(n - 6)(n + 2)$ $\qquad\qquad$ $n^2 - 4n - 12$

d. $(p - 8)(p + 10)$ $\qquad\quad$ $p^2 + 2p - 80$

e. $(q - 5r)(q + 2r)$ $\qquad\quad$ $q^2 - 3qr - 10r^2$

f. $(s + 3)^2$ $\qquad\qquad\qquad$ $s^2 + 6s + 9$

g. $(t - 4)^2$ $\qquad\qquad\qquad$ $t^2 - 8t + 16$

h. $(3u + 5)^2$ $\qquad\qquad\quad$ $9u^2 + 30u + 25$

i. $(5v - 4)^2$ $\qquad\qquad\quad$ $25v^2 - 40v + 16$

j. $(ax + by)^2$ $\qquad\qquad\quad$ $a^2x^2 + 2abxy + b^2y^2$

k. $(be - ma)^2$ $\qquad\qquad$ $b^2e^2 - 2\,beam + m^2a^2$

l. $(w + x)(w - x)$ $\qquad\quad$ $w^2 - x^2$

m. $(a - 11)(a + 11)$ $\qquad\quad$ $a^2 - 121$

n. $(am - 7)(am + 7)$ $a^2m^2 - 49$

o. $(a^2b + c)(a^2b - c)$ $a^4b^2 - c^2$

p. $3(x + 5)(x - 2)$ $3x^2 + 9x - 30$

q. $-4(2x - 5)(3x - 4)$ $-24x^2 + 92x - 80$

r. $x(2x - 5)(4x + 7)$ $8x^3 - 6x^2 - 35x$

s. $5(x - 5)(x + 5)$ $5x^2 - 125$

Let's do some exercises.

Exercise 1: $x^2 - y^2 = 24; 3(x + y)(x - y) =$

A. 8   D. 72

B. 24   E. 13,824

C. 27

Exercise 2: $x + y = m; x - y = \dfrac{1}{m}; x^2 - y^2 =$

A. m^2 D. $\dfrac{1}{m}$

B. m E. $\dfrac{1}{m^2}$

C. 1

Exercise 3: $\left(x + \dfrac{1}{x}\right)^2 = 64; x^2 + \dfrac{1}{x^2} =$

A. 9   D. 65

B. 62   E. 66

C. 64

Exercise 4: $x^2 + y^2 = 20$ and $xy = -6.$ Then $(x + y)^2 =$

A. 8   D. 26

B. 14   E. 32

C. 20

Exercise 5: $(x - y)^2 + 4xy =$

A. $x^2 + 8x + y^2$ D. $(x + y)^2$

B. $x^2 + 4x + y^2$ E. $x^2 + y^2$

C. $x^2 - y^2$

 Let's look at the answers.

Answer 1:   D: $3(x + y)(x - y) = 3(x^2 - y^2) = 3(24) = 72$.

Answer 2:   C: $(x + y)(x - y) = x^2 - y^2 = \dfrac{m}{1} \times \dfrac{1}{m} = 1$.

Answer 3:   B: $\left(x + \dfrac{1}{x}\right)\left(x + \dfrac{1}{x}\right) = x^2 + 2(x)\left(\dfrac{1}{x}\right) + \dfrac{1}{x^2} = x^2 + \dfrac{1}{x^2} + 2 = 64$. So

$x^2 + \dfrac{1}{x^2} = 64 - 2 = 62$.

Answer 4:   A: $(x + y)^2 = x^2 + 2xy + y^2 = x^2 + y^2 + 2xy = 20 + 2(-6) = 8$.

Answer 5:   D: $x^2 - 2xy + y^2 + 4xy = x^2 + 2xy + y^2 = (x + y)^2$.

Let's go on to factoring.

FACTORING

Factoring is the reverse of the distributive law. There are three types of factoring you need to know: largest common factor, difference of two squares, and trinomial factorization.

If the distributive law says $x(y + z) = xy + xz$, then taking out the largest common factor says $xy + xy = x(y + z)$. Let's demonstrate a few factoring examples.

Example 7:   Factor:

Problem	Answer	Explanation
a. $4x + 6y - 8$	$2(2x + 3y - 4)$	2 is the largest common factor.
b. $8ax + 12ay - 40az$	$4a(2x + 3y - 10z)$	4 is the largest common factor; a is also a common factor

c. $10a^4y^6z^3 - 15a^7y$ $5a^4y(2y^5z^3 - 3a^3)$ The largest common factor and the lowest power of each common variable is factored out: a^4 and y, but not z because it is not in both terms.

d. $x^4y - xy^3 + xy$ $xy(x^3 - y^2 + 1)$ Factor out the lowest power of each common variable. Three terms in the original give three terms in parentheses. Note that $1 \times xy = xy$.

e. $9by + 12be + 4ye$ prime   Some expressions cannot be factored.

Difference of Two Squares

Because $(a + b)(a - b) = a^2 - b^2$, factoring tells us that $a^2 - b^2 = (a + b)(a - b)$.

Example 8:

Problem	Answer	Explanation
a. $x^2 - 25$	$(x + 5)(x - 5)$ or $(x - 5)(x + 5)$	Either order is OK.
b. $x^2 - 121$	$(x + 11)(x - 11)$	
c. $9a^2 - 25b^2$	$(3a + 5b)(3a - 5b)$	
d. $5a^3 - 20a$	$5a(a^2 - 4) = 5a(a + 2)(a - 2)$	Factor out the largest common factor first, then use the difference of two squares.
e. $x^4 - y^4$	$(x^2 + y^2)(x^2 - y^2) =$ $(x^2 + y^2)(x + y)(x - y)$	This is the difference of two squares where the square roots in the factors are also squares. Sum of two squares doesn't factor, but use the difference of two squares again.

Example 9:   Factor completely:

Problem	Solution
a. $12am + 18an$	$6a(2m + 3n)$
b. $6at - 18st + 4as$	$2(3at - 9st + 2as)$
c. $10ax + 15ae - 16ex$	Prime
d. $18a^5c^6 - 27a^3c^8$	$9a^3c^6(2a^2 - 3c^2)$
e. $25a^4b^7c^9 - 75a^8b^9c^{10}$	$25a^4b^7c^9(1 - 3a^4b^2c)$
f. $a^4b^5 + a^7b - ab$	$ab(a^3b^4 + a^6 - 1)$
g. $9 - x^2$	$(3 + x)(3 - x)$
h. $x^4 - 36y^2$	$(x^2 + 6y)(x^2 - 6y)$
i. $2x^3 - 98x$	$2x(x + 7)(x - 7)$
j. $a^4 - 81b^2$	$(a^2 + 9b)(a^2 - 9b)$
k. $x^2 - 49$	$(x + 7)(x - 7)$
l. $5z^2 - 25$	$5(z^2 - 5)$
m. $a^4 - c^8$	$(a^2 + c^4)(a + c^2)(a - c^2)$
n. $2a^9 - 32a$	$2a(a^4 + 4)(a^2 + 2)(a^2 - 2)$

(Q) Let's do some exercises.

Exercise 6: $8x + 6y = 30$. Then $20x + 15y =$

A. 15   D. 75

B. 30   E. 150

C. 60

Exercise 7: $x^2 - 4 = 47 \times 43; x =$

       A. 41   **D.** 47

       B. 43   **E.** 49

       C. 45

 Let's look at the answers.

Answer 6:   **D:** $8x + 6y = 2(4x + 3y) = 30$; so $4x + 3y = 15$. $20x + 15y = 5(4x + 3y)$ $= 5 \times 15 = 75$.

Answer 7:   **C:** $x^2 - 4 = (x + 2)(x - 2) = 47 \times 43$, or $(45 + 2)(45 - 2)$. So $x = 45$.

Later in this chapter and in later chapters, we will see more ACT comparison questions. For now, let's do trinomial factoring.

Factoring Trinomials

Factoring trinomials is a puzzle, a game, which is rarely done well in high school and even more rarely practiced. Let's learn the factoring game.

First, let's rewrite the first four parts of Example 5 backward and look at them.

a. $x^2 + 11x + 28 = (x + 7)(x + 4)$

b. $x^2 - 7x + 10 = (x - 5)(x - 2)$

c. $x^2 + 3x - 18 = (x + 6)(x - 3)$

d. $x^2 - 2x - 48 = (x + 6)(x - 8)$

Each term starts with x^2 ($= +1x^2$), so the first sign is $+$. We'll call the sign in front of the x term the middle sign, and we'll call the sign in front of the number term the last sign.

Let's look at **a** and **b** above to state some rules of the game:

1. If the last sign (in the trinomial) is $+$, then both signs (in the parentheses) must be the same. The reason? $(+) \times (+) = +$, and $(-) \times (-) = +$.

2. Only if the last sign is $+$, look at the sign of the middle term. If it is $+$, both factors have a $+$ sign (as in a); if it is $-$, both factors have a $-$ sign (as in b).

3. If the last sign is $-$, the signs in the two factors must be different (See c and d.).

Now, let's play the game,

Example 10: Factor: $x^2 - 16x + 15$.

Solution:
1. The last sign $+$ means both signs are the same. The middle sign $-$ means both are $-$.

2. The only factors of x^2 are $(x)(x)$. Look at the number term 15. The factors of 15 are $(3)(5)$ and $(1)(15)$. So $(x - 5)(x - 3)$ and $(x - 15)(x - 1)$ are the only possibilities. We have chosen the first and last terms to be correct, so we only do the middle term. The first, $-8x$, is wrong; the second, $-16x$, is correct.

3. The answer is $(x - 15)(x - 1)$. If neither worked, the trinomial couldn't be factored.

Example 11: Factor completely: $x^2 - 4x - 21$.

Solution:
1. The last sign negative means the signs of the factors are different.

2. $x^2 = x(x)$ and the factors of 21 are 7 and 3 or 21 and 1. We want the pair that totals the middle number (-4), so -7 and 3 are correct. Note that the larger factor (7) gets the minus sign because the middle number is negative.

3. The answer is $(x - 7)(x + 3)$.

Note *If you multiply the inner and outer terms and get the right number but the wrong sign, both signs in the parentheses must be changed.*

The game gets more complicated if the coefficient of x^2 is not 1.

Example 12: Factor completely: $4x^2 + 4x - 15$.

Solution:
1. The last sign is $-$, so the signs of the factors must be different.

2. The factors of $4x^2$ are $(4x)(x)$ or $(2x)(2x)$.

3. The factors of 15 are 3 and 5, or 1 and 15. Let's write out all the possibilities and the resulting middle terms. We are looking for terms whose difference is $4x$.

   $(4x \quad 3)(x \quad 5)$; middle terms are $3x$ and $20x$, no way to get $4x$.

   $(4x \quad 5)(x \quad 3)$; middle terms are $5x$ and $12x$, and again, there is no way to get $4x$.

   $(4x \quad 15)(x \quad 1)$; middle terms are $15x$ and $4x$, wrong!

(4x   1)(x   15); middle terms are 1x and 60x, the next county.

(2x   1)(2x   15); middle terms are 2x and 30x, wrong again!

(2x   3) (2x   5); middle terms are 6x and 10x, correct, whew!

4. The minus sign goes in front of the 3 and the plus sign goes in front of the 5 to get the middle coefficent of +4, so the answer is $(2x - 3)(2x + 5)$.

Example 13: Factor completely: $3x^2 + 15x + 12$.

Solution: Take out the common factor first.

$3x^2 + 15x + 12 = 3(x^2 + 5x + 4) = 3(x + 4)(x + 1)$.

Example 14. Factor completely; coefficients may be integers only.

Problem	Solution
a. $x^2 + 11x + 24$	$(x + 3)(x + 8)$
b. $x^2 - 11x - 12$	$(x - 12)(x + 1)$
c. $x^2 + 5x - 6$	$(x + 6)(x - 1)$
d. $x^2 - 20x + 100$	$(x - 10)^2$
e. $x^2 - x - 2$	$(x - 2)(x + 1)$
f. $x^2 - 15x + 56$	$(x - 7)(x - 8)$
g. $x^2 + 8x + 16$	$(x + 4)^2$
h. $x^2 - 6x - 16$	$(x - 8)(x + 2)$
i. $x^2 - 17x + 42$	$(x - 14)(x - 3)$
j. $x^2 + 5xy + 6y^2$	$(x + 2y)(x + 3y)$
k. $3x^2 - 6x - 9$	$3(x - 3)(x + 1)$
l. $4x^2 + 16x - 20$	$4(x + 5)(x - 1)$
m. $x^3 - 12x^2 + 35x$	$x(x - 7)(x - 5)$

n. $2x^8 + 8x^7 + 6x^6$ $2x^6(x + 3)(x + 1)$

o. $x^4 - 10x^2 + 9$ $(x + 3)(x - 3)(x + 1)(x - 1)$

p. $x^4 - 8x^2 - 9$ $(x^2 + 1)(x + 3)(x - 3)$

q. $2x^2 - 5x + 3$ $(2x - 3)(x - 1)$

r. $2x^2 + 5x - 3$ $(2x - 1)(x + 3)$

s. $5x^2 - 11x + 2$ $(5x - 1)(x - 2)$

t. $9x^2 + 21x - 8$ $(3x + 8)(3x - 1)$

u. $3x^2 - 8x - 3$ $(3x + 1)(x - 3)$

v. $6x^2 - 13x + 6$ $(3x - 2)(2x - 3)$

w. $6x^2 + 35x - 6$ $(6x - 1)(x + 6)$

x. $9x^2 + 71x - 8$ $(9x - 1)(x + 8)$

y. $9x^4 + 24x^3 + 12x^2$ $3x^2(3x + 2)(x + 2)$

Ⓠ   Let's do a couple of exercises.

Exercise 8:   If $x^2 + 5x + 4 = 27$, then $3(x + 1)(x + 4) =$

A. 9   D. 81

B. 24   E. 243

C. 30

Exercise 9:   If $(x - 6)$ is a factor of $x^2 + kx - 48$, $k =$

A. -288 D. 2

B. -14 E. 14

C. -2

Let's look at the answers.

Answer 8:   D: $x^2 + 5x + 4 = (x + 1)(x + 4) = 27$; $3(x + 1)(x + 4) = 3(27) = 81$.

Answer 9:   D: $(-6)(?) = -48$; $? = 8$; $8 + (-6) = 2 = k$. To check, $(x - 6)(x + 8) = x^2 + 2x - 48$.

Again, later on, we will present more problems involving trinomial factoring.

ALGEBRAIC FRACTIONS

Except for adding and subtracting, the techniques for algebraic fractions are easy to understand. They must be practiced, however.

Reducing Fractions

Factor the top and bottom; cancel factors that are the same.

Example 15:   Reduce the following fractions:

<u>Problem</u>	<u>Solution</u>
a. $\dfrac{x^2 - 9}{x^2 - 3x}$	$\dfrac{(x + 3)(x - 3)}{x(x - 3)} = \dfrac{x + 3}{x}$
b. $\dfrac{2x^3 + 10x^2 + 8x}{x^4 + x^3}$	$\dfrac{2x(x + 4)(x + 1)}{x^3(x + 1)} = \dfrac{2(x + 4)}{x^2}$
c. $\dfrac{x - 9}{9 - x}$	$\dfrac{(x - 9)}{-1(x - 9)} = -1$

 Let's do a few more exercises.

Exercise 10: $\dfrac{16x + 4}{4} =$

A. $4x$

B. $4x + 1$

C. $12x$

D. $12x + 1$

E. $16x + 1$

Exercise 11: $\dfrac{x^2 - 16}{x - 4} =$

A. $x + 4$
B. $x - 4$
C. $2x + 4$
D. $2x - 4$
E. $x^2 - x - 12$

Exercise 12: $\dfrac{2x^2 + 10x + 12}{2x + 6} =$

A. x
B. $x + 1$
C. $x + 2$
D. $11x + 2$
E. $11x + 6$

A Let's look at the answers.

Answer 10: B: $\dfrac{16x + 4}{4} = \dfrac{4(4x + 1)}{4} = 4x + 1$. Another way to do this problem is

$$\dfrac{16x + 4}{4} = \dfrac{16x}{4} + \dfrac{4}{4} = 4x + 1.$$

Answer 11: A: $\dfrac{(x + 4)(x - 4)}{x - 4} = x + 4.$

Answer 12: C: $\dfrac{2(x + 2)(x + 3)}{2(x + 3)} = \dfrac{2(x + 2)}{2} = x + 2.$

Multiplication and Division of Fractions

Algebraic fractions use the same principles as multiplication and division of numerical fractions except we factor all tops and bottoms, canceling one factor in any top with its equivalent in any bottom. In a division problem, we must remember to invert the second fraction first and then multiply.

Example 16: $\dfrac{x^2 - 25}{(x + 5)^3} \times \dfrac{x^3 + x^2}{x^2 - 4x - 5} =$

Solution: $\dfrac{(x + 5)(x - 5)}{(x + 5)(x + 5)(x + 5)} \times \dfrac{x^2(x + 1)}{(x - 5)(x + 1)} = \dfrac{x^2}{(x + 5)^2}$

Example 17: $\dfrac{x^4 + 4x^2}{x^6} \div \dfrac{x^4 - 16}{x^2 + 3x - 10} =$

Solution: $\dfrac{x^2(x^2 + 4)}{x^6} \times \dfrac{(x + 5)(x - 2)}{(x^2 + 4)(x - 2)(x + 2)} = \dfrac{x + 5}{x^4(x + 2)}$

Adding and Subtracting Algebraic Fractions

It might be time to review the section in Chapter 2 on adding and subtracting fractions. Follow these steps:

1. If the bottoms are the same, add the tops, reducing if necessary.

2. If the bottoms are different, factor the denominators.

3. The LCD is the product of the most number of times a prime appears in any one denominator.

4. Multiply top and bottom by "what's missing."

5. Add (subtract) and simplify the numerators; reduce, if possible.

Example 18: $\dfrac{x}{36 - x^2} - \dfrac{6}{36 - x^2} =$

Solution: $\dfrac{x - 6}{36 - x^2} = \dfrac{x - 6}{(6 - x)(6 + x)} = \dfrac{-1}{x + 6}$

Example 19: $\dfrac{5}{12xy^3} + \dfrac{9}{8x^2y} =$

Solution: $\dfrac{5}{2 \times 2 \times 3xyyy} + \dfrac{9}{2 \times 2 \times 2xxy}$

$= \dfrac{5(2x)}{2 \times 2 \times 2 \times 3xxyyy} + \dfrac{9(3yy)}{2 \times 2 \times 2 \times 3xxyyy} = \dfrac{10x + 27y^2}{24x^2y^3}$

Example 20: $\dfrac{2}{x^2 + 4x + 4} + \dfrac{3}{x^2 + 5x + 6} =$

Solution: $\dfrac{2}{(x + 2)(x + 2)} + \dfrac{3}{(x + 2)(x + 3)}$

$= \dfrac{2(x + 3)}{(x + 2)(x + 2)(x + 3)} + \dfrac{3(x + 2)}{(x + 2)(x + 3)(x + 2)} = \dfrac{5x + 12}{(x + 2)(x + 2)(x + 3)}$

Simplifying Complex Fractions

The ACT seems to like questions about complex fractions, but mostly with numbers.

Example 21: Simplify $\dfrac{2 - \frac{5}{6}}{\frac{2}{3} + \frac{7}{8}}$.

Solution: Find the LCD of all the terms (24) and multiply each term by it.

$$\frac{\frac{2}{1} \times \frac{24}{1} - \frac{5}{6} \times \frac{24}{1}}{\frac{2}{3} \times \frac{24}{1} + \frac{7}{8} \times \frac{24}{1}} = \frac{48 - 20}{16 + 21} = \frac{28}{37}$$

Note   *When you multiply each term by 24, all the fractions disappear except for the major one.*

Example 22: Simplify $\dfrac{1 - \frac{25}{x^2}}{1 - \frac{10}{x} + \frac{25}{x^2}}$.

Solution: The LCD is x^2.

$$\frac{x^2\left(1 - \frac{25}{x^2}\right)}{x^2\left(1 - \frac{10}{x} + \frac{25}{x^2}\right)} = \frac{x^2 - 25}{x^2 - 10x + 25} = \frac{(x+5)(x-5)}{(x-5)(x-5)} = \frac{x+5}{(x-5)}$$

Q   **Let's do some more exercises.**

Exercise 13: The reciprocal of $2 - \dfrac{1}{4}$ is

    A. $\dfrac{1}{2} - 4$ D. $\dfrac{4}{9}$

    B. $-\dfrac{4}{7}$ E. $\dfrac{4}{7}$

    C. $-\dfrac{4}{9}$

Exercise 14: $y = \dfrac{1}{x}$. Then $\dfrac{1-x}{1-y} =$

    A. $-x$ D. $(1-x)$

    B. x E. $(x-1)$

    C. 1

Exercise 15: $\dfrac{2\frac{1}{5} + \frac{3}{5}}{2\frac{1}{5} - \frac{3}{5}} =$

    A. -1 **D.** $\dfrac{7}{4}$

    B. 1 **E.** $\dfrac{14}{5}$

    C. $\dfrac{7}{5}$

 Let's look at the answers.

Answer 13: E: $2 - \dfrac{1}{4} = \dfrac{7}{4}$. Its reciprocal is $\dfrac{4}{7}$.

Answer 14: A: $\dfrac{1-x}{1-y} = \dfrac{1-x}{1-\frac{1}{x}} = \dfrac{x(1-x)}{x(1-\frac{1}{x})} = \dfrac{x(1-x)}{x-1} = -x$. The answer is A because

$$\dfrac{1-x}{x-1} = -1.$$

Answer 15: D: The top is $\dfrac{11}{5} + \dfrac{3}{5} = \dfrac{14}{5}$; the bottom is $\dfrac{11}{5} - \dfrac{3}{5} = \dfrac{8}{5}$. So the fraction

simplifies to $\dfrac{\frac{14}{5}}{\frac{8}{5}}$; the 5's cancel, and $\dfrac{14}{8} = \dfrac{7}{4}$.

SHORT AND LONG DIVISION

Short division is the opposite of adding fractions with like denominators.
In symbols, for example, $\dfrac{a+b-c}{d} = \dfrac{a}{d} + \dfrac{b}{d} - \dfrac{c}{d}$, where d is a single term, a monomial.

Example 23: Problem　　　　　　　　　Solution

    a. $\dfrac{12x - 18}{6}$ $2x - 3$

    b. $\dfrac{8x^{10} - 12x^8 - 20x^7}{4x^4}$ $2x^6 - 3x^4 - 5x^3$

    c. $\dfrac{abc - abd - ab}{ab}$ $c - d - 1$

For completeness we will do algebraic long division. First, let's review long division with numbers.

Suppose we have $6\sqrt{2371}$. How would we do this problem?

1. Divide 6 into 23 and get 3.

2. $3 \times 6 = 18$.

3. $23 - 18 = 5$.

4. Bring down the 7 to get 57. Repeat.

5. Divide 6 into 57 and get 9.

6. $9 \times 6 = 54$.

7. $57 - 54 = 3$.

8. Bring down the 1 to get 31. Repeat.

9. Divide 6 into 31 and get 5.

10. $5 \times 6 = 30$.

11. $31 - 30 = 1$. The remainder is 1.

12. The answer is $395\frac{1}{6}$.

$$
\begin{array}{r}
395\ \frac{1}{6} \\
6\overline{)\ 2371} \\
\underline{18} \\
57 \\
\underline{54} \\
31 \\
\underline{30} \\
1
\end{array}
$$

Note *The 6 is called the **divisor**; 2371 is called the **dividend**; $395\frac{1}{6}$ is called the **quotient**.*

The procedure for **algebraic long division** is the same.

Example 24: Divide $4x^3 - 2x^2 + 8x - 11$ by $2x - 4$

$$
\begin{array}{r}
29 \\
2x^2 + 3x + 10 + \overline{2x - 4} \quad x \neq 2 \\
2x - 4\overline{)\ 4x^3 - 2x^2 + 8x - 11} \\
\underline{\overset{-}{\oplus}\,4x^3\,\overset{+}{\ominus}\,8x^2} \\
6x^2 + 8x \\
\underline{\overset{-}{\oplus}\,6x^2\,\overset{+}{\ominus}\,12x} \\
20x - 11 \\
\underline{\overset{-}{\oplus}\,20x\,\overset{+}{\ominus}\,40} \\
29
\end{array}
$$

Solution:

1. If the divisor and/or the dividend are not arranged from the highest exponent to the lowest, rearrange the terms. In this problem they are already arranged highest to lowest.

2. Divide the highest power term of the divisor into the highest power term of the dividend. $\dfrac{4x^3}{2x} = 2x^2$.

3. Multiply $2x^2$ by the entire divisor: $2x^2(2x - 4) = 4x^3 - 8x^2$.

4. Subtract: $4x^3 - 2x^2 + 80 - 11 - (4x^3 - 8x^2) = 6x^2 + 8x - 11$. Repeat.

Note *We have already brought down the next term.*

The first terms must cancel; otherwise, there is a mistake.

5. $\dfrac{6x^2}{2x} = 3x$; $3x(2x - 4) = 6x^2 - 12x$; $6x^2 + 8x - 11 - (6x^2 - 12x)$
   $= 20x - 11$. Repeat.

6. $\dfrac{20x}{2x} = 10$; $10(2x - 4) = 20x - 40$; $20x - 11 - (20x - 40) = 29$;
   the remainder is 29.

7. The final answer is $2x^2 + 3x + 10 + \dfrac{29}{2x - 4}$; $x \neq 2$ because you
   cannot divide by 0.

Although the problem could be a lot messier in several ways, this is as much (or more) than you need for the ACT.

 If the remainder had been 0 in this problem, that would have meant $2x - 4$ would have been a factor of the original polynomial.

Let's go on to equations.

CHAPTER 6: *Equations and Inequalities*

"*The equations here are the equations for life. Master them, and it will bring you joy.*"

FIRST-DEGREE EQUATIONS

In high school, the topic of first-degree equations was probably the most popular of all. The ACT asks questions that are usually not too long and usually not too tricky. To review, here are the steps to solving first-degree equations. If you get good at these, you will know when to use the steps in another order.

To solve for *x*, follow these steps (believe it or not, it took a long time to get the phrasing of this list just right):

1. Multiply by the LCD to get rid of fractions. Cross-multiply if there are only two fractions.

2. If the "*x*" term appears only on the right, switch the sides.

3. Multiply out all parentheses by using the distributive law.

4. On each side, combine like terms.

5. Add the opposite of the *x* term on the right to each side.

6. Add the opposite of the non-*x* term(s) on the left to each side.

7. Factor out the *x*. This step occurs only if there is more than one letter in a problem.

8. Divide each side by the whole coefficient of *x*, including the sign.

Note *The **opposite** of a term is the same term with its opposite sign. So the opposite of 3x is −3x, the opposite of −7y is + 7y, and the opposite of 0 is 0. The technical name for opposite is **additive inverse**.*

Note *In the following four examples, the step numbers will refer to the list of steps shown above. For each example, several numbered steps may be omitted because they are not needed to find the solution.*

Example 1:   Solve for x: $7x - 2 = 10x + 13$

Solution:

$7x - 2 = 10x + 13$	Step 5: Add $-10x$ to each side.
$-3x - 2 = +13$	Step 6: Add $+2$ to each side.
$-3x = 15$	Step 8: Divide each side by -3.
$x = -5$	Solution

Example 2:   Solve for x: $7 = 2(3x - 5) - 4(x - 6)$

Solution:

$7 = 2(3x - 5) - 4(x - 6)$	Step 2: Switch sides.
$2(3x - 5) - 4(x - 6) = 7$	Step 3: Multiply out the parentheses.
$6x - 10 - 4x + 24 = 7$	Step 4: Combine like terms on each side.
$2x + 14 = 7$	Step 6: Add -14 to each side.
$2x = -7$	Step 8: Divide each side by 2.
$x = -\dfrac{7}{2}$	The answer doesn't have to be an integer.

Example 3:   Solve for x: $\dfrac{x}{4} + \dfrac{x}{6} = 1$

Solution:

$\dfrac{x}{4} + \dfrac{x}{6} = 1$	Step 1: Multiply each term by 12.
$3x + 2x = 12$	Step 4: Combine like terms.
$5x = 12$	Step 8: Divide each side by 5.
$x = \dfrac{12}{5}$	Solution

Example 4:   Solve for x: $y = \dfrac{3x - 5}{x - 7}$

Solution: Write $y = \dfrac{y}{1}$: $\dfrac{y}{1} = \dfrac{3x - 5}{x - 7}$ Step 1: Cross-multiply.

$(x - 7)y = 1(3x - 5)$ Step 3: Distribute.

$xy - 7y = 3x - 5$ Step 5: Add $-3x$ to each side.

$xy - 3x - 7y = -5$ Step 6: Add $7y$ to each side.

$xy - 3x = 7y - 5$ Step 7: Factor out the x from the left.

$x(y - 3) = 7y - 5$ Step 8: Divide each side by $y - 3$.

$x = \dfrac{7y - 5}{y - 3}$

Ⓠ Let's do some ACT-type exercises.

Exercise 1: $2x - 6 = 4$; $x + 3 =$

A. 5   D. 8

B. 6   E. 9

C. 7

Exercise 2: $x - 9 = 9 - x$; $x =$

A. 0   D. 13.5

B. 4.5   E. 18

C. 9

Exercise 3: $4x - 17 = 32$; $12x - 51 =$

A. $12\dfrac{1}{4}$ D. 96

B. $36\dfrac{3}{4}$ E. 288

C. 64

Exercise 4: $\dfrac{xy}{y-x} = 1; x =$

A. $\dfrac{1}{2}$ D. $\dfrac{y}{y-1}$

B. 1 E. $\dfrac{y}{1-y}$

C. $\dfrac{y}{y+1}$

 Let's look at the answers.

Answer 1:   **D:** $x = 5$, but the question asks for $x + 3 = 8$. *Note:* Tests such as the ACT often ask for $x +$ something instead of just x. Be careful—give what the test asks for.

Answer 2:   **C:** $2x = 18$; $x = 9$. The answer is C. It actually can be solved just by looking because $9 - 9 = 9 - 9$ (or $0 = 0$).

Answer 3:   **D:** We do not solve this equation. We recognize that $12x - 51 = 3(4x - 17) = 3(32) = 96$.

Answer 4:   **C:** By cross-multiplying, we get $xy = y - x$. Then $xy + x = y$, which factors to $x(y + 1) = y$. Therefore, $x = \dfrac{y}{y+1}$.

The ACT does ask questions like Exercise 4. I know I keep mentioning it, but you must be able to do this without paper and pencil.

LINEAR INEQUALITIES

To review some facts about inequalities:

$a < b$ (read, "a is less than b") means a is to the left of b on the number line.

$a > b$ (read, "a is greater than b") means a is to the right of b on the number line.

$x > y$ is the same as $y < x$.

The notation $x \geq y$ (read, "x is greater than or equal to y") means $x > y$ or $x = y$.

Similarly, $x \leq y$ (read, "x is less than or equal to y"), means $x < y$ or $x = y$.

We solve linear inequalities ($<$, $>$, $\leq$, $\geq$) the same way we solve linear equalities, except when we multiply or divide by a negative, the order reverses.

Example 5:   Solve for x: $6x + 2 < 3x + 10$

Solution: $3x < 8$, so $x < \dfrac{8}{3}$. The inequality does not switch because both sides are divided by a positive number (3).

Example 6:   Solve for x: $-2(x - 3) \leq 4x - 3 - 7$

Solution: $-2x + 6 \leq 4x - 10$, or $-6x \leq -16$. Thus, $x \geq \dfrac{-16}{-6} = \dfrac{8}{3}$. Here the inequality switches because we divided both sides by a negative number (-6).

Example 7:   Solve for x: $8 > \dfrac{x - 2}{-3} \geq 5$

Solution: We multiply through by -3, and both inequalities switch. We get $-24 < x - 2 \leq -15$. If we add 2 to each part to get a value for x alone, the final answer is $-22 < x \leq -13$.

(Q)   **Now, let's do some more exercises.**

Exercise 5:   If $3x + 4 > 17$, $3x + 7 >$

A. $\dfrac{13}{3}$ D. 17

B. $\dfrac{22}{3}$ E. 20

C. 14

Exercise 6:   If $3x + 4y < 5$, $x <$

A. $5 - 4y - 3$ D. $\dfrac{5 - 4y}{3}$

B. $\dfrac{5}{4}y - 3$ E. $\dfrac{5}{3} - 4y$

C. $\dfrac{5}{12}y$

Exercise 7: $x > 0$ and $y > 0$. The number of ordered pairs of whole numbers (x, y) such that $2x + 3y < 9$ is

A. 1   D. 4

B. 2   E. 5

C. 3

 Let's look at the answers.

Answer 5:   E: We don't actually have to solve this one. $3x + 7 = (3x + 4) + 3 > 17 + 3$, or 20.

Answer 6:   D: $3x + 4y < 5$ is the same as $3x < 5 - 4y$. Dividing by 3, we get $\dfrac{5 - 4y}{3}$.

Answer 7:   C: We must substitute numbers. (1, 1) is okay because $2(1) + 3(1) < 9$; (2, 1) is okay because $2(2) + 3(1) < 9$; (1, 2) is okay because $2(1) + 3(2) < 9$; and that's all.

We will do more on ordered pairs later in the book. As we have seen already, some questions overlap more than one topic.

ABSOLUTE VALUE EQUALITIES

Absolute value is the magnitude, without regard to sign. You should know the following facts about absolute value:

$|3| = 3, |-7| = 7$, and $|0| = 0$

$|u| = 6$ means that $u = 6$ or -6.

$|u| = 0$ always means $u = 0$.

$|u| = -17$ has no solutions because the absolute value is never negative.

Example 8:   Solve for x: $|2x - 5| = 7$

Solution: Either $2x - 5 = 7$ or $2x - 5 = -7$. So $x = 6$ or $x = -1$.

Note   *This kind of problem always has two answers.*

Example 9:   Solve for x: $|5x + 11| = 0$.

Solution: $5x + 11 = 0$; $x = -\dfrac{11}{5}$.

Note   *This type of problem (absolute value equals 0) always has one answer.*

Those of you with some math background know there is a lot more to absolute value. This section and the next, however, are all you need for the ACT.

Q   **Let's do a few more exercises.**

Exercise 8: $|2x + 1| = |x + 5|$; $x =$

A. -2

D. 4 and -2

B. 0

E. 0 and 4

C. 4

Exercise 9: $|x - y| = |y - x|$. This statement is true

A. for no values

D. only for all integers

B. only if $x = y = 0$

E. for all real numbers

C. only if $x = y$

Exercise 10:   If $4|2x + 3| = 11$, $8|2x + 3| + 5 =$

A. $\dfrac{11}{4}$

D. 27

B. $\dfrac{31}{4}$

E. 110

C. 22

A   **Let's look at the answers.**

Answer 8:   D: $2x + 1 = x + 5$ or $2x + 1 = -(x + 5)$, for which the answers are 4 and -2, respectively.

Answer 9:   E: For example, if $x = 3$ and $y = -2$, $|3 - (-2)| = |-2-3| = 5$.

Answer 10:   D: We don't have to solve this for x at all. If $4|2x + 3| = 11$, then $8|2x + 3| = 2(11) = 22$. Adding 5, we get 27.

ABSOLUTE VALUE INEQUALITIES

If we talk about integers $|u| \leq 3$, we have $|u| = -3, -2, -1, 0, 1, 2,$ and 3. So $|u| \leq a$ means $-a \leq u \leq a$, where $a > 0$.

Example 10: Solve for x: $|2x - 3| < 11$

Solution: $-11 < 2x - 3 < 11$. Adding 3 to each piece means $-8 < 2x < 14$. Dividing by 2 gives $-4 < x < 7$.

If we talk about integers $|u| \geq 4$, we have $u = 4, 5, 6, \ldots$ and $-4, -5, -6, \ldots$. So $|u| \geq a$ means $u \geq a$ or $u \leq -a, a > 0$.

Example 11: Solve for x: $|x - 7| > 4$.

Solution: $x - 7 > 4$ or $x - 7 < -4$. The two parts of the answer are $x > 11$ or $x < 3$.

Ⓠ **Let's do some more exercises:**

Exercise 11: If $5 \leq |x| \leq 5$, $x =$

        A. 0   **D.** no values

        B. 5   **E.** all values

        C. −5 and 5

Exercise 12: $|x - 5| \geq -5$ if $x =$

        A. 0   **D.** no values

        B. 5   **E.** all values

        C. −5 and 5

Exercise 13: $|x + 5| \leq -5$ if $x =$

        A. 0   **D.** no values

        B. 5   **E.** all values

        C. −5 and 5

Let's look at the answers.

Answer 11:   C: Both $|-5|$ and $|5|$ equal 5.

Answer 12:   E: The absolute value is always greater than any negative number because it is always greater than or equal to zero.

Answer 13:   D: The absolute value can't be less than a negative number.

QUADRATIC EQUATIONS

Quadratic equations, equations involving the square of the variable, can be solved in three principal ways: factoring, taking the square root, and using the quadratic formula. Another name for the solution of any equation is a **root**.

Solving Quadratics by Factoring

Solving quadratic equations by factoring is based on the fact that if $a \times b = 0$, then either $a = 0$ or $b = 0$.

Example 12:   Solve for all values of x: $x(x - 3)(x + 7)(2x + 1)(3x - 5)(ax + b)(cx - d) = 0$.

Solution: Setting each factor equal to 0 (better if you can do it just by looking), we get $x = 0, 3, -7, -\dfrac{1}{2}, \dfrac{5}{3}, -\dfrac{b}{a}$, and $\dfrac{d}{c}$.

Solving Quadratics by Taking the Square Root

If the equation is of the form $x^2 = c$, with no x term, we just take the square root: $x = \pm\sqrt{c}$.

 Remember that $\sqrt{9} = 3$, $-\sqrt{9} = -3$, $\sqrt{-9}$ is not real, and if $x^2 = 9$, then $x = \pm 3$!

Example 13:   Solve for all values of x:

a. $x^2 - 7 = 0$

b. $ax^2 - b = c$, where $a, b, c > 0$.

Solutions: a. $x^2 = 7$; $x = \pm\sqrt{7}$

b. $ax^2 = b + c$; $x^2 = \dfrac{b + c}{a}$, so $x = \pm\sqrt{\dfrac{b + c}{a}}$, or $\pm\dfrac{\sqrt{a(b + c)}}{a}$

Q **Let's do some more exercises:**

Exercise 14: The solutions to $x^2 - 3x - 4 = -6$ are

    A. $x = 4$ and $x = -1$ **D.** $x = 1$ and $x = 2$

    B. $x = 4$ and $x = 1$ **E.** $x = 5$ and $x = -2$

    C. $x = 1$ and $x = -1$

Exercise 15: If $x = 6$ and $x = -9$ are the answers to a quadratic equation, the original quadratic equation is

    A. $x^2 + 15x - 54 = 0$ **D.** $x^2 + 3x - 54 = 0$

    B. $x^2 - 15x - 54 = 0$ **E.** $x^2 - 54x + 54 = 0$

    C. $x^2 - 3x - 54 = 0$

Exercise 16: $x = 2a$ and $x = -5b$ are solutions to a quadratic equation. The quadratic equation is

    A. $x^2 - 2ab - 10ab = 0$ **D.** $x^2 - (2a - 5b)x - 10ab = 0$

    B. $x^2 + 2ab - 10ab = 0$ **E.** $x^2 + (2x - 5b)x + 10ab = 0$

    C. $x^2 + (2a - 5b)x - 10ab = 0$

 Let's look at the answers.

Answer 14: **D:** Add 6 to both sides and factor to get $x^2 - 3x + 2 = (x - 2)(x - 1) = 0$. Then set each factor equal to 0.

Answer 15: **D:** If 6 is a solution, $(x - 6)$ is a factor, and if -9 is a solution, $(x + 9)$ is a factor. So $(x - 6)(x + 9) = x^2 + 3x - 54 = 0$.

Answer 16: **D:** $(x - 2a)(x + 5b) = x^2 - 2ax + 5bx - 10ab = x^2 - (2a - 5b)x - 10ab = 0$.

Solving Quadratics by Using the Quadratic Formula

The quadratic formula states that if $ax^2 + bx + c = 0$, then

$$x = \frac{-b \pm \sqrt{b^2 - 4ac}}{2a},$$

where a is the coefficient of the x^2 term, b is the coefficient of the x term, and c is the number term.

Example 14: Solve $3x^2 - 5x + 2 = 0$ by using the quadratic formula.

Solution: $a = 3, b = -5, c = 2.$ $x = \dfrac{-(-5) \pm \sqrt{(-5)^2 - 4(3)(2)}}{2(3)} = \dfrac{5 \pm 1}{6}. x_1$ (read

as "x sub one," the first answer) $= \dfrac{5 + 1}{6} = 1; x_2$ (read, "x sub two," the

second answer) $= \dfrac{5 - 1}{6} = \dfrac{2}{3}.$

Example 15: Solve $3x^2 - 5x + 2 = 0$ by factoring.

Solution: This is the same problem as Example 14. $3x^2 - 5x + 2 = (3x - 2)(x - 1)$
$= 0,$ so $x = \dfrac{2}{3}$ or $1.$

Factoring is preferred; using the quadratic formula takes too long.

Before we go to the next set of exercises, I suppose most of you know the quadratic formula, but few have seen it shown to be true. The teacher in me has to show you, even if you don't care.

$ax^2 + bx + c = 0$ — The coefficient of x^2 must be 1.

$x^2 + \dfrac{b}{a}x = -\dfrac{c}{a}$ — Complete the square; this means taking half the coefficient of x, squaring it, and adding it to both sides.

$x^2 + \dfrac{b}{a}x + \left(\dfrac{b}{2a}\right)^2 = \left(\dfrac{b}{2a}\right)^2 - \dfrac{c}{a}$ — Factor the left side and do the algebra on the right side.

$\left(x + \dfrac{b}{2a}\right)^2 = \dfrac{b^2}{4a^2} - \dfrac{c(4a)}{a(4a)} = \dfrac{b^2 - 4ac}{4a^2}$ — Multiply the last term by $\dfrac{4a}{4a}$ and combine terms.

$\left(x + \dfrac{b}{2a}\right)^2 = \dfrac{b^2}{4a^2} - \dfrac{4ac}{4a^2} = \dfrac{b^2 - 4ac}{4a^2}$ — Take the square root of both sides.

$x + \dfrac{b}{2a} = \dfrac{\pm\sqrt{b^2 - 4ac}}{2a}$ — Solve for x and simplify.

$x = -\dfrac{b}{2a} \pm \dfrac{\sqrt{b^2 - 4ac}}{2a} = \dfrac{-b \pm \sqrt{b^2 - 4ac}}{2a}$

The quadratic formula is really true!

The quadratic equation has been included here for completeness. Quadratics on the ACT can usually be solved by factoring or taking the square root.

Let's go on.

CHAPTER 7: *Problems with Words*

"It is necessary to study the words of math. Only then can you truly understand all."

I consider word problems a most important part of the ACT. Most of the questions on this test will have some kind of words in them, even if they are not "problems with words."

There are some sections that the ACT does not seem to require. They include consecutive integer problems, age problems, and interest problems. However, I feel that the ACT might put in problems concerning these topics, so I included them in this book. Included are other problems the ACT specifically requires: ratio problems, everyday problems (nobody really gets these problems in everyday life), speed (distance) problems, and mixture problems. Finally, I talk a little about measurements.

Let's get going!

BASICS

As we know, the answer in **addition** is the **sum**. Other words that indicate addition are **plus**, **more**, **more than**, **increase**, and **increased by**. You can write all sums in any order because addition is commutative.

The answer in **multiplication** is the **product**. Another word that is used is **times**. Sometimes the word **of** indicates multiplication, as we shall see shortly. **Double** means to multiply by two, and **triple** means to multiply by three. Because multiplication is also commutative, we can write any product in any order.

Division's answer is called the **quotient**. Another phrase that is used is **divided by**.

The answer in **subtraction** is called the **difference**. Subtraction can present a reading problem because $4 - 6 \neq 6 - 4$, so we must be careful to subtract in the correct order. Example 1 shows how some subtraction phrases are translated into algebraic expressions.

Example 1: <u>Phrases</u>   <u>Expressions</u>

    a. The difference between 9 and 5 $9 - 5$

        The difference between m and n $m - n$

    b. Five minus two $5 - 2$

        m minus n $m - n$

    c. Seven decreased by three $7 - 3$

        m decreased by n $m - n$

    d. Nine diminished by four $9 - 4$

        m diminished by n $m - n$

    e. Ten less two $10 - 2$

        m less n $m - n$

    f. Ten less than two $2 - 10$

        m less than n $n - m$

    g. Three from five $5 - 3$

        m from n $n - m$

 One word can make a big difference. In parts e and f of Example 1, m less n means m − n; and m less than n means n − m. In addition, m is less than n means m < n. You must read carefully!

The following words usually indicate an equal sign: *is, am, are, was, were, the same as, equal to.*

You also must know the following phrases for inequalities: at least ($\geq$), not more than ($\leq$), over ($>$), and under ($<$).

Example 2: Write the following in symbols:

Problem	Solution
a. m times the sum of q and r	$m(q + r)$
b. Six less the product of x and y	$6 - xy$
c. The difference between c and d divided by f	$\dfrac{c - d}{f}$
d. b less than the quotient of r divided by s	$\dfrac{r}{s} - b$
e. The sum of d and g is the same as the product of h and r	$d + g = hr$
f. x is at least y	$x \geq y$
g. Zeb's age n is not more than 21	$n \leq 21$
h. I am over 30 years old, where "I" represents "my age."	$I > 30$
i. Most people are under seven feet tall, where "p" represents "most people"	$p < 7$

COMMON AND EVERYDAY PROBLEMS

Example 3: In spring at a recent school board election, Ms. Johnson received 50 more votes than Ms. Smith for president of the school board. If 892 votes were cast, how many votes did each get?

Solution: In most problems, it is better to let $x =$ the smaller number—in this case Ms. Smith's vote total. Ms. Johnson received $x + 50$ votes. Then $x + (x + 50) = 892$; $2x = 842$; so $x = 421$, the number of Ms. Smith's votes. Ms. Johnson received $421 + 50 = 471$ votes.

Example 4:   Two numbers total 40. The sum of twice one of them and triple the other is 105. Find the numbers.

Note   *If two numbers total 40 and one is 11, the other is 40 − 11 (or 29). If two numbers total 40 and one is unknown, x, the other is 40 − x.*

Solution: Let one number $= x$; the other number is $40 - x$. The sum (add) of twice one number, $2x$, and triple the other number, $3(40 - x)$, is 105. The equation is $2x + 3(40 - x) = 105$; $2x + 120 - 3x = 105$; $x = 15$ and, because both numbers were asked for, $40 - x = 40 - 15 = 25$ is the number.

Example 5:   The sum of two numbers is 20. Five times the larger less the smaller is 70. Find the larger number.

Solution: Let $x =$ the number you are looking for—in this case, the larger number. Then $20 - x$ is the smaller number. *Less* means "subtract," so don't change the order. The equation is $5x - (20 - x) = 70$; $6x - 20 = 70$; $x = 15$.

RATIOS

The comparison of two numbers is called a **ratio**. The ratio of 3 to 5 is written two ways: $\frac{3}{5}$ or 3 : 5 (read, "the ratio of 3 to 5").

Example 6:   Find the ratio of 5 ounces to 2 pounds.

Solution: The ratio is $\frac{5}{32}$, because 16 ounces are in a pound, and a ratio should have the same measurements.

Example 7:   A board is cut into two pieces that are in the ratio of 3 to 4. If the board is 56 inches long, how long is the longer piece?

Solution: If the pieces are in the ratio 3 : 4, we let one piece equal $3x$ and the other $4x$. The equation, then, is $3x + 4x = 56$; so $x = 8$; and the longer piece is $4x = 32$ inches.

I have asked this problem many, many times. Almost no one has ever gotten it correct—not because it is difficult, but because no one does problems like this anymore.

CONSECUTIVE INTEGERS

If there are any "fun" word problems, they would have to do with consecutive integers. Let's recall the following facts about integers, most of which you know without having to even think about them: Integers: $-3, -2, -1, 0, 1, 2, 3, 4, \ldots$.

Evens: $-6, -4, -2, 0, 2, 4, 6, 8, \ldots$.

Odds: $-5, -3, -1, 1, 3, 5, 7, \ldots$.

If we let $x =$ an integer, then $x + 1$ represents the next consecutive integer, and $x + 2$ represents the next consecutive integer after that. Then $x + (x + 1) + (x + 2) = 3x + 3$ is the sum of three consecutive integers, where x is the smallest and $x + 2$ is the largest in the group.

If $y =$ an even integer, then $y + 2$ is the next consecutive *even* integer; $y + 4$ and $y + 6$ are the next consecutive even integers after that. Then the sum of four consecutive even integers is $y + (y + 2) + (y + 4) + (y + 6) = 4y + 12$.

Similarly, if z is an odd integer, the next three odd integers are $z + 2$, $z + 4$, and $z + 6$. This is the same as for integers, except we start out letting z be odd instead of even.

Example 8: The sum of three consecutive integers is twice the smallest. What is the smallest integer?

Solution: We have $x + (x + 1) + (x + 2) = 2x$, which simplifies to $3x + 3 = 2x$. So $x = -3$. The integers are -3, -2, and -1; the smallest is -3.

 Integers can be negative!

Most consecutive integer problems are done by using tricks, as the next few examples show.

Example 9: The sum of five consecutive even integers is 210. What is the sum of the smallest two?

Solution: If we have an odd number of consecutive, consecutive even, or consecutive odd integers, the middle number is the average (the mean); So the middle number is given by $\dfrac{210}{5} = 42$. Once we know that, count backward and forward to get the others. The five numbers are 38, 40, 42, 44, and 46. The sum of the two smallest is $38 + 40 = 78$.

Example 10: The sum of four consecutive integers is -50. What is the sum of the two largest?

Solution: Dividing -50 by 4, we get -12.5. The four consecutive integers are the closest integers to -12.5, namely, -14, -13, -12, and -11. The sum of the two largest, -12 and -11, is -23.

AGE

Similar to consecutive integer problems are age problems. We just have to think about them logically.

Example 11: p years ago, Mary was q years old; in r years, she will be how many years old?

Solution: The secret is age now. If Mary was q years old p years ago, now she is $p + q$. Then r years in the future, she will be $p + q + r$. If necessary, substitute numbers for p, q, and r to see how this works.

SPEED

We are familiar with speed being given in miles per hour (mph), so it is easy to remember that $\text{speed} = \dfrac{\text{distance}}{\text{time}}$, or $r = \dfrac{d}{t}$, where r stands for rate (the speed). Use this relationship, or the equivalent ones: $d = rt$ or $t = \dfrac{d}{r}$, to do word problems involving speed.

Example 12: Sue drives for 2 hours at 60 mph and 3 hours at 70 mph. What is her average speed?

Solution: Sue's average speed for the whole trip is given by $r = \dfrac{d}{t}$, where d is the total distance and t is the total time. Note that her average speed is *not* the average of the speeds. Use $d = rt$ for each part of her trip to get the total distance. The total distance is $60(2) + 70(3) = 330$ miles. The total time is 5 hours. So Sue's average speed is $r = \dfrac{330}{5}$ mph $= 66$ mph.

Example 13: Don goes 40 mph in one direction and returns at 60 mph. What is his average speed?

Solution: Notice that the problem doesn't tell the distance. It doesn't have to; the distance in each direction is the same, because it is a round trip.

We can take any distance, so let's choose 120 miles, the LCM of 40 and 60. Then the time going is $\frac{120}{40} = 3$ hours, and the time returning is $\frac{120}{60} = 2$ hours. The average speed is the total distance divided by the total time, $\frac{2(120)}{3+2} = \frac{240}{5} = 48$ mph.

We actually don't have to choose a number for the distance, however. We could use x. Just for learning's sake, we will do this same problem (Example 13) using x as the distance. The time going is $\frac{x}{40}$, and the time returning is $\frac{x}{60}$. Then we have:

$$\text{Total speed} = \frac{\text{total distance}}{\text{total time}} = \frac{2x}{\frac{x}{40} + \frac{x}{60}} = \frac{120(2x)}{120(\frac{x}{40} + \frac{x}{60})} = \frac{240x}{5x} = 48 \text{ mph}$$

Example 14: A plane leaves Indianapolis traveling west. At the same time, a plane traveling 30 mph faster leaves Indianapolis going east. After two hours the planes are 2,000 miles apart. What is the speed of the faster plane?

Solution: A chart and a picture are best for problems like this.

	r	t	d
W	x	2	$2x$
E	$x + 30$	2	$2(x + 30)$

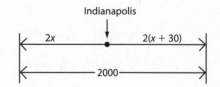

We let $x =$ the speed of the plane going west; then $x + 30$ is the speed of the eastern-going plane. The time for each is 2 hours. Because $rt = d$, the distances are as shown in the above chart. According to the picture, $2x + 2(x + 30) = 2000$. So $x = 485$; $x + 30 = 515$ mph.

The problem is the same if the planes are starting at the ends and flying toward each other.

Let's do some basic exercises.

Exercise 1: Four more than a number is seven less than triple the number. The number is

A. 4   D. 9

B. 5.5   E. 11

C. 7

Note *The word* number *does not necessarily mean an integer or even necessarily a positive number.*

Exercise 2: Mike must have at least an 80 average but less than a 90 average to get a *B*. If he received scores of 98, 92, and 75 on the first three tests, which of these grades on the fourth test will give him a *B*?

A. 42   D. 98

B. 54   E. 100

C. 66

Exercise 3: Nine less than a number is the same as the difference between nine and the number. The number is

A. 18   D. −9

B. 9   E. All numbers are correct.

C. 0

Exercise 4: Seven consecutive odd numbers total −77. The sum of the largest three is

A. −21   D. −39

B. −27   E. −45

C. −33

Exercise 5: For three consecutive integers, the sum of the squares of the first two equals the square of the largest. There are two sets of answers. The sum of all six integers is

A. 0   D. 12

B. 3   E. 24

C. 6

Exercise 6: Ed goes 20 mph in one direction and 50 mph on the return trip. His average speed is

A. 25 mph

B. $27\frac{2}{7}$ mph

C. $28\frac{4}{7}$ mph

D. 30 mph

E. $30\frac{6}{7}$ mph

Exercise 7: The angles of a triangle are in the ratio of 3 : 5 : 7. The largest angle is

A. 12°

B. 36°

C. 60°

D. 84°

E. 108°

Exercise 8: b years in the future, I will be c years old. How old was I six years in the past?

A. $b - c - 6$

B. $c - b - 6$

C. $c - b + 6$

D. $b - c + 6$

E. $b + c - 6$

Exercise 9: The value of d dimes and q quarters in pennies is

A. $d + q$

B. dq

C. $250dq$

D. $10d + 25q$

E. $35dq$

Exercise 10: A car leaves Chicago at 2 P.M. going west. A second car leaves Chicago at 5 P.M., going west at 30 mph faster. At 7 P.M., the faster car hits the slower one. The accident occurred after how many miles?

A. 200

B. 100

C. 60

D. 40

E. 20

Exercise 11: Meg is six times as old as Peg. In 15 years, Meg will be three times as old as Peg. Meg's age now is

A. 10

B. 25

C. 60

D. 75

E. 90

Exercise 12: A fraction, when reduced, is $\frac{2}{3}$. If 6 is added to the numerator and 14 is added to the denominator, the fraction reduces to $\frac{3}{5}$. The sum of the original numerator and denominator is

A. 60   D. 90

B. 70   E. 100

C. 80

 Let's look at the answers.

Answer 1:   **B:** Let's break this one down into small pieces. Four more than a number is written as $n + 4$ (or $4 + n$). Seven less than triple the number is $3n - 7$ (the only correct way). *Is* means "equals," so the equation is $n + 4 = 3n - 7$. Solving, we get $n = 5.5$.

Answer 2:   **C:** The "setup" to do this problem is $80 \leq \dfrac{(98 + 92 + 75 + x)}{4} < 90$.

However, $80(4) = 320$ total points for a minimum, and it must be less than $90(4) = 360$ points. So far, Mike has $98 + 92 + 75 = 265$ points; $265 + 66 = 321$ points. (However, answer choices D or E will result in a grade of A, and I'm sure Mike wouldn't object to that.)

Answer 3:   **B:** $x - 9 = 9 - x$; $x = 9$.

Answer 4:   **A:** The middle one is $-\dfrac{77}{7} = -11$. The three largest ones are thus -9, -7, -5, and their sum is -21.

Answer 5:   **D:** $x^2 + (x + 1)^2 = (x + 2)^2$, which simplifies to $x^2 - 2x - 3 = 0$; $(x - 3)(x + 1) = 0$. The solution set is $x = 3$ or $x = -1$. For $x = 3$, the integers are 3, 4, 5; for $x = -1$, the integers are $-1, 0, 1$. The sum of all six is $3 + 4 + 5 + (-1) + 0 + 1 = 12$.

Answer 6:   C: If we assume a 100-mile distance, the original trip was 5 hours, and the return trip was 2 hours. $r = \dfrac{d}{t} = \dfrac{200}{7} = 28\dfrac{4}{7}$ mph.

Answer 7:   D: $3x + 5x + 7x = 180$, so $x = 12°$. The largest angle is $7x = 84°$.

Answer 8:   B: My age now is $c - b$, so six years ago it was $(c - b) - 6$.

Answer 9:   D: Dimes are 10 cents each, so the value is $10d$, where d is the number of dimes. Similarly, the value of quarters is $25q$, where q is the number of quarters.

Answer 10:   B: Let's construct a chart and picture.

	r	t	d
Slower	x	5	$5x$
Faster	$x + 30$	2	$2(x + 30)$

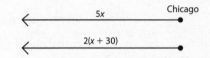

The rate of the slower car is x, and the time of the slower car is 7 P.M. -2 P.M., or 5 hours. The rate of the faster car is $x + 30$; and its time is 7 P.M. -5 P.M., or 2 hours. When they crashed, their distances were equal, so $5x = 2(x + 30)$. Then $x = 20$; and the total distance is $5(20)$ or $2(20 + 30) = 100$ miles.

Answer 11:   C:

	Age now	Age in 15 years
Peg	x	$x + 15$
Meg	$6x$	$6x + 15$

We let $x =$ Peg's (the younger one's) age. Meg's age is thus $6x$. In 15 years, Meg's age ($6x + 15$) will be (equal) three times Peg's age ($3(x+15)$). So the equation is $6x + 15 = 3x + 45$, and $x = 10$. Meg's age now is $6x = 60$.

Answer 12:   A: The fraction can be written as $\dfrac{2x}{3x}$. So $\dfrac{2x + 6}{3x + 14} = \dfrac{3}{5}$. Cross-multiplying, we get $5(2x + 6) = 3(3x + 14)$, so $x = 12$. The original numerator is $2x = 24$ and the original denominator is $3x = 36$, and their sum is $24 + 36 = 60$.

MIXTURES

Mixture problems are easier done with charts.

Example 15: Walnuts selling at $6.00 a pound are mixed with 24 pounds of almonds at $9.00 a pound to give a mixture selling at $7.00 a pound. How many pounds of walnuts are used?

Solution:

	Cost per Pound	× Number of Pounds	= Total Cost
Walnuts	6	x	$6x$
Almonds	9	24	216
Mixture	7	$x + 24$	$7(x + 24)$

We set up a chart for the cost. The columns are cost per pound, the number of pounds, and the total cost. We let x equal the number of pounds of walnuts. The total pounds of walnuts plus the total pounds of almonds is the total weight of the mixture. The equation is the cost of the walnuts plus the cost of the almonds equals the cost of the mixture: $6x + 216 = 7(x + 24)$, so $x = 48$ pounds of walnuts.

Coin problems are just like mixture problems, except we are working with money, not walnuts and almonds.

Example 16: There are 40 coins in nickels and dimes totaling $2.80. How many nickels are there?

Solution:

	Value per Coin	× Number of Coins	= Total Value
Nickels	5	x	$5x$
Dimes	10	$40 - x$	$10(40 - x)$
Mixture	—	40	280

The problem is done in pennies. The total number of coins is 40. If there are x nickels, there are $40 - x$ dimes. The value of x nickels is $5x$. The value of $40 - x$ dimes is $10(40 - x)$. The values of nickels plus dimes is the total value: $5x + 400 - 10x = 280$, so $x = 24$ nickels.

The problem also could be done by trial and error. Twenty of each coin would mean $3.00, so we need more nickels. It must be an even number because the total is $2.80. If we first try 22 and then 24, we would get the correct answer.

Q **Let's do some more exercises.**

Exercise 13: The sum of two numbers is 18 and their difference is 4. The larger number is

A. 14   D. 11

B. 13   E. 10

C. 12

Exercise 14: Adult tickets cost $10 and children's tickets cost $5. If 100 tickets are sold and $800 is taken in, how many adult tickets are sold?

A. 50   D. 75

B. 60   E. 80

C. 70

Exercise 15: Sid is twice as old as Rex. Ten years ago, Sid was four times as old as Rex. How old is Sid today?

A. 5   D. 30

B. 10   E. 60

C. 20

Exercise 16: The number of quarters is four more than twice the number of dimes. If the total is $7.00, how many dimes are there?

A. 10   D. 24

B. 16   E. 34

C. 20

Exercise 17: Fred leaves Fort Worth by car traveling north. Two hours later, Jim also leaves Fort Worth going north, but 20 mph slower. After six more hours, they are 260 miles apart. Fred's speed is

A. 40 mph   D. 70 mph

B. 50 mph   E. 80 mph

C. 60 mph

Exercise 18: The difference in the cost between two books is $8. Together they cost $50. The cost of the less expensive book is

A. $21   **D.** $27

B. $23   **E.** $29

C. $25

 Let's look at the answers.

Answer 13: **D:** x, the larger number, minus $(18 - x)$, the smaller number, is 4; so $x - (18 - x) = 4$, or $2x - 18 = 4$; so $x = 11$. You might do this by trial and error: $14 - 4$, wrong; $13 - 5$, wrong; $12 - 6$; wrong; $11 - 7$; right!

Answer 14:

	Value per Tickets	×	Number of Tickets	=	Total Value
Adult	10		x		$10x$
Child	5		$100 - x$		$5(100 - x)$
Mixture	—		100		800

B: As the chart indicates, this is similar to the mixture problem, Example 15 in this chapter. The equation is $10x + 500 - 5x = 800$, so $x = 60$.

Answer 15:

	Age now	Age 10 years ago
Sid	$2x$	$2x - 10$
Rex	x	$x - 10$

D: According to the chart and the problem, $2x - 10 = 4(x - 10)$, so $x = 15$. Sid's age is $2x = 30$.

Answer 16: **A:** A chart is probably unnecessary. We have x dimes and $(2x + 4)$ quarters. The equation is $10x + 25(2x + 4) = 700$, so $x = 10$.

Answer 17:

	r	×	t	=	d
Fred	x		8		$8x$
Jim	$x - 20$		6		$6(x - 20)$

D: Fred goes at x mph for 8 hours. Jim goes at $x - 20$ mph for 6 hours. Because they are going in the same direction, we get $8x - 6(x - 20) = 260$, or $x = 70$. Notice that 260 is the *difference* in their distances, not the distance they traveled, so we use subtraction.

Answer 18: A: Let x = the less expensive book, so $x + 8$ = the more expensive one; $x + (x + 8) = 50$, so $x = 21$. If you were looking for the more expensive book, you could let x = the more expensive book; then $x - 8$ would be the less expensive one!

MEASUREMENTS

You might want to review some basic measurements and how to convert a few.

Linear: 12 inches = 1 foot; 3 feet = 1 yard; 5,280 feet = 1 mile.

Liquid: 8 ounces = 1 cup; 2 cups = 1 pint; 2 pints = 1 quart; 4 quarts = 1 gallon.

Weight: 16 ounces = 1 pound; 2,000 pounds = 1 ton.

Dry measure: 2 pints = 1 quart; 8 quarts = 1 peck; 4 pecks = 1 bushel. If I love you a bushel and a peck, it would be 5 pecks or 40 dry quarts.

Metric: 1,000 grams in a kilogram; 1,000 milligrams in a gram; 1,000 liters in a kiloliter; 1,000 meters in a kilometer;

1,000 millimeters = 1 meter; 100 centimeters = 1 meter; 10 millimeters = 1 centimeter.

When doing conversions, we pay particular attention to the units, canceling them when doing the multiplication. Sometimes, however, there is confusion about what conversion to use, for example, whether to multiply by $\dfrac{12 \text{ inches}}{1 \text{ foot}}$ or by $\dfrac{1 \text{ foot}}{12 \text{ inches}}$. To avoid this confusion, check to see what units are called for in the answer, and then make sure those units are in the correct place in the conversions.

Example 17: Change 30 kilograms 20 grams to milligrams.

Solution: The solution is in milligrams, so be sure milligrams is in the numerator (top) of the conversions. If you need further conversions, such as converting kilograms to grams here, be sure the units will cancel with the conversion for milligrams:

$$\frac{30 \text{ kg}}{1} \times \frac{1000 \text{ g}}{1 \text{ kg}} \times \frac{1000 \text{ mg}}{1 \text{ g}} + \frac{20 \text{ g}}{1} \times \frac{1000 \text{ mg}}{1 \text{ g}} = 30,000,000 + 20,000 = 30,020,000 \text{ mg}$$

Note *Notice how the measurements (g, kg) cancel.*

Example 18:   Change 90 miles per hour into feet per second.

Solution: The answer is in feet per second, so feet should be in the numerator (top) of any conversion, and seconds should be in the denominator (bottom) of any conversion:

$$\frac{90 \text{ miles}}{\text{hour}} \times \frac{1 \text{ hour}}{60 \text{ minutes}} \times \frac{1 \text{ minute}}{60 \text{ seconds}} \times \frac{5280 \text{ feet}}{1 \text{ mile}} = \frac{132 \text{ feet}}{\text{sec}}$$

 Each fraction after the first is equivalent to 1. When we multiply by 1, the value doesn't change. Again, the measurements cancel, and we wind up with feet per second.

INTEREST

Last, we need to talk a little about simple interest. We know that the interest is equal to the principal times (annual) rate times time (in years). In symbols $i = prt$. The total amount of money is the principal plus the interest, or $A = p + i = p + prt = p(1 + rt)$.

Example 19:   Suppose we invest $20,000 at simple interest at 12% for 3 months. How much money do we have?

Solution: $A = p + prt = 20,000 + 20,000(.12)\left(\dfrac{1}{4}\right) = \$20,600$. Of course, we wouldn't normally invest at simple interest. However, a safe 12% interest would be great.

Example 20:   Suppose we invest $10,000 at 10% for a year, compounded every six months. How much do we have after a year?

Solution: For the first six months, or half a year, $A = p + prt = 10,000 + 10,000(.10)\left(\dfrac{1}{2}\right) = \$10,500$. After the second six months, $A = p + prt = 10,500 + 10,500(.10)\left(\dfrac{1}{2}\right) = \$11,025$, the amount after one year. This is $25 more than if we had simple interest for the full year. That is why compounding continuously is most desirable—we literally earn interest on our interest.

CHAPTER 8:   *Working with Two or More Unknowns*

"Understanding more complex problems will be gratifying to you."

SOLVING SIMULTANEOUS EQUATIONS

We can solve two equations in two unknowns, also known as **simultaneous equations**, in five basic ways. Only two are practical for the ACT: **substitution** and **elimination**. Sometimes, we use a combination of these two.

Substitution

In substitution, we find an unknown with a coefficient of 1, solve for that variable, and substitute it in the other equation.

Example 1:   Solve for x and y:

$$3x + 4y = 4 \qquad (1)$$

$$x - 5y = 14 \qquad (2)$$

Solution: In equation (2) $x = 5y + 14$. Substituting this into equation (1), we get $3(5y + 14) + 4y = 4$. Solving, we get $y = -2$; $x = 5y + 14 = 5(-2) + 14 = 4$. The answer is $x = 4$ and $y = -2$.

We can check by substituting these values into the original equations to see that they are solutions to both equations.

If the coefficient of none of the terms is 1, the elimination method is better.

Elimination

There are several ways to eliminate one of the variables, as seen in the following examples. Once we have eliminated one of the variables, we can solve for the other variable by using substitution.

Example 2: $2x + 3y = 12$

$5x - 3y = 9$

Solution: If we add the equations, term by term, we can eliminate the y term. We get $7x = 21$, so $x = 3$; substituting $x = 3$ into either equation, we get $y = 2$. So the answer is $x = 3, y = 2$.

If addition doesn't work, try subtraction.

Example 3: $5x + 4y = 14$

$5x - 2y = 8$

Solution: By subtracting, we get $6y = 6$, so $y = 1$; then by substituting, we get $x = 2$.

If adding or subtracting doesn't work, we must find two numbers that, when we multiply the first equation by one of them and the second equation by the other, and then add (or subtract) the resulting equations, one letter is eliminated.

Example 4: $5x + 3y = 11$ (1)

$4x - 2y = 22$ (2)

Solution: To eliminate x, multiply equation (1) by 4 and equation (2) by -5; then add.

$$4(5x + 3y) = 4(11) \quad \text{or} \quad 20x + 12y = 44$$

$$-5(4x - 2y) = -5(22) \quad \text{or} \quad -20x + 10y = -110$$

Adding, we get $22y = -66$; so $y = -3$. We could substitute now, but we could also eliminate y by multiplying the original equation (1) by 2 and equation (2) by 3. Let's do that.

$$2(5x + 3y) = 2(11) \quad \text{or} \quad 10x + 6y = 22$$

$$3(4x - 2y) = 3(22) \quad \text{or} \quad 12x - 6y = 66$$

Adding, we get $22x = 88$, so $x = 4$. The answer is $x = 4, y = -3$.

Practice in Solving Simultaneous Equations

For those of you who are curious, the other three basic ways of solving simultaneous equations are by using graphs, matrices, or determinants. We will do graphing in the next chapter.

Q **Let's do some exercises.**

Exercise 1: If $x = y + 3$ and $y = z + 7$, x (in terms of z) =

A. $z - 10$ D. $z + 4$

B. $z - 4$ E. $z + 10$

C. z

Exercise 2: Two apples and 3 pears cost 65 cents, and 5 apples and 4 pears cost $1.10. Find the cost, in cents, of one pear:

A. 10   D. 25

B. 15   E. 30

C. 20

Exercise 3: As in Exercise 2, 2 apples and 3 pears cost 65 cents, and 5 apples and 4 pears cost $1.10. Find the cost, in cents, of one pear and one apple together:

A. 10   D. 25

B. 15   E. 30

C. 20

Exercise 4: Find $x + y$:

$7x + 4y = 27$

$x - 2y = -3$

A. 1   D. 7

B. 3   E. 9

C. 5

Exercise 5: For lunch, Ed buys 3 hamburgers and 1 soda for $12.50, and Mei buys 1 hamburger and 1 soda for $5.60. How much does Ed pay for his hamburgers?

A. $2.15   D. $10.35

B. $3.45   E. $18.10

C. $6.90

Exercise 6:   The product of 4 and the sum of x and y is at least as large as the quotient of a divided by b. This can be written as

A. $4x + y - \dfrac{a}{b} \geq 0$ D. $\dfrac{a}{b} - 4x + 4y < 0$

B. $x + 4y - \dfrac{a}{b} > 0$ E. $4(x + y) + \dfrac{a}{b} \geq 0$

C. $4(x + y) - \dfrac{a}{b} \geq 0$

(A)   **Let's look at the answers.**

Answer 1:   E: $x = y + 3 = (z + 7) + 3 = z + 10$.

Answer 2:   B:

$2a + 3p = 65$

$5a + 4p = 110$

In solving for p, eliminate a by multiplying the top equation by 5 and the bottom by -2.

$5(2a + 3p) = 5(65)$ or $10a + 15p = 325$

$-2(5a + 4p) = -2(110)$ or $-10a - 8p = -220$

Adding, we get $7p = 105; p = 15$.

Answer 3:   D: Much more often, we get a problem like this. The equations are the same as in Exercise 2, but rather than asking for the cost of one apple or the cost of one pear, this exercise asks for the cost of one apple plus one pear. The trick is simply to add the original equations. We then get $7a + 7p = 175$. Dividing both sides by 7, we get $a + p = 25$.

Answer 4:   C: Less frequently, when adding doesn't work, try subtracting. If we subtract, the difference becomes $6x + 6y = 30$. So $x + y = 5$.

Answer 5:   D: The equations are

$3h + s = 12.50$

$h + s = 5.60$

Subtracting, we get $2h = 6.90$, so $h = 3.45$. Ed's three hamburgers cost $10.35.

Answer 6:   C: $4(x + y) \geq \dfrac{a}{b}$. After rearranging, only answer choice C is correct.

Let's take a break from algebra, and take a look at points, lines, and shapes.

"Your journey began from a single point. You travel in a straight line; sometimes the slope may be steep and the distance seems far, but you are now at the midpoint. The endpoint is in sight."

This topic used to be part of a course called analytic geometry (algebraic geometry). We'll start at the beginning.

POINTS IN THE PLANE

We start with a **plane**—a two-dimensional space, like a piece of paper. On this plane, we draw two perpendicular lines, or **axes**. The *x*-axis is horizontal; the *y*-axis is vertical. Positive *x* is to the right; negative *x* is to the left. Positive *y* is up; negative *y* is down. Points in the plane are indicated by **ordered pairs** (*x, y*). The *x* number, called the **first coordinate** or **abscissa**, is always given first; the *y* number, called the **second coordinate** or **ordinate**, is always given second. Here are some points on the plane.

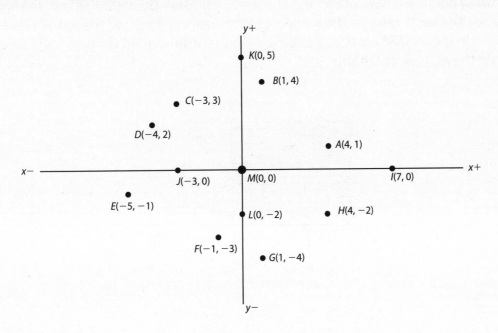

Note the following:

- For any point on the x-axis, the y coordinate always is 0.

- For any point on the y-axis, the x coordinate is 0.

- The point where the two axes meet, (0, 0), is called the **origin**.

- The axes divide the plane into four **quadrants**, usually written with roman numerals, starting in the upper right quadrant and going counterclockwise.

  - In quadrant I, $x > 0$ and $y > 0$.

  - In quadrant II, $x < 0$ and $y > 0$.

  - In quadrant III, $x < 0$ and $y < 0$.

  - In quadrant IV, $x > 0$ and $y < 0$.

In the following figure, we have drawn the line $y = x$. For every point on this line, the first coordinate has the same value as the second coordinate, or $y = x$. If we shade the area above this line, $y > x$ in the shaded portion. Similarly, $x > y$ in the unshaded portion. Sometimes, questions on the ACT ask about this.

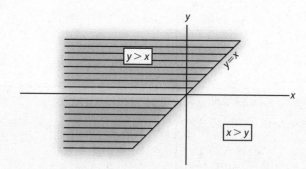

The following figure shows symmetry about the *x*-axis, *y*-axis, and the origin. Suppose (a, b) is in quadrant I. Then $(-a, b)$ would be in quadrant II, $(-a, -b)$ would be in quadrant III, and $(a, -b)$ would be in quadrant IV, as pictured.

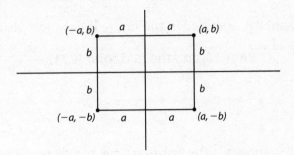

LINES

Distance and Midpoint

The formulas for distance and midpoint look a little complicated, but they are fairly easy to use. It just takes practice.

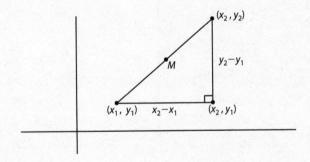

To find the **distance** between two points (x_1, y_1) and (x_2, y_2) on a plane, we must use the distance formula:

$$d = \sqrt{(x_2 - x_1)^2 + (y_2 - y_1)^2}$$

The distance formula is just the Pythagorean Theorem (discussed in the next chapter).

Distances are always positive. You may be six feet tall, but you cannot be minus six feet tall.

The **midpoint** of a line between two points (x_1, y_1) and (x_2, y_2) on a plane is given by the coordinates

$$M = \left(\frac{x_1 + x_2}{2}, \frac{y_1 + y_2}{2} \right)$$

In one dimension, if the line is horizontal, these formulas simplify to $d = |x_2 - x_1|$ and $M = \dfrac{x_1 + x_2}{2}$.

Similarly, if the line is vertical, these formulas simplify to $d = |y_2 - y_1|$ and $M = \dfrac{y_1 + y_2}{2}$.

For example, for the horizontal line shown in the figure below, the distance between the points is $d = |x_2 - x_1| = |7 - (-3)| = 10$, and the midpoint is $M = \dfrac{x_1 + x_2}{2} = \dfrac{-3 + 7}{2} = 2$.

Similarly, for the vertical line shown in the figure below, the distance between the points is $d = |y_2 - y_1| = |-3 - (-7)| = 4$, and the midpoint is $M = \dfrac{y_1 + y_2}{2} = \dfrac{(-7) + (-3)}{2} = -5$.

Slope

The **slope** of a line tells by how much the line is "tilted" compared to the x-axis. The formula for the slope of a line is

$$m = \frac{\text{rise}}{\text{run}} = \frac{\text{change in } y}{\text{change in } x} = \frac{y_2 - y_1}{x_2 - x_1},$$

where (x_1, y_1) and (x_2, y_2) are any two points on the line.

Note the following facts about the slope of a line, as shown in the figure below:

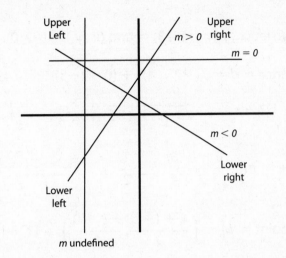

- The slope is positive if the line goes from the lower left to the upper right.
- The slope is negative if it goes from the upper left to the lower right.
- Horizontal lines have zero slope.
- Vertical lines have no slope or undefined slope or "infinite" slope.

Example 1: Find the distance, slope, and midpoint for the line segment joining these points:

a. (2, 3) and (6, 8)　　c. (7, 3) and (4, 3)

b. (4, −3) and (−2, 0)　　d. (2, 1) and (2, 5)

Solutions:

a. We let $(x_1, y_1) = (2, 3)$ and $(x_2, y_2) = (6, 8)$, although the other way around is also okay.

Then

$$\text{Distance} = d = \sqrt{(x_2 - x_1)^2 + (y_2 - y_1)^2} = \sqrt{(6-2)^2 + (8-3)^2} = \sqrt{41}$$

$$\text{Slope} = m = \frac{y_2 - y_1}{x_2 - x_1} = \frac{8-3}{6-2} = \frac{5}{4}$$

$$\text{Midpoint} = M = \left(\frac{x_1 + x_2}{2}, \frac{y_1 + y_2}{2}\right) = \left(\frac{2+6}{2}, \frac{3+8}{2}\right) = (4, 5.5)$$

Notice that the slope is positive; the line segment goes from the lower left to the upper right.

b. We let $(x_1, y_1) = (4, -3) =$ and $(x_2, y_2) = (-2, 0)$.

Distance $= d = \sqrt{(-2 - 4)^2 + (0 - (-3))^2} = \sqrt{45}$

$$= \sqrt{3 \times 3 \times 5} = 3\sqrt{5}$$

Slope $= m = \dfrac{0 - (-3)}{-2 - 4} = -\dfrac{1}{2}$

Midpoint $= M = \left(\dfrac{4 + (-2)}{2}, \dfrac{-3 + 0}{2}\right) = (1, -1.5)$

Notice that the slope is negative; the line segment goes from the upper left to the lower right.

c. We let $(x_1, y_1) = (7, 3) =$ and $(x_2, y_2) = (4, 3)$.

It is a one-dimensional distance, so $d = |4 - 7| = 3$

Slope $= m = \dfrac{3 - 3}{4 - 7} = \dfrac{0}{-3} = 0$

Midpoint $= M = \left(\dfrac{7 + 4}{2}, \dfrac{3 + 3}{2}\right) = (5.5, 3)$

Notice that the horizontal line segment has slope $m = 0$.

d. We let $(x_1, y_1) = (2, 1) =$ and $(x_2, y_2) = (2, 5)$.

Again, this is a one-dimensional distance, so $d = |5 - 1| = 4$

Slope $= m = \dfrac{5 - 1}{2 - 2} = \dfrac{4}{0}$, undefined

Midpoint $= M = \left(\dfrac{2 + 2}{2}, \dfrac{5 + 1}{2}\right) = (2, 3)$

Notice that the slope of the vertical line segment is undefined.

Q **Now let's do some exercises.**

Exercise 1:   The coordinates of *P* are (*j*, *k*). If *s* < *k* < *j* < *r*, which of the points shown in the figure could have the coordinates (*r*, *s*)?

A. A   D. D

B. B   E. E

C. C

Use the figure below for Exercises 2 and 3.

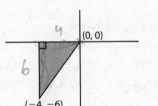

Exercise 2:   Which of the following points is inside the triangle?

A. (−3, 6)   D. (−3, −4)

B. (−5, −5)   E. (−1, −3)

C. (−2, −5)

Exercise 3:   The area of the triangle is

A. 6   D. 24

B. 12   E. 48

C. 18

Exercise 4:   *M* is the midpoint of line segment *AB*. If the coordinates of *A* are (*m*, −*n*), then the coordinates of *B* are

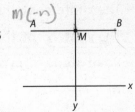

A. (*m*, *n*)   D. (*n*, *m*)

B. (−*m*, *n*)   E. (−*n*, −*m*)

C. (−*m*, −*n*)

Exercise 5:   In the given figure, $AB \parallel x$-axis and $PQ = AB$.
The coordinates of point A are

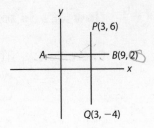

A. $(-1, 2)$ **D.** $(9, 0)$

B. $(1, 2)$ **E.** $(-9, 2)$

C. $(9, -8)$

 Let's look at the answers.

Answer 1:   **C:** For points C, D, and E, the x value is bigger than the x value of P; only point C has a y value less than the y value of P.

Answer 2:   **D:** You can do this by sight.

Answer 3:   **B:** We really haven't gotten to this, but I asked it because we have the picture. The area of the triangle is half the area of the rectangle.

$$A = \frac{1}{2}bh = \frac{1}{2} \times 4 \times 6 = 12$$

Answer 4:   **C:** Slightly tricky. Point B has the same y value as A, but its x value is the negative of the x value for A. Note that the actual values for m and n are negative numbers.

Answer 5:   **A:** The length of $PQ = 10$. For the length of AB to be 10, A must be $(-1, 2)$ since $|9 - (-1)| = 10$.

Standard Equation of a Line

Let's go over the facts we need.

- **Standard form** of the line: $Ax + By = C$; A, B both $\neq 0$.

- The **x-intercept**, the point at which the line hits the x-axis, occurs when $y = 0$.

- The **y-intercept**, the point at which the line hits the y-axis, occurs when $x = 0$.

- **Point-slope form** of a line: Given slope m and point (x_1, y_1), the point-slope form of a line is $m = \dfrac{y - y_1}{x - x_1}$.

- **Slope-intercept form** of a line: $y = mx + b$, where m is the slope and $(0, b)$ is the y-intercept.

- Lines of the form:

  $y = $ constant, such as $y = 2$, are lines parallel to the x-axis; the equation of the x-axis is $y = 0$.

  $x = $ constant, such as $x = -3$, are lines parallel to the y-axis; the equation of the y-axis is $x = 0$.

  $y = mx$ are lines that pass through the origin.

  Example 2: For $Ax + By = C$, find the x and y intercepts.

  Solution: The y-intercept means $x = 0$; so $y = \dfrac{C}{B}$, and the y intercept is $\left(0, \dfrac{C}{B}\right)$.

  The x-intercept means $y = 0$; so $x = \dfrac{C}{A}$, and the x intercept is $\left(\dfrac{C}{A}, 0\right)$.

  Example 3: For $3x - 4y = 7$, find the x and y intercepts.

  Solution: For the y-intercept, $x = 0$; so $y = \dfrac{7}{-4}$, and the y-intercept is $\left(0, -\dfrac{7}{4}\right)$.

  For the x-intercept, $y = 0$; $x = \dfrac{7}{3}$, and the x-intercept is $\left(\dfrac{7}{3}, 0\right)$.

  Example 4: Given $m = \dfrac{3}{2}$ and point $(5, -7)$, write the equation of the line in standard form.

  Solution: $m = \dfrac{y - y_1}{x - x_1}$, so $\dfrac{3}{2} = \dfrac{y - (-7)}{x - 5}$. Cross-multiplying, we get $3(x - 5) = 2(y + 7)$, or $3x - 2y = 29$.

  Example 5: Given points $(3, 6)$ and $(7, 11)$ on a line, write the equation of the line in slope-intercept form.

  Solution: $y = mx + b$. $m = \dfrac{11 - 6}{7 - 3} = \dfrac{5}{4}$, and we will use point $(3, 6)$, so $x = 3$ and $y = 6$. Therefore, $6 = \dfrac{5}{4}(3) + b$, and $b = \dfrac{9}{4}$. So the line is $y = \dfrac{5}{4}x + \dfrac{9}{4}$.

Example 6:   Sketch lines $x = -3$, $y = 8$, and $y = \dfrac{2}{3}x$.

Solution:

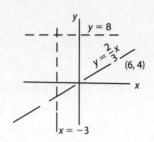

Ⓠ **Let's do a few more exercises.**

Exercise 6:   A line with the same slope as the line $y = \dfrac{2}{3}x - 5$ is

   A. $2x = 18 - 3y$ **D.** $-2x - 3y = 14$

   B. $2x + 3y = 6$ **E.** $2y = 12 - 3x$

   C. $2x - 3y = 6$

Exercise 7:   Find the area of the triangle formed with the positive x-axis, positive y-axis, and the line though the point $(3, 4)$ with slope -2. The area is

   A. 5   **D.** 50

   B. 15   **E.** 10

   C. 25

Ⓐ **Let's look at the answers.**

Answer 6:   C: We have to solve for y in each case, but we are interested in only the coefficient of x. The only answer choice that works is C.

Answer 7:   C: You must visualize the figure.

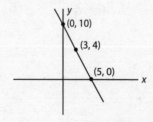

The area of the triangle is one-half the x-intercept times the y-intercept.

The equation of the line is $-2 = \dfrac{y-4}{x-3}$. If we let $x = 0$, the y-intercept is 10. If we let $y = 0$, the x-intercept is 5. Area $= \dfrac{1}{2}ab = \dfrac{1}{2} \times 5 \times 10 = 25$.

Solving Two Equations in Two Unknowns by Graphing

It may be necessary to solve two equations in two unknowns by graphing. What you must do is graph each line. The point where they meet is the solution to the problem.

Example 7:　Solve by graphing: $2x + y = 8$
　　　　　　　　　　　　　　　　$2x + 3y = 12$

Solution:　　We graph using intercepts.

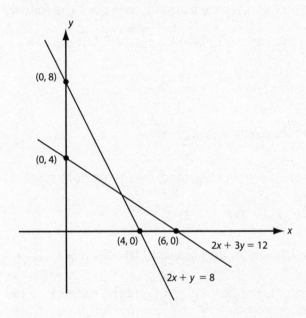

$2x + y = 8$: If $x = 0$, then $y = 8$, so the y-intercept is $(0, 8)$; if $y = 0$, then $x = 4$, so the x-intercept is $(4, 0)$. Graph the line through these two points.

$2x + 3y = 12$: If $x = 0$, then $y = 4$, and the y-intercept is $(0, 4)$; if $y = 0$, then $x = 6$, and the x-intercept is $(6, 0)$. Graph the line through these two points. The lines meet at the point $(3, 2)$. You can check $x = 3$ and $y = 2$ in both equations. On the actual ACT, you can rarely check anything due to time constraints.

EQUATION OF A CIRCLE

We will do an algebraic version of the circle. We will do more, like in your geometry class, in Chapter 12.

A circle is the set of all points (x, y) at a given distance r (called the radius) from a given point (h, k) called the center.

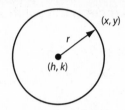

Finding the radius means using the distance formula, so we get the following:

$$r = \sqrt{(x - h)^2 + (y - k)^2}$$

Note (h, k) is the center, a fixed point.

Note (x, y) is any point on the circumference.

Note   No one uses this form of the circle. Instead, we square both sides.

So the equation of the circle is $(x - h)^2 + (y - k)^2 = r^2$.

Example 8:   What is the center and radius of the circle $(x - 5)^2 + (y + 6)^2 = 11$.

Solution: The center is the point $(5, -6)$ and the radius is $\sqrt{11}$.

Example 9:   Write the equation of a circle with radius 7 and center $(-8, 9)$.

Solution: Substituting directly into the equation of a circle, we get $(x + 8)^2 + (y - 9)^2 = 49$.

Note   *If you get any questions on these last two topics, especially circles, draw the picture. You'll be surprised how many times the picture will give you the answer.*

Let's finally get to angles and triangles.

CHAPTER 10: *All Kinds of Angles and All About Triangles*

" *Understanding the area and its perimeter will enhance your chances for success.* "

Before I wrote this chapter, I formulated in my head how the chapter would go. Too many of the questions on angles had to do with triangles. So I decided to write the chapters together. Let's start with some definitions.

TYPES OF ANGLES

There are several ways to classify angles, such as by angle measure, as shown here:

Acute angle: An angle of less than 90°.

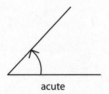

acute

Right angle: A 90° angle. As we will see, some other words that indicate a right angle or angles are perpendicular (⊥), altitude, and height.

right

Obtuse angle: An angle of more than 90° but less than 180°.

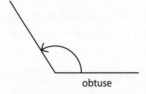

obtuse

113

Straight angle: An angle of 180°.

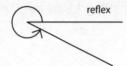

straight

Reflex angle: An angle of more than 180° but less than 360°.

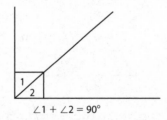

reflex

Angles are also named for their relation to other angles, such as:

Supplementary angles: Two angles that total 180°. $\angle 1 + \angle 2 = 180°$.

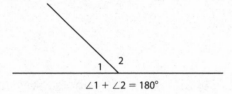

$\angle 1 + \angle 2 = 180°$

Complementary angles: Two angles that total 90°. $\angle 1 + \angle 2 = 90°$.

$\angle 1 + \angle 2 = 90°$

You probably learned that angles are congruent and measures of angles are equal. I am using what I learned; it is simpler and makes understanding easier. So "angle 1 equals angle 2" (or $\angle 1 = \angle 2$) means the angles are both congruent and equal in degrees.

ANGLES FORMED BY PARALLEL LINES

Let's look at angles formed when a line crosses two parallel lines. In the next figure, $\ell_1 \| \ell_2$, and t is a **transversal**, a line that cuts two or more lines. It is not important that you know the names of these angles, although many of you will. It is important only to know that angles formed by a line crossing parallel lines that look equal are equal. The angles that are not equal add to 180°. In this figure, $\angle 1 = \angle 4 = \angle 5 = \angle 8$ and $\angle 2 = \angle 3 = \angle 6 = \angle 7$. Any angle from the first group added to any angle from the second group totals 180°.

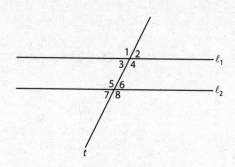

Vertical angles, which are the opposite angles formed when two lines cross, are equal. In the figure below, $\angle 1 = \angle 3$ and $\angle 2 = \angle 4$. Also, $\angle 1 + \angle 2 = \angle 2 + \angle 3 = \angle 3 + \angle 4 = \angle 4 + \angle 1 = 180°$.

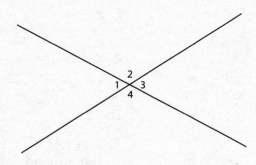

Q **Let's do some exercises.**

Exercise 1: $\angle b =$

      A. 45°   **D.** 105°

      B. 60°   **E.** 135°

      C. 90°

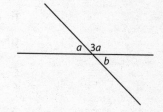

Exercise 2: $\ell_1 \parallel \ell_2.\ m - n =$

      A. 30°   **D.** 90°

      B. 50°   **E.** 180°

      C. 65°

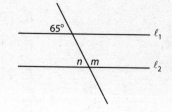

Exercise 3: $y + z =$

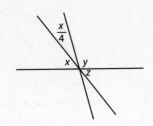

A. $180° - x$

D. $90° + \dfrac{5x}{4}$

B. $180° - \dfrac{x}{4}$

E. $90° - \dfrac{5x}{4}$

C. $45° - \dfrac{x}{4}$

Exercise 4: $180° - w =$

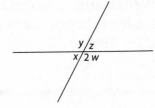

A. $x + w$

D. $y - z$

B. $x + y$

E. $z - w$

C. $y + z$

Exercise 5: $b =$

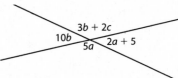

A. $5.5°$

D. $12.5°$

B. $7°$

E. Cannot be determined

C. $10°$

Exercise 6: y (in terms of x) $=$

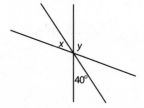

A. x

D. $140° + x$

B. $x + 40°$

E. $320° - x$

C. $140° - x$

Exercise 7: $\angle x =$

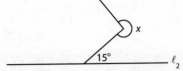

A. $70°$

D. $290°$

B. $110°$

E. $345°$

C. $210°$

Exercise 8:   The ratio of $a°$ to $(a + b)°$ is 3 to 8; $a =$

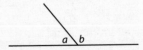

A. $60°$

D. $108°$

B. $67.5°$

E. $112.5°$

C. $72°$

Now let's look at the answers.

Answer 1:   A: $3a + a = 180°$; $a = 45°$ and $b = a = 45°$.

Answer 2:   B: $n = 65°$ and $n + m = 180°$; so $m = 115°$, and $m - n = 50°$.

Answer 3:   B: $\frac{x}{4} + y + z = 180°$, so $y + z = 180° - \frac{x}{4}$.

Answer 4:   A: Below the line, $x + 2w = x + w + w = 180°$, so $x + w = 180° - w$.

Answer 5:   A: This is a toughie. Don't look at vertical angles, look at the supplementary angles. On the bottom, we have $5a + 2a + 5° = 180°$, so $7a = 175°$, and $a = 25°$. Then, on the left, $10b + 5a = 180°$. Substituting $a = 25°$, we get $10b = 180° - 125° = 55°$, or $b = 5.5°$.

If we had looked at the vertical angles after we determined that $a = 25°$, then $10b = 2a + 5° = 2(25°) + 5° = 55°$, so $b = 5.5°$.

Answer 6:   C: $x + y + 40° = 180°$; so $y = 140° - x$.

Answer 7:   D: Draw $\ell_3 \parallel \ell_1$ and ℓ_2.

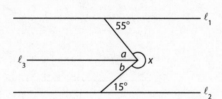

Then $\angle b = 15°$ and $\angle a = 55°$, so

$\angle x = 360° - (15° + 55°) = 290°$.

Answer 8:   B: One way to answer this exercise is to say $a = \left(\frac{3}{8}\right) \times 180$. You will notice that if you divide 8 into 180, you will have a fraction (or a decimal). So only answer choices B or E could be correct. Because B is < 90, B must be the correct answer. Using logic on the ACT could save you a lot of time and give you more correct answers quickly.

So many angle questions on the ACT involve triangles that we ought to look at triangles next.

TRIANGLES

Basics about Triangles

A **triangle** is a polygon with three sides. Angles are usually indicated with capital letters. The side opposite the angle is indicated with the same letter, only lowercase.

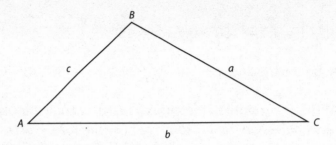

You should know the following general facts about triangles.

- The **sum of the angles** of a triangle is 180°.

- The **altitude**, or **height** (*h*), of ΔABC shown below is the line segment drawn from a vertex perpendicular to the base, extended if necessary. The **base** of the triangle is *AC* = *b*.

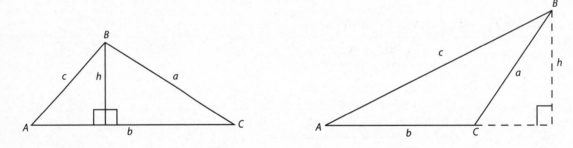

- The **perimeter of a triangle** is the sum of the three sides: $p = a + b + c$.

- The **area of a triangle** is $A = \dfrac{1}{2}bh$. The reason is that a triangle is half a rectangle. Because the area of a rectangle is base times height, a triangle is half a rectangle, as shown in the figure below.

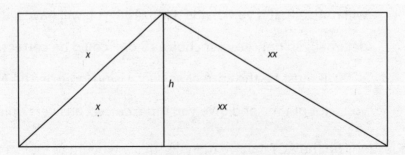

- An **angle bisector** is a line that bisects an angle in a triangle. In the figure below, *BD* bisects ∠*ABC* if ∠1 = ∠2.

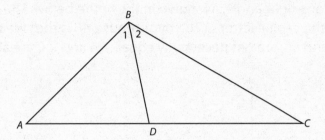

- A **median** is a line drawn from any angle of a triangle to the midpoint of the opposite side. In the figure below, *BD* is a median to side *AC* if *D* is the midpoint of *AC*.

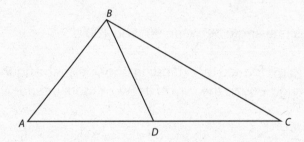

There are many kinds of triangles. One way to describe them is by their sides.

- A **scalene** triangle has three unequal sides and three unequal angles.

- An **isosceles** triangle has at least two equal sides. In the figure below, side *BC* (or *a*) is called the **base**; it may be equal to, greater than, or less than any other side. The **legs**, *AB* = *AC* (or *b* = *c*) are equal. Angle *A* is the **vertex angle**; it may equal the others, or be greater than or less than the others. The **base angles** are equal: ∠*B* = ∠*C*.

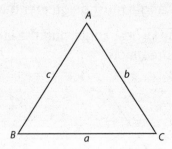

- An **equilateral** triangle is a triangle with all equal sides. All angles equal 60°, so this triangle is sometimes called an **equiangular** triangle. For an equilateral triangle of side *s*, the perimeter *p* = 3*s*, and the area $A = \dfrac{s^2\sqrt{3}}{4}$. This formula seems to be very popular lately, and you may see it on the ACT.

Triangles can also be described by their angles.

- An **acute** triangle has three angles that are less than 90°.

- A **right** triangle has one right angle, as shown in the figure below. The **right angle** is usually denoted by the capital letter C. The **hypotenuse** AB is the side opposite the right angle. The **legs**, AC and BC, are not necessarily equal. ∠A and ∠C are always **acute** angles.

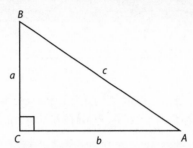

- An **obtuse** triangle has one angle between 90° and 180°.

An **exterior angle** of a triangle is formed by extending one side. In the figure below, ∠1 is an exterior angle. An exterior angle equals the sum of its two remote interior angles: ∠1 = ∠A + ∠B.

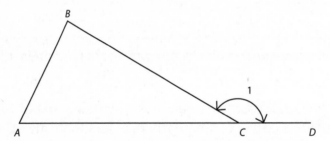

There are three other facts about triangles you should know:

1. The sum of any two sides of a triangle must be greater than the third side.

2. The largest side lies opposite the largest angle, and the largest angle lies opposite the largest side, as shown in the figure below.

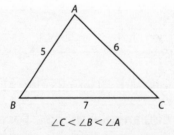

∠C < ∠B < ∠A

3. A line segment joining the midpoints of two sides of a triangle is parallel to the third side and equals half of the third side.

Example 1:   Give one set of angles for a triangle that satisfies the following descriptions:

Description	**Solution**
a. Scalene, acute	50°, 60°, 70°
b. Scalene, right	30°, 60°, 90°. We will deal with this one soon.
c. Scalene, obtuse	30°, 50°, 100°
d. Isosceles, acute	20°, 80°, 80°
e. Isosceles, right	Only one: 45°, 45°, 90°. We will deal with this one soon also.
f. Isosceles, obtuse	20°, 20°, 140°
g. Equilateral	Only one: three 60° angles

Let's first do some exercises with angles. Then we'll turn to area and perimeter exercises. We'll finish the chapter with our famous friend Pythagoras and his famous theorem.

 Let's do some more exercises.

Exercise 9:   Two sides of a triangle are 4 and 7. If only integer measures are allowed for the sides, the third side must be taken from which set?

   A. {5, 6, 7, 8, 9, 10, 11}   **D.** {3, 4, 5, 6, 7, 8, 9, 10, 11}

   B. {4, 5, 6, 7, 8, 9, 10}   **E.** {1, 2, 3, 4, 5, 6, 7, 8, 9, 10, 11}

   C. {3, 4, 5, 6, 7, 8, 9, 10}

Exercise 10:   Arrange the sides in order, largest to smallest, for the figure shown at right.

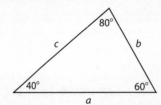

   A. $a > b > c$ **D.** $b > c > a$

   B. $a > c > b$ **E.** $c > a > b$

   C. $b > a > c$

Exercise 11: $x = 2y; z =$

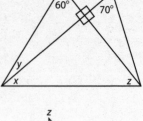

        A. 30°   **D.** 60°

        B. 40°   **E.** 90°

        C. 50°

Exercise 12: WX bisects $\angle ZXY; \angle Z =$

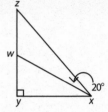

        A. 20°   **D.** 60°

        B. 40°   **E.** 70°

        C. 50°

Exercise 13: $\angle TVW = 10x; x$ could be

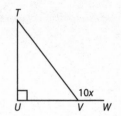

        A. 3°   **D.** 16°

        B. 6°   **E.** 20°

        C. 9°

Exercise 14:   Write b in terms of a:

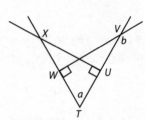

        A. $a + 90°$ **D.** $180° - a$

        B. $2a$ **E.** $180° - 2a$

        C. $2a + 90°$

Exercise 15: $a + b + c + d =$

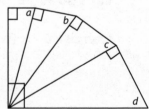

        A. 90°   **D.** 360°

        B. 180°   **E.** 450°

        C. 270°

Exercise 16:   The largest angle is

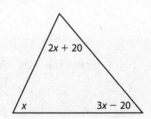

        A. 30°   **D.** 80°

        B. 50°   **E.** 90°

        C. 70°

Exercise 17: $\ell_1 \parallel AB; y =$

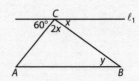

        A. 40°   **D.** 80°

        B. 60°   **E.** Cannot be
                           determined

        C. 70°

Exercise 18: $\ell_1 \parallel AB$; $y =$

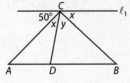

     A. 40°

     B. 60°

     C. 70°

     D. 80°

     E. Cannot be determined

Use $\triangle ABC$ for Exercises 19 and 20.

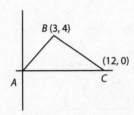

Exercise 19:   The area of $\triangle ABC$ is

     A. 18

     B. 24

     C. 36

     D. 48

     E. 60

Exercise 20:   The perimeter of $\triangle ABC$ is

     A. $17 + \sqrt{97}$

     B. 27

     C. 32

     D. $\sqrt{266}$

     E. $10\sqrt{10}$

For Exercises 21 and 22, use this figure of a square with an equilateral triangle on top of it, $AE = 20$.

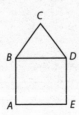

Exercise 21:   The perimeter of $ABCDE$ is

     A. 50

     B. 100

     C. 120

     D. 160

     E. 200

Exercise 22:   The area of *ABCDE* is

        A. 600   **D.** 800

        B. $100(4 + \sqrt{2})$ **E.** 1,000

        C. $100(4 + \sqrt{3})$

For Exercises 23 and 24, use $\triangle ABC$ with midpoints *X*, *Y*, and *Z*.

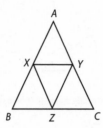

Exercise 23:   If the perimeter of $\triangle ABC$ is 1, the perimeter of $\triangle XYZ$ is

        A. $\dfrac{1}{16}$ **D.** $\dfrac{1}{2}$

        B. $\dfrac{1}{8}$ **E.** 1

        C. $\dfrac{1}{4}$

Exercise 24:   If the area of $\triangle ABC$ is 1, the area of $\triangle XYZ$ is

        A. $\dfrac{1}{16}$ **D.** $\dfrac{1}{2}$

        B. $\dfrac{1}{8}$ **E.** 1

        C. $\dfrac{1}{4}$

Exercise 25:   In the figure shown, $BC = \dfrac{1}{3}BD$. If the area of $\triangle ABC = 10$, the area of rectangle *ABDE* is

        A. 30   **D.** 120

        B. 40   **E.** Cannot be determined

        C. 60

Ⓐ **Let's look at the answers.**

Answer 9: **B:** The third side *s* must be greater than the difference and less than the sum of the other two sides, or $> 7 - 4$ and $< 7 + 4$. Thus the third side must be between 3 and 11.

Answer 10: **B:** Judge the relative lengths of the sides by the size of the angles opposite them. Then $a > c > b$.

Watch out for the words "Not drawn to scale." If it is a simple figure, "not drawn to scale" usually means it is not drawn to scale, and you cannot assume relative sizes without being given actual measurements. However, if it is a semi-complicated or complicated figure, the figure probably *is* drawn to scale.

Answer 11: **A:** Look at the individual right triangles whose two acute angles must total 90°. $y = 30°$; $x = 60°$; and $z = 30°$.

Answer 12: **C:** $\angle ZXY = 40°$, so $\angle Z$ must be 50°.

Answer 13: **D:** $\angle TVW$ must be between 90° and 180°, so $9° < x < 18°$.

Answer 14: **A:** This is really tricky. *UX* is drawn to confuse you. In ΔTVW, *b* is the exterior angle, so $b = a + 90°$.

Answer 15: **C:** The sum of 4 triangles is $4 \times 180° = 720°$. The sum of 5 right angles (don't forget the one in the lower left of the figure, which is the sum of four acute angles of the triangles) is 450°; so $a + b + c + d = 720° - 450° = 270°$.

Answer 16: **D:** $x + 2x + 20 + 3x - 20 = 180$, or $6x = 180$, so $x = 30$. $2x + 20 = 80$ and $3x - 20 = 70$. The largest angle is 80°.

Answer 17: **A:** $2x + x + 60 = 180$; $x = 40°$. But $y = x = 40°$ (because $\ell_1 \parallel AB$).

Answer 18: **E:** *y* cannot be determined. The ACT occasionally asks a question for which there is no answer. However, I've never seen two in a row and I've seen thousands of similar questions.

Answer 19: **B:** $A = \dfrac{1}{2}bh = \dfrac{1}{2} \times 12 \times 4 = 24$.

Answer 20: **A:** Use the distance formula to find sides *AB* and *BC*. $p = AC + AB + BC = 12 + \sqrt{4^2 + 3^2} + \sqrt{(3 - 12)^2 + (4 - 0)^2} = 12 + \sqrt{25} + \sqrt{97} = 17 + \sqrt{97}$.

Answer 21: **B:** Do not include BD; $p = 5 \times 20 = 100$.

Answer 22: **C:** Area $= s^2 + \dfrac{s^2\sqrt{3}}{4} = 20^2 + \dfrac{20^2\sqrt{3}}{4} = 400 + 100\sqrt{3} = 100\,(4 + \sqrt{3})$

Answer 23: **D:** If the perimeter of $\triangle ABC$ is 1, and all the sides of $\triangle XYZ$ are half of those of $\triangle ABC$, so is the perimeter.

Answer 24: **C:** If the sides of $\triangle XYZ$ are half of those of $\triangle ABC$, the area of $\triangle XYZ$ is $\left(\dfrac{1}{2}\right)^2 A = \dfrac{1}{4}A = \dfrac{1}{4}$.

Answer 25: **C:** If we draw lines parallel to DE to divide the original rectangle into three congruent rectangles, and then divide each rectangle into two triangles, we see that each triangle is one-sixth of the rectangle. So the area of the rectangle is $6(10) = 60$.

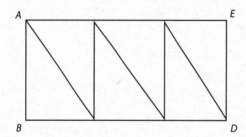

We'll have more of these type of exercises as part of Chapter 12, where we discuss circles.

Let's go on to good old Pythagoras.

PYTHAGOREAN THEOREM

This is perhaps the most famous math theorem of all. Most theorems have one proof. A small fraction have two. This theorem, however, has more than a hundred, including three by past presidents of the United States. We've had some smart presidents who actually knew some math.

The Pythagorean Theorem simply states:

In a right triangle, the hypotenuse squared is equal to the sum of the squares of the legs.

In symbols,

$$c^2 = a^2 + b^2.$$

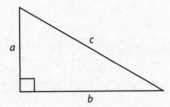

As a teacher, I must show you one proof.

Proof:

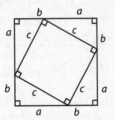

In this figure, the larger square equals the smaller square plus the four congruent triangles. In symbols, $(a + b)^2 = c^2 + 4\left(\dfrac{1}{2}ab\right)$.

Multiplying this equation out, we get $a^2 + 2ab + b^2 = c^2 + 2ab$. Then canceling $2ab$ from both sides, we get $c^2 = a^2 + b^2$. The proof is complete.

There are two basic problems you need to know how to do: finding the hypotenuse and finding one of the legs of the right triangle.

    Example 2:   Solve for *x*:

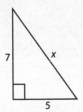

    Solution: $x^2 = 7^2 + 5^2$; $x = \sqrt{74}$.

Example 3:   Solve for *x*:

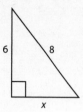

Solution: $8^2 = 6^2 + x^2$, or $x^2 = 64 - 36 = 28$. So $x = \sqrt{28} = \sqrt{2 \times 2 \times 7} = 2\sqrt{7}$.

Notice that the hypotenuse squared is always by itself, whether it is a number or a letter.

Pythagorean Triples

Although the ACT allows calculators, it is a good idea to memorize these triples. The ACT seems to love, love, love them. Below are the sides of the most important right triangles. The hypotenuse is always listed third in each group.

The 3-4-5 group: 3-4-5, 6-8-10, 9-12-15, 12-16-20, 15-20-25

The 5-12-13 group: 5-12-13, 10-24-26

The rest: 8-15-17, 7-24-25, 20-21-29, 9-40-41, 11-60-61

Special Right Triangles

You ought to know two other special right triangles, the isosceles right triangle (with angles 45°-45°-90°) and the 30°-60°-90° right triangle. The facts about these triangles can all be found by using the Pythagorean Theorem.

1. The 45°-45°-90° isosceles right triangle:

   * The legs are equal.

   * To find a leg given the hypotenuse, divide the hypotenuse by $\sqrt{2}$ (or multiply by $\frac{\sqrt{2}}{2}$).

   * To find the hypotenuse given a leg, multiply the leg by $\sqrt{2}$.

   Example 4:   Find *x* and *y* for this isosceles right triangle.

   Solution: $x = 5$ (the legs are equal); $y = 5\sqrt{2}$.

Example 5:   Find x and y for this isosceles right triangle.

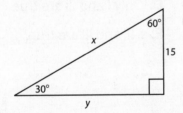

Solution: $x = y = \dfrac{18}{\sqrt{2}} = 18 \times \dfrac{\sqrt{2}}{2} = 9\sqrt{2}$.

2. The 30°-60°-90° right triangle.

*   If the shorter leg (opposite the 30° angle) is not given, get it first. It is always half the hypotenuse.

*   To find the short leg given the hypotenuse: divide the hypotenuse by 2.

*   To find the hypotenuse given the short leg: multiply the short leg by 2.

*   To find the short leg given the long leg: divide the long leg by $\sqrt{3}$ (or multiply by $\dfrac{\sqrt{3}}{3}$).

*   To find the long leg given the short leg: multiply the short leg by $\sqrt{3}$.

Example 6:   Find x and y for this right triangle.

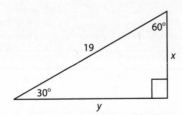

Solution: The short leg is given (15); $x = 2(15) = 30$; $y = 15\sqrt{3}$.

Example 7:   Find x and y for this right triangle.

Solution: $x = \dfrac{19}{2} = 9.5$; $y = 9.5\sqrt{3}$.

Example 8:   Find x and y for this right triangle.

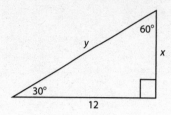

Solution: $x = \dfrac{12}{\sqrt{3}} = 12\dfrac{\sqrt{3}}{3} = 4\sqrt{3}$; $y = 2(4\sqrt{3}) = 8\sqrt{3}$.

Q   **Let's do a few exercises.**

Exercise 26:   Two sides of a right triangle are 3 and $\sqrt{5}$.

    I: The third side is 2.

    II: The third side is 4.

    III: The third side is $\sqrt{14}$.

    Which of the following choices is correct?

    A. Only II is true.   **D.** Only I and III are true.

    B. Only III is true.   **E.** I, II, and III are true.

    C. Only I and II are true.

Exercise 27:   The area of square $ABCD =$

    A. 50   **D.** 576

    B. 100   **E.** 625

    C. 225

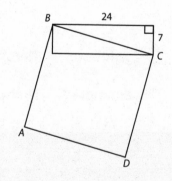

Exercise 28: $x =$

    A. 16   **D.** 22

    B. 18   **E.** 24

    C. 20

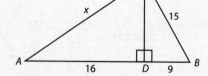

Exercise 29: $c^2 - b^2 =$

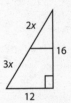

    A. 72   **D.** 194

    B. 144   **E.** 288

    C. 216

Exercise 30: $x =$

    A. 1   **D.** 4

    B. 2   **E.** 4.5

    C. 3

Exercise 31:   A 25-foot ladder is leaning on the floor. Its base is 15 feet from the wall. If the ladder is pushed until it is only 7 feet from the wall, how much farther up the wall is the ladder pushed?

    A. 4 feet   **D.** 20 feet

    B. 8 feet   **E.** 24 feet

    C. 12 feet

 Let's look at the answers.

Answer 26:   D: Try the Pythagorean Theorem with various combinations of 3, $\sqrt{5}$, and x (the third side). The only ones that work are Statement I: $2^2 + \left(\sqrt{5}\right)^2 = 3^2$; and Statement III: $3^2 + \left(\sqrt{5}\right)^2 = \left(\sqrt{14}\right)^2$.

Answer 27:   E: We recognize the right triangle as a 7-24-25 triple, so side $BC = 25$. The area of the square is $(25)^2 = 625$.

Answer 28:   C: This is a 15-20-25 triple, so $x = 20$.

Answer 29:   D: We see that MN is the side of two triangles. By the Pythagorean Theorem, we get $c^2 - b^2 = x^2 + y^2 = \left(5\sqrt{2}\right)^2 + 12^2 = 50 + 144 = 194$.

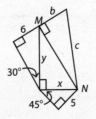

Answer 30:   D: This triangle is a 12-16-20 triple, so $3x + 2x = 5x = 20$, and $x = 4$.

Answer 31:   A: The first figure is a 15-20-25 right triangle with the ladder 20 feet up the wall. The second figure is a 7-24-25 triple with the ladder 24 feet up the wall. The ladder is pushed another $24 - 20 = 4$ feet up the wall.

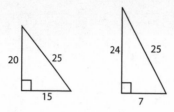

SIMILAR TRIANGLES

Two triangles are similar if corresponding angles are congruent and corresponding sides are in proportion.

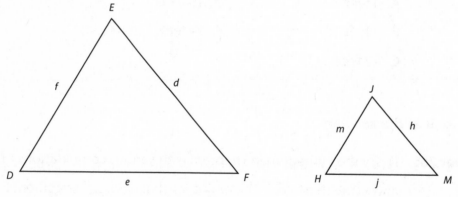

In the above figure, it means $\angle D \cong \angle H$, $\angle E \cong \angle J$, and $\angle F \cong \angle M$ and $\dfrac{f}{m} = \dfrac{d}{h} = \dfrac{e}{j}$.

$\dfrac{f}{m} = \dfrac{d}{h} = \dfrac{e}{j}$ is called the **ratio of similarity**.

Example 9:   For the figure below,

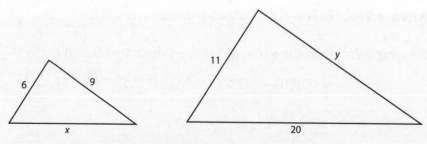

a. What is the ratio of similarity?

b. Find *x* and *y*.

c. What is the ratio of their areas?

Solutions: **a.** The left sides in each triangle are given. The ratio of similarity is $\frac{6}{11}$.

b. $\frac{6}{11} = \frac{x}{20}$; $11x = 120$; $x = \frac{120}{11}$; $\frac{6}{11} = \frac{9}{y}$; $6y = 99$; $y = \frac{99}{6}$ or $\frac{33}{2}$. Once you start with the length of the smallest side of the first triangle on the top of a fraction, the corresponding smallest side of the second triangle must always be on the top of the ratio.

c. The ratio of the areas is the square of the ratio of similarity. In this case the ratio of the areas would be $\frac{36}{121}$.

 For three-dimensional similar figures, the ratio of their volumes would be the cube of the ratio of similarity.

That's all for angles and triangles for now. We will see more when circles are discussed in Chapter 12. For now, though, let's look at rectangles and other polygons.

"*Mastering all shapes and sizes will enhance your journey.*"

We now deal with the rest of the polygons (closed figures with line-segment sides).

QUADRILATERALS

Parallelograms

A **parallelogram** is a **quadrilateral** (four-sided polygon) with parallel opposite sides.

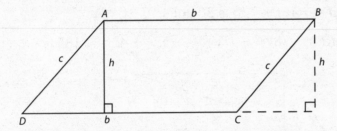

You should know the following properties about parallelograms:

- The opposite angles are equal. $\angle DAB = \angle BCD$ and $\angle ADC = \angle ABC$.

- The consecutive angles are supplementary. $\angle DAB + \angle ABC = \angle ABC + \angle BCD = \angle BCD + \angle CDA = \angle CDA + \angle DAB = 180°$.

- The opposite sides are equal. $AB = CD$ and $AD = BC$.

- The diagonals bisect each other. $AE = EC$ and $DE = EB$.

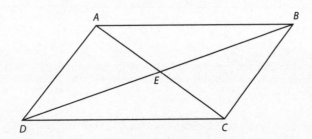

- Area $= A = bh$.
- Perimeter $= p = 2b + 2c$.

Example 1:   For parallelogram *RSTU* shown in the figure below, find the following if *RU* = 10:

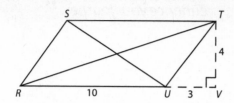

a. The area

c. Diagonal *RT*

b. The perimeter

d. Diagonal *SU*

Solutions: **a.** $A = bh = (10)(4) = 40$ square units. The whole test should be this easy!

b. We have to find the length of *RS* = *TU*. *TU* = 5 because it is the hypotenuse of a 3-4-5 right triangle. So the perimeter is $p = 2(10) + 2(5) = 30$ units.

c. $RT = \sqrt{(RV)^2 + (TV)^2} = \sqrt{13^2 + 4^2} = \sqrt{185}$

d.

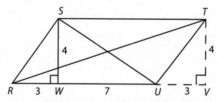

To find diagonal *SU*, draw the other altitude *SW* as pictured.

$SU = \sqrt{WU^2 + SW^2} = \sqrt{7^2 + 4^2} = \sqrt{65}$

Example 2: For parallelogram *WXYZ* with altitudes *XM* and *YN*, find the following in terms of *a*, *b*, and *c*:

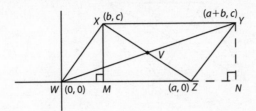

a. The coordinates of point *M*

b. The coordinates of point *N*

c. The coordinates of point *V*

d. The perimeter

e. The area

Solutions:

a. *M* has the same *x*-coordinate as point *X* and the same *y*-coordinate as point *W*, so the coordinates of *M* are $(b, 0)$.

b. *N* has the same *x*-coordinate as point *Y* and the same *y*-coordinate as point *W*, so the coordinates of *N* are $(a + b, 0)$.

c. *V* is halfway between *W* and *Y*, so use the formula for the midpoint between $Y(a + b, c)$ and $W(0, 0)$: Midpoint $V = \left(\dfrac{(a + b) + 0}{2}, \dfrac{c + 0}{2} \right) = \left(\dfrac{a + b}{2}, \dfrac{c}{2} \right)$.

d. $WZ = XY$ is length a. By the distance formula, $WX = ZY = \sqrt{(b - 0)^2 + (c - 0)^2} = \sqrt{b^2 + c^2}$. Therefore, the perimeter is $p = 2a + 2\sqrt{b^2 + c^2}$.

e. Area $= A =$ base $\times$ height $= ac$.

Example 3: For parallelogram *EFGH*, find the smaller angle.

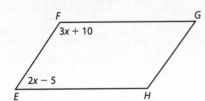

Solution: Consecutive angles of a parallelogram are supplementary. Therefore, $(3x + 10)° + (2x - 5)° = 180°$; $x = 35°$; so the smaller angle is $2(35°) - 5° = 65°$. Be careful to give the answer the ACT wants. Two other, but incorrect, answer choices would be $35°$ and $115°$, for those who do not read carefully!!!

Rhombus

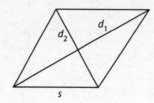

A **rhombus** is an equilateral parallelogram.

Thus, a rhombus has all of the properties of a parallelogram plus the following:

- All sides are equal.
- The diagonals are perpendicular bisectors of each other.
- Perimeter = $p = 4s$.
- Area = $A = bh = \dfrac{1}{2} \times d_1 \times d_2$, the area equals half the product of its diagonals.

Example 4: For the rhombus given below with side $s = 13$ and larger diagonal $BD = 24$, find the other diagonal and the area.

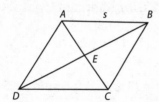

Solution: $AB = 13$ and $BD = 24$. Because the diagonals bisect each other, $BE = 12$.

The diagonals are perpendicular to each other, so $\triangle ABE$ is a 5-12-13 right

triangle, and $AE = 5$. Therefore, the other diagonal $AC = 10$. The area is

$A = \dfrac{1}{2} \times BD \times AC = \dfrac{1}{2}(24)(10) = 120$ square units.

Example 5: Find the area of a rhombus with side 10 and smaller interior angle of 60°.

Solution: If we draw the diagonal through the two larger angles, we will have two congruent equilateral triangles. The area of this rhombus is twice the area of each triangle, or $2 \times \dfrac{s^2\sqrt{3}}{4}$. Because $s = 10$, the area is

$$A = 2 \times \dfrac{10^2\sqrt{3}}{4} = 50\sqrt{3} \text{ square units.}$$

Now let's go on to more familiar territory.

Rectangle

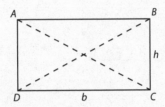

A **rectangle** is a parallelogram with right angles.

Therefore, it has all of the properties of a parallelogram plus the following:

- All angles are 90°.
- Diagonals are equal (but *not* perpendicular).
- Perimeter $= p = 2b + 2h$.
- Area $= A = bh$. This is a **postulate** (law taken to be true without proof) from which we get the area of all other figures with sides that are line segments.

The easier the shape, the more likely the ACT will have a problem or problems about it.

Example 6: One base of a rectangle is 8, and one diagonal is 9. Find all the sides and the other diagonal. Find the perimeter and area.

Solution: The top base and bottom base are both 8. Both diagonals are 9. The other two sides are each $\sqrt{9^2 - 8^2} = \sqrt{17}$. So the perimeter is $p = 16 + 2\sqrt{17}$ units; and the area is $A = 8\sqrt{17}$ square units.

Example 7: $AB = 10$, $BC = 8$, $EF = 6$, and $FG = 3$. Find the area of the shaded region of the figure below.

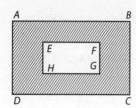

Solution: The area of the shaded region is the area of the outside rectangle minus the area of the inside one. $A = (10)(8) - (6)(3) = 62$ square units.

Example 8:   In polygon $ABCDEF$, $BC = 30$, $AF = 18$, $AB = 20$, and $CD = 11$. Find the perimeter and area of the polygon.

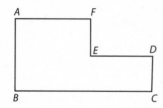

Solution: Draw a line through DE, hitting AB at point G. Then $AF = GE$ and $BC = GD$. Because $DG = 30$ and $GE = 18$, $DE = 12$. $AB = CD + EF$. $AB = 20$ and $CD = 11$, so $EF = 9$. This gives the lengths of all the sides. The perimeter thus is $p = AB + BC + CD + DE + EF + AF = 20 + 30 + 11 + 12 + 9 + 18 = 100$ units.

The area of rectangle $BCDG$ is $BC \times CD = (30)(11) = 330$. The area of rectangle $AFEG$ is $AF \times FE = (18)(9) = 162$. Therefore, the total area is $330 + 162 = 492$ square units. There are other ways to find this area, as you might be able to see.

Example 9:   The areas of the pictured rectangle and triangle are the same.

If $\dfrac{LW}{4} = 20$, what is bh?

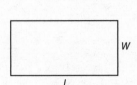

Solution: $\dfrac{LW}{4} = 20$; so $LW = 80$, which is the area of the rectangle. Because that

also is the area of the triangle, $\dfrac{1}{2}bh = 80$. So $bh = 160$.

Square

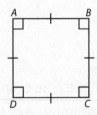

A **square** is a rectangle with equal sides, or it can be thought of as a rhombus with four equal 90° angles.

Therefore, it has all of the properties of a rectangle and a rhombus:

- All sides are equal.

- All angles are 90°.

- Both diagonals bisect each other, are perpendicular to each other, and are equal.

- Each diagonal $d = d_1 = d_2 = s\sqrt{2}$, where $s =$ a side.

- Perimeter $= p = 4s$.

- Area $= A = \dfrac{d^2}{2} = s^2$.

Example 10: What is the area of this square?

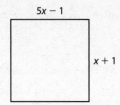

Solution: Because it is a square, $5x - 1 = x + 1$, so $x = \dfrac{1}{2}$ and $x + 1 = 1\dfrac{1}{2}$. Then $A = \left(1\dfrac{1}{2}\right)^2 = 2\dfrac{1}{4}$.

Example 11: The area of square C is 36; the area of square B is 25. What is the area of square A?

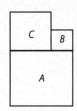

Solution: The side of square C must be 6, and the side of square B must be 5. Therefore, the side of square A is 11, and the area of square A is $11^2 = 121$.

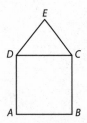

The figure above is a square surmounted by an equilateral triangle. (I've always wanted to write that word.) $AB = 10$. Use this figure for Examples 12 and 13.

Example 12: What is the perimeter of the figure?

Solution: The perimeter is $5(10) = 50$. Note that CD is *not* part of the perimeter.

Example 13: What is the area of the figure?

Solution: $A = s^2 + \dfrac{s^2\sqrt{3}}{4} = 10^2 + \dfrac{10^2\sqrt{3}}{4} = 100 + 25\sqrt{3} = 25(4 + \sqrt{3})$.

Trapezoid

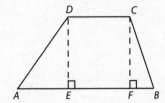

A **trapezoid** is a quadrilateral with exactly one pair of parallel sides.

Because a trapezoid is *not* a type of parallelogram, it has its own unique set of properties, as follows:

- The parallel sides, *AB* and *CD*, are called **bases**.

- The heights, *DE* and *CF*, are equal.

- The legs, *AD* and *BC*, may or may not be equal.

- The diagonals, *AC* and *BD*, may or may not be equal.

- Perimeter $= p = AB + BC + CD + AD$.

- Area $= A = \frac{1}{2}h(b_1 + b_2)$, where b_1 and b_2 are the bases and *h* is the height.

Note   *If we draw one of the diagonals, we see that a trapezoid is the sum of two triangles. Factoring out $\frac{1}{2}h$, we get the formula for the area of the trapezoid.*

If the legs are equal, the trapezoid is called an **isosceles trapezoid**, shown below.

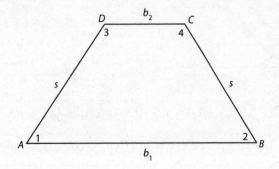

An isosceles trapezoid has the following additional properties:

- Perimeter $= p = b_1 + b_2 + 2s$.

- The diagonals are equal, $AC = BD$.

- The base angles are equal, $\angle 1 = \angle 2$ and $\angle 3 = \angle 4$.

Example 14: Find the area and the perimeter of Figure *ABCD*.

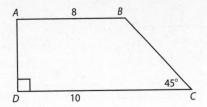

Solution: Draw the height from point *B*, *BG*, as shown below.

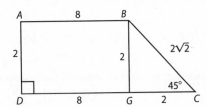

DG = 8; *CG* = 2. Because $\triangle BGC$ is an isosceles right triangle, the height

BG (and *AD*) = 2; *BC*, the hypotenuse of the isosceles right triangle, is

therefore $2\sqrt{2}$. Therefore, the perimeter is $p = 10 + 2 + 8 + 2\sqrt{2} =$

$20 + 2\sqrt{2}$, and the area is $A = \frac{1}{2}h(b_1 + b_2) = \frac{1}{2}(2)(8 + 10) = 18$.

Example 15: Given trapezoid *ORST*, with *RS* ∥ *OT*, find the coordinates of point *S*. Find
the perimeter and the area of trapezoid *ORST*.

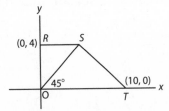

Solution: Because $\triangle ORS$ is a 45°-45°-90° triangle, *OR* = *RS* = 4, so *S* is the point

(4, 4). The length of *OT* = 10. By the distance formula, the length of

$ST = \sqrt{(10 - 4)^2 + (0 - 4)^2} = \sqrt{52} = 2\sqrt{13}$. Therefore, the perimeter is

$p = 10 + 4 + 4 + 2\sqrt{13}$, or, to be fancy, $2(9 + \sqrt{13})$. Area $= \frac{1}{2}h(b_1 + b_2)$

$= \frac{1}{2}(4)(10 + 4) = 28$. In a multiple-choice question, the ACT would ask

about either the area or perimeter, but not both. But sometimes the ACT

is fancy, like here.

Example 16: Find the area of isosceles trapezoid *EFGH*.

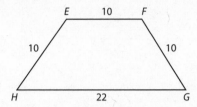

Solution: Draw in the two heights for the trapezoid.

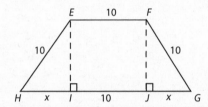

The two bases of the triangles formed are equal because it is an

isosceles trapezoid. From the figure, $2x + 10 = 22$, so $x = 6$. Each of the

triangles is a 6-8-10 Pythagorean triple, so the height of the trapezoid is

8. Therefore, $A = \frac{1}{2}(8)(10 + 22) = 128$.

POLYGONS

Let's talk about polygons in general. Most of the time we deal with **regular** polygons. A regular polygon has all sides equal and all angles equal. A square and an equilateral triangle are examples of regular polygons we have already discussed.

Any *n*-sided polygon has the following properties.

- The sum of all the interior angles is $(n - 2)180°$, where *n* is the number of sides (or angles) in the polygon.

- The sum of all exterior angles always equals 360°.

- An interior angle plus its exterior angle always add to 180°.

- The number of diagonals is $\frac{n(n - 3)}{2}$.

If the polygon is regular, it has the following additional properties:

- Each exterior angle $= \frac{360°}{n}$.

- Each interior angle $= \frac{(n - 2)180°}{n}$.

Polygons are named for the number of sides they have.

A **pentagon** is a 5-sided polygon.

A **hexagon** is a 6-sided polygon.

A **heptagon** is a 7-sided polygon.

An **octagon** is an 8-sided polygon.

A **nonagon** is a 9-sided polygon.

A **decagon** is a 10-sided polygon.

A **dodecagon** is a 12-sided polygon.

An **n-gon** is an n-sided polygon.

Example 17:   An octagon has a perimeter of 27. If 5 is added to each side, what is the perimeter of the new octagon?

Solution: It doesn't matter how long each side is! If 5 is added to each of 8 sides, 40 is added to the perimeter. The new perimeter is $27 + 40 = 67$.

Example 18:   The side of a regular hexagon is 4. Find its area.

Solution: A regular hexagon is made up of six equilateral triangles. The side of each triangle is 4, and the area is $A = 6\dfrac{s^2\sqrt{3}}{4} = 6\dfrac{4^2\sqrt{3}}{4} = 24\sqrt{3}$.

Example 19:   The sum of the interior angles of a polygon is $720°$. Find the number of sides, the number of degrees in one exterior angle, and the number of degrees in one interior angle.

Solution: $(n - 2)(180) = 720$. Divide each side of this equation by 180 to simplify: $n - 2 = 4$, so $n = 6$ sides. One exterior angle $= \dfrac{360°}{6} = 60°$. An interior angle is supplemental to its external angle, by definition, so $180° - 60° = 120°$ for each interior angle.

We'll get more ACT-looking questions at the end of the chapter on circles, which is next.

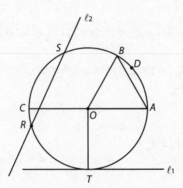

"*Although sometimes it seems you are going in circles, you are really heading toward your goal.*"

Circles

Circles are a favorite topic of the ACT. Circles allow for many short questions that can be combined with the other geometric shapes. Let's get started.

PARTS OF A CIRCLE

We all know what a circle looks like, but maybe we're not familiar with its "parts."

O is the **center** of the circle. *A* circle is often named by its center, so this is circle *O*.

OA, *OT*, *OC*, and *OB* are **radii** (singular: radius); a radius is a line segment from the center to the **circumference**, or edge, of the circle.

Note *All radii (r) of a circle are equal. This is a postulate or axiom, a law taken to be true without proof.*

It is probably a good idea to tell you there are no proofs on the ACT, as there probably were when you took geometry.

AC is the **diameter**, *d*, the distance from one side of the circle through the center to the other side; $d = 2r$ and $r = \dfrac{d}{2}$.

ℓ_1 is a **tangent**, a line that touches a circle in one and only one point.

T is a **point of tangency**, the point where a tangent touches the circle. The radius to the point of tangency (*OT*) is always perpendicular to the tangent, so $OT \perp \ell_1$.

ℓ_2 is a **secant**, a line that passes through a circle in two places.

RS is a **chord**, a line segment that has each end on the circumference of the circle. The diameter is the longest chord in a circle.

OADBO is a **sector** (a pie-shaped part of a circle). There are a number of sectors in this figure; others include *BOCSB* and *OATRCSBO*. We will see these again soon.

An **arc** is any distance along the circumference of a circle.

> Arc *ADB* is a **minor arc** because it is less than half a circle. Arc *BDATRC* is a **major arc** because it is more than half a circle.
>
> Arc *ATRC* is a **semicircle** because it is exactly half a circle. Arc *ADBSC* is also a semicircle.

Whew! Enough! However, we do need some more facts about circles.

The following are mostly theorems, or proven laws. Again, there are no proofs on the ACT, but you need to be aware of these facts.

AREA AND CIRCUMFERENCE

Area of a circle:

$$A = \pi r^2$$

Circumference (perimeter of a circle):

$$C = 2\pi r \text{ or } \pi d$$

SECTORS

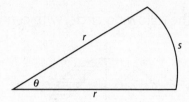

Area of a sector:

$$A = \frac{\theta}{360°} \pi r^2,$$

where θ (theta) is the angle of the sector in degrees.

Arc length of a sector:

$$s = \frac{\theta}{360°} \times 2\pi r$$

Perimeter of a sector:

$$p = s + 2r,$$

where s is the arc length.

Example 1:   Find the area and perimeter of a 60° sector of a circle of diameter 12.

Solution:

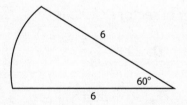

If the diameter is 12, the radius is 6. The sector is pictured above. Its area is $A = \frac{60°}{360°} \times \pi 6^2 = 6\pi$ square units. Although you should know that pi (π) is about 3.14, I've never seen a problem for which you had to multiply 6 times 3.14. The answer is left in terms of π. The perimeter of the sector is $s = 2(6) + \frac{60°}{360°} \times 2\pi(6) = 12 + 2\pi$ units.

Q   **Let's do some exercises.**

For Exercises 1 through 5, refer to the following circle, with center O.

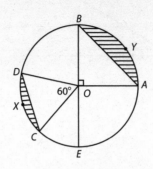

Exercise 1:   If the area of △AOB is 25, the area of circle O is

A. 12.5π   D. 100π

B. 25π   E. 200π

C. 50π

Exercise 2:   If OA = 8, the area of the shaded region BAYB is

A. 16(π − 2)   D. 64(π − 1)

B. 16(π − 1)   E. 32(π − 2)

C. 8(2π − 1)

Exercise 3:   If CD = 10, the perimeter of sector DOCXD is

A. $30 + \dfrac{10\pi}{3}$ D. $20 + \dfrac{20\pi}{3}$

B. $30 + \dfrac{20\pi}{3}$ E. $30 + 30\pi$

C. $20 + \dfrac{10\pi}{3}$

Exercise 4:   If OC = 2, the area of the shaded portion DCXD is

A. $\pi - \sqrt{3}$ D. $\dfrac{2\pi - 3\sqrt{3}}{3}$

B. $2\pi - \sqrt{3}$ E. $\dfrac{8\pi - 3\sqrt{3}}{3}$

C. $4\pi - \sqrt{3}$

Exercise 5:   If the area of $\triangle COD$ is $25\sqrt{3}$, the perimeter of semicircle *EOBDXCE* is

  A. 10π **D.** $10(2\pi + 1)$

  B. $10(\pi + 1)$ **E.** $20(\pi + 1)$

  C. $10(\pi + 2)$

I guess you get the idea already.

 Let's look at the answers.

Answer 1:   C: $A = \dfrac{1}{2}(r)(r) = \dfrac{1}{2}r^2 = 25$, so $r^2 = 50$. The area of the circle is thus

$\pi r^2 = 50\pi$. Notice that once we have a value for r^2, we don't have to

find r to do this problem.

Answer 2:   A: The area of region *BAYB* is the area of one-fourth of a circle minus the

area of $\triangle AOB$. So the area is $A = \dfrac{1}{4}\pi 8^2 - \dfrac{1}{2}(8)(8) = 16\pi - 32 = 16(\pi - 2)$.

Answer 3:   C: The perimeter of sector *DOCXD* $= 2r + s$, where s is the length of arc

CXD. $\triangle COD$ is equilateral, so $CD = CO = DO = r = 10$. $s = \dfrac{60°}{360°}2\pi(10) =$

$\dfrac{10\pi}{3}$. So the perimeter of sector *CODXD* is $p = 20 + \dfrac{10\pi}{3}$.

Answer 4:   D: The area of region *DCXD* is the area of sector *ODXCO* minus the area

of $\triangle DOC$, when $OC = 2$. So the area is

$A = \dfrac{60°}{360°}\pi 2^2 - \dfrac{2^2\sqrt{3}}{4} = \dfrac{2\pi}{3} - \sqrt{3} = \dfrac{2\pi - 3\sqrt{3}}{3}$.

Answer 5:   C: We must first find the radius. The area of equilateral $\triangle COD =$

$\dfrac{s^2\sqrt{3}}{4} = 25\sqrt{3}$. So $s^2 = 100$, and $s = r = 10$. The perimeter of the

semicircle is $\dfrac{1}{2}(2\pi r) + 2r = \pi r + 2r = 10\pi + 20 = 10(\pi + 2)$.

There are a few more things we need to know. When we talked about two intersecting line segments earlier, we saw that, for the figure below, *CE* might equal *ED*; however, if the description of the figure doesn't say so, you cannot assume it. Also, *ED* might be perpendicular to *AB*, but if it doesn't say so, you cannot assume it, either. In fact, we can say *CD* **bisects** *AB* at *E* only if we know that *AE* = *EB* or *E* is the **midpoint** of *AB*.

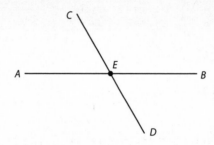

Now, however, we consider two intersecting line segments in a circle, such as chord *AB* and radius *CO* in circle *O*.

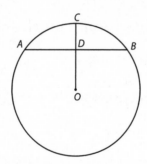

If one of the following facts is true, all are true:

1. *OD* ⊥ *AB*

2. *CDO* bisects *AB*

3. *CO* bisects $\overparen{ACB}$ (read "arc *ACB*")

 *When the ACT says "distance to a chord," distance always means **perpendicular** distance. Sometimes the ACT shows the perpendicular. When it doesn't, you have to know it is perpendicular.*

Let's do some more exercises

For Exercises 6 and 7, use this figure, which is a triangle-semicircle shape.

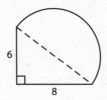

Exercise 6: The perimeter of this figure is

A. $14 + 5\pi$ D. $24 + 10\pi$

B. $14 + 10\pi$ E. $12 + 10\pi$

C. $24 + 5\pi$

Exercise 7: The area of this figure is

A. $24 + \dfrac{25\pi}{2}$ D. $48 + 25\pi$

B. $24 + 25\pi$ E. $48 + 50\pi$

C. $24 + 50\pi$

Exercise 8: A circle is **inscribed** in (inside and touching) figure *MNPQ*, which has all right angles. Diameter $AB = 10$. The area of the shaded portion is

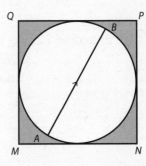

A. $100 - 12.5\pi$ D. $40 - 5\pi$

B. $100 - 25\pi$ E. $100 - 100\pi$

C. $40 - 10\pi$

Exercise 9: If $AB = 10$, the area of the shaded portion in the figure is

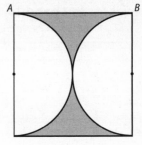

A. $100 - 12.5\pi$ D. $40 - 5\pi$

B. $100 - 25\pi$ E. $100 - 100\pi$

C. $40 - 10\pi$

For Exercises 10 and 11, use this figure. The perimeter of the 16 semicircles is 32π.

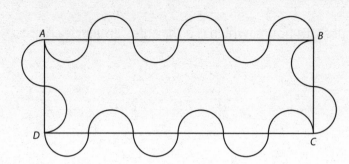

Exercise 10: The area of rectangle *ABCD* is

     A. 64   D. 16π

     B. 128   E. Cannot be determined

     C. 192

Exercise 11: The area inside the region formed by the semicircular curves from *A* to *B* to *C* to *D* and back to *A* is

     A. 64   D. 16π

     B. 128   E. Are you for real??!!

     C. 192

Exercise 12: In the figure, $EF = CD = 12$, B is the midpoint of OD, and A is the midpoint of CO. The area of the shaded portion is

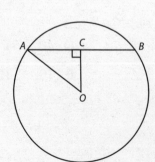

     A. $36(4\sqrt{3} - \pi)$ D. $72(3\sqrt{3} - \pi)$

     B. $6(6\sqrt{3} - \pi)$ E. $36(6\sqrt{3} - \pi)$

     C. $144(\pi - 3)$

For Exercises 13 and 14, use this figure.

Exercise 13:   If the diameter = 20, $OC \perp AB$, and $\angle A = 30°$, $AB =$

A. 10   D. $10\sqrt{3}$

B. 5   E. $5\sqrt{2}$

C. $5\sqrt{3}$

Exercise 14:   If OC bisects AB, $AB = 16$, and $OC = 6$, the area of circle O is

A. 10π D. 100π

B. 20π E. 400π

C. 40π

 Let's look at the answers.

Answer 6:   A: The figure includes a 6-8-10 Pythagorean triple, but 10 is not part of the perimeter. $p = 6 + 8 + \frac{1}{2}2\pi(5) = 14 + 5\pi$.

Answer 7:   A: $A = \frac{1}{2}bh + \frac{1}{2}\pi r^2 = \frac{1}{2}6 \times 8 + \frac{1}{2}\pi 5^2 = 24 + \frac{25\pi}{2}$.

Answer 8:   B: The area is the area of the square minus the area of the circle. $A = s^2 - \pi r^2 = 10^2 - \pi 5^2 = 100 - 25\pi$.

Answer 9:   B: Answer 8 and Answer 9 are exactly the same problems. In Answer 8, we could also say the square **circumscribes** the circle.

Answer 10:   C: Each semicircle has arc length $\frac{180°}{360°}\pi d$, and there are 16 semicircles, so $16\left(\frac{1}{2}\pi d\right) = 32\pi$, or $8\pi d = 32\pi$, so $d = 4$. The rectangle's dimensions are thus 8 and 24. The area is $A = b \times h = 8(24) = 192$.

Answer 11:   C: Believe it or not, Exercise 11 is exactly the same as Exercise 10! We can think of the areas of the "outer" semicircles as canceling out the areas of the "inner" semicircles, and we are left with only the area of rectangle *ABCD*.

Answer 12:   **B:** The information is enough to tell us the triangle is equilateral and $\angle AOB$ = 60°. The shaded area is the area of $\triangle COD$ minus the area of sector $OABO$. Thus, $A = \dfrac{s^2\sqrt{3}}{4} - \dfrac{1}{6}\pi r^2 = \dfrac{12^2\sqrt{3}}{4} - \dfrac{1}{6}\pi 6^2 = 36\sqrt{3} - 6\pi = 6(6\sqrt{3} - \pi)$.

Answer 13:   **D:** AO, the radius, is 10; CO, the side opposite the 30° angle, is 5; and AC, the side opposite the 60° angle, is $5\sqrt{3}$. $AB = 2(AC) = 2(5\sqrt{3}) = 10\sqrt{3}$.

Answer 14:   **D:** To find the area of the circle, we need to find the radius OA. We know AC is 8 and OC is 6. We have a 6-8-10 right triangle, so $AO = r = 10$. The area is $\pi(10)^2 = 100\pi$.

Okay. Now let's go from two dimensions to three dimensions.

"*Many dimensions in your trip will add to your ultimate success.*"

This chapter is relatively short. There are only a few figures we need to know. Because these are three-dimensional figures, we discuss their volumes and surface areas (areas of all of the sides). The diagonal is the distance from one corner internally to an opposite corner.

BOX

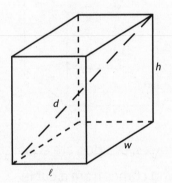

This figure is also known as a **rectangular solid**, and if that isn't a mouthful enough, its correct name is a **rectangular parallelepiped**. But essentially, it's a **box**.

- Volume = $V = \ell wh$
- Surface area = $SA = 2\ell w + 2\ell h + 2wh$
- Diagonal = $d = \sqrt{\ell^2 + w^2 + h^2}$, known as the 3-D Pythagorean Theorem

Example 1: For the given figure, find V, SA, and d.

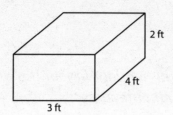

2 ft

4 ft

3 ft

Solution: $V = \ell w h = (3)(4)(2) = 24$ cubic feet; $SA = 2\ell w + 2\ell h + 2wh = 2(3)(4) + 2(3)(2) + 2(4)(2) = 52$ square feet; $d = \sqrt{\ell^2 + w^2 + h^2} = \sqrt{3^2 + 4^2 + 2^2} = \sqrt{29} \approx 5.4$ feet

CUBE

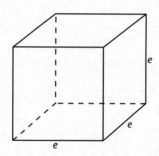

e

e

e

A **cube** is a box for which all of the faces, or sides, are equal squares.

- $V = e^3$ (read as "e cubed"). Cubing comes from a cube!
- $SA = 6e^2$
- $d = e\sqrt{3}$
- A cube has 6 faces, 8 vertices, and 12 edges.

Example 2: For a cube with an edge of 10 meters, find V, SA, and d.

Solution: $V = 10^3 = 1,000$ cubic meters; $SA = 6e^2 = 6(10)^2 = 600$ square meters; $d = e\sqrt{3} = 10\sqrt{3} \approx 17.32$ meters

CYLINDER

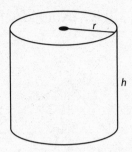

A cylinder is shaped like a can. The curved surface is considered as a side, and the top and bottom are equal circles.

- $V = \pi r^2 h$

- $SA = \text{top} + \text{bottom} + \text{curved surface} = 2\pi r^2 + 2\pi rh$

Once a neighbor of mine wanted to find the area of the curved part of a cylinder. He wasn't interested in why, just the answer. Of course, being a teacher, I had to explain it to him. I told him that if he cut a label off a soup can and unwrapped it, the figure is a rectangle; neglecting the rim, the height is the height of the can and the width is the circumference of the circle. Multiply this height and width, and the answer is $2\pi r \times h$. He waited patiently and then soon moved. (Just kidding!)

In general, the volume of any figure for which the top is the same as the bottom is $V = Bh$, where B is the area of the base. If the figure comes to a point, the volume is $\left(\dfrac{1}{3}\right)Bh$. The surface area is found by adding up all the sides.

Example 3:   Find V and SA for a cylinder of height 10 yards and diameters of 8 yards.

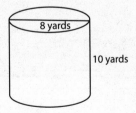

8 yards

10 yards

Solution: We see that, because $d = 8$, $r = 4$. Then $V = \pi r^2 h = \pi(4^2 \times 10) = 160\pi$ cubic yards; $SA = 2\pi r^2 + 2\pi rh = 2\pi 4^2 + 2\pi(4)(10) = 112\pi$ square yards.

Q **Let's do some exercises.**

Use this figure for Exercises 1 through 3. It is a pyramid with a square base. $WX = 8$, $BV = 3$, and B is in the middle of the base.

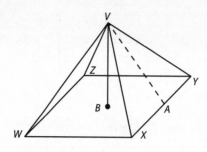

Exercise 1: The volume of the pyramid is

A. 192   D. 32

B. 96   E. 16

C. 64

Exercise 2: The surface area of the pyramid is

A. 72   D. 224

B. 112   E. 448

C. 144

Exercise 3: $VY =$

A. 6   D. 9

B. $\sqrt{41}$ E. $\sqrt{89}$

C. 7

Exercise 4: In the given rectangular solid, the perimeter of $\triangle ABC =$

A. $\sqrt{325} = 5\sqrt{13}$ D. 37

B. 30   E. 41

C. $27 + \sqrt{261}$

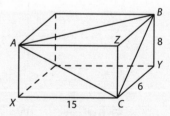

Exercise 5: The volume of the cylinder shown is:

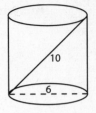

    A. 640π **D.** 144π

    B. 320π **E.** 72π

    C. 288π

Exercise 6: *ABKL* is the face of a cube with *AB* = 10, and box *BCFG* has a square front with *BC* = 6. The surface area that can be viewed in this configuration is

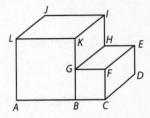

    A. 300   **D.** 400

    B. 356   **E.** 1360

    C. 396

Exercise 7: A cylinder has volume *V*. If we triple its radius, what do we multiply the height by in order for the volume to stay the same?

    A. $\dfrac{1}{9}$ **D.** 3

    B. $\dfrac{1}{3}$ **E.** 9

    C. 1

 Let's look at the answers.

Answer 1: C: $V = \left(\dfrac{1}{3}\right)Bh = \dfrac{1}{3}s^2h = \dfrac{1}{3}(8^2)(3) = 64$.

Answer 2: C: $SA = s^2 + 4\left(\dfrac{1}{2}bh\right)$. $AB = \left(\dfrac{1}{2}\right)WX = 4$; $\triangle ABV$ is a 3-4-5 right triangle with $AB = 4$ and $BV = 3$, so $AV = 5$. AV is the height of each triangular side, h, and $b = XY = 8$. So $SA = 8^2 + 2(8)(5) = 144$.

Answer 3: B: $\triangle AVY$ is a right triangle with right angle at A. $AY = 4$ and $AV = 5$, so $VY = \sqrt{4^2 + 5^2} = \sqrt{41}$.

Answer 4:   **C:** In the given figure, we have to use the 2-D Pythagorean Theorem three times to find the sides of $\triangle ABC$. $\triangle BCY$ is a 6-8-10 triple, so $BC = 10$, and $\triangle ACX$ is a 8-15-17 triple, so $AC = 17$. For $\triangle ABZ$, we actually have to calculate the missing side $\sqrt{6^2 + 15^2} = \sqrt{261}$. So the perimeter is $10 + 17 + \sqrt{261} = 27 + \sqrt{261}$.

Answer 5:   **E:** The diameter of the base is 6, and again we have a Pythagorean triple; so $h = 8$. The volume is $\pi(3^2)(8) = 72\pi$.

Answer 6:   **C:** The areas are: $ABKL = 100$; $IJLK = 100$; $BCFG = 36$; $CDEF = 60$; $EFGH = 60$; $GHIK = 40$. The total is 396.

Answer 7:   **A:** The volume $V = \pi r^2 h$. For simplicity, let $r = 1$ and $h = 1$. So $V = \pi$. If we triple the radius, $V = \pi(3)^2 h$. For the original volume to still be π, $9h = 1$, or $h = \dfrac{1}{9}$.

CHAPTER 14: *Other Algebraic Topics*

"At this point, your probability of success has greatly increased."

FUNCTIONS

A most important part of algebra is the study of functions. Let's give it its due.

Function: To each element in set *D*, we assign one and only one element. The set *D* is called the **domain**. On the ACT you should think of the *x* values. The assignment is called the **map**; the set of numbers that are assigned is called the **range**. On the ACT you should think of the *y* values.

Note *If you are unfamiliar with sets and elements, see Chapter 16.*

Example 1: Let $f(x) = x^2 + 3x + 22$; find the following:

Problem	Solution
a. $f(4)$	$4^2 + 3(4) + 22 = 50$
b. $f(-3)$	$(-3)^2 + 3(-3) + 22 = 22$
c. $f(0)$	$0^2 + 3(0) + 22 = 22$
d. $f(x + h)$	$(x + h)^2 + 3(x + h) + 22 =$ $x^2 + 2xh + h^2 + 3x + 3h + 22$
e. $f(\text{pigs})$	$(\text{pigs})^2 + 3\text{pigs} + 22$

Example 2: Let $g(x) = x^2 + 7x$; let $D = \{-3, 4, 7\}$. Find the range.

Solution: Range $= \{f(-3), f(4), f(7)\} = \{-12, 44, 98\}$

Note *Functions (the maps) are usually indicated by f(x), g(x), F(x), and G(x). However, any letter can be used.*

A graph is a function if any time you draw a vertical line, the line crosses the graph only once. All lines (except a vertical line) are functions; a circle is not a function.

PIECEWISE FUNCTIONS

Sometimes a function has more than one piece. Let's give an example; we'll do it the longer way for understanding, the shorter way, and how the ACT might ask the question.

Example 3:   Graph $f(x) = \begin{cases} x + 6 & \text{if} & x < 0 \\ x^2 & \text{if} & 0 \le x \le 3 \\ 5 - x & \text{if} & x > 3 \end{cases}$

Solution: We make a table of values: $x = -3, -2, -1, 0^-, 0, 1, 2, 3, 3^+, 4, 5, \ldots$

When $x < 0$, we use the first part of the definition, $f(-3) = (-3) + 6 = 3$, and we have the point $(-3, 3)$.

Similarly, $f(-2) = (-2) + 6 = 4$, and we have the point $(-2, 4)$; $f(-1) = (-1) + 6 = 5$ yields the point $(-1, 5)$; $f(0^-) = 0^- + 6 = 6^-$ (or a little less than 0, like $-.0001$; plus 6 equals a little less than 6). The point is $(0^-, 6^-)$—on a graph this is an open dot because the graph doesn't quite hit $(0, 6)$.

For the second part of the definition, $f(0) = 0^2 = 0$ yields the point $(0, 0)$; $f(1) = 1^2 = 1$ gives $(1, 1)$; $f(2) = 2^2 = 4$ gives $(2, 4)$; and $f(3) = 9$ gives $(3, 9)$.

For the third part of the definition, $f(3^+) = 5 - 3^+ = 2^-$ (5 minus a little more than 3 equals a little less than 2, or 2^-), which yields the point $(3^+, 2^-)$ with an open dot on $(3, 2)$; $f(4) = 5 - 4 = 1$ gives $(4, 1)$; and $f(5) = 5 - 5 = 0$ gives $(5, 0)$.

The graph would look like this:

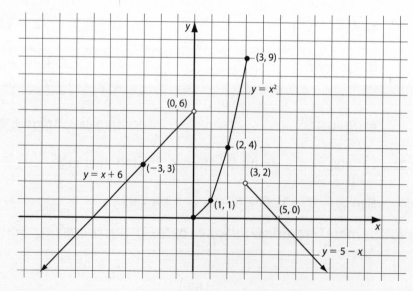

To be able to do this same problem the short way, you must know or be able to get the graph really quickly.

We graph $y = x + 6$, but we are interested only in the part of the line where $x < 0$.

We graph $y = x^2$, but we are interested only in the part of the graph between 0 and 3, inclusive.

We graph $y = 5 - x$, but we are interested only in the part of the graph where $x > 3$.

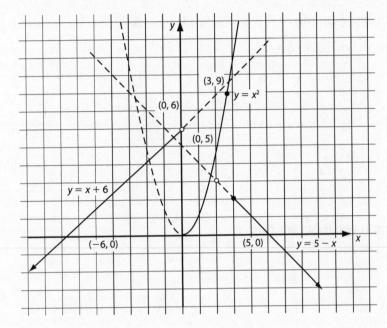

The ACT could provide a value for $f(x)$ and you would have to know what part of the definition of a piecewise function holds and find x.

The ACT will have a question with 5 answer choices, one of which tells what x is.

Q **Let's look at an exercise that the ACT could ask.**

Exercise 1: Referring to the figure above, if $f(x) = 4$, x could be

A. 2 only

B. −2 only

C. 2, −2 only

D. 1 and 2 only

E. 1, 2, and 4 only

A   **Let's look at the answer.**

Answer 1:   **C:** If $f(x) = x + 6 = 4$; $x = -2$; because $-2 < 0$, $x = -2$ is okay. If $f(x) = x^2 = 4$; $x = 2$ and $x = -2$; only 2 is between 0 and 3; so $x = 2$ is okay. If $f(x) = 5 - x = 4$, $x = 1$; because 1 is not > 3, $x = 1$ is not okay.

PARABOLAS

The parabola you will see on the ACT is of the form $y = ax^2 + bx + c$, where a cannot be 0.

- If $a > 0$, the graph will look like this:

vertex

- If $a < 0$, the graph will look like this:

vertex

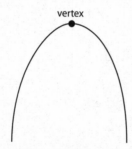

The vertex is the lowest or highest point of the parabola. Its x value is found by setting $x = -\dfrac{b}{2a}$.

Example 4:   Sketch $y = x^2 - 4x - 5$.

Solution: We sketch by finding the vertex, x-intercept(s) and y-intercept.

Vertex: $x = -\dfrac{b}{2a} = -\dfrac{-4}{2} = 2$; $y = (2)^2 - 4(2) - 5 = -9$: $(2, -9)$

x-intercept(s): $y = 0$; $x^2 - 4x - 5 = (x - 5)(x + 1) = 0$: $(5, 0)$ and $(-1, 0)$.

y-intercept: $x = 0$; $y = -5$: $(0, -5)$.

The sketch looks like this:

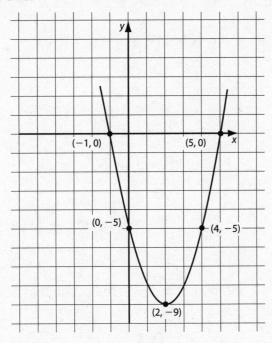

Example 5:   Sketch $y = 18 - 2x^2$.

Solution: We sketch by finding the vertex, x-intercept(s), and y-intercept.

Vertex: $x = -\dfrac{b}{2a} = -\dfrac{0}{2(2)} = 0$; $y = 18$: $(0, 18)$. It is also the y-intercept.

x-intercepts: $y = 0$; $18 - 2x^2 = -2(x^2 - 9) = -2\,(x + 3)(x - 3) =$

0: $(-3, 0)$ and $(3, 0)$.

The sketch looks like this:

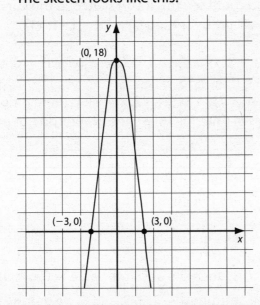

Note   *With no x term, the parabola is symmetric with respect to the y-axis.*

Let's try a few exercises:

Exercise 2: $f(x) = (x + 5)^2$, $g(x) = (x + 11)^2$, and $g(x) = f(x)$; $x =$

A. 16   D. −8

B. 8   E. −16

C. 0

Exercise 3: If $f(x) = x^2 + 2x + 3$ and $f(x) = 2$, then $x =$

A. 11   D. −1

B. 1   E. more than one value

C. 0

Exercise 4: If $f(x) = x^2 + 1$ and $g(x) = -x^2 - 1$; the number of points where $f(x)$ meets $g(x)$ is

A. 0   D. 3

B. 1   E. more than 3

C. 2

A **Let's look at the answers.**

Answer 2: D: The answer is halfway between the two; halfway between −5 and −11 is −8. You could see this if you sketched the curve. Or you could solve it algebraically by setting $(x + 5)^2 = (x + 11)^2$.

Answer 3: D: $x^2 + 2x + 3 = 2$; $x^2 + 2x + 1 = (x + 1)(x + 1) = 0$; so $x = -1$.

Answer 4: A: $x^2 + 1 = -x^2 - 1$; so $2x^2 = -2$; $x^2 = -1$; there is no real solution (we will look at this in Chapter 16), so the graphs do not meet.

ABSOLUTE VALUE GRAPH

Example 6: Let's graph $y = |x - 4|$.

Solution: The vertex occurs when the absolute value = 0, or when $x = 4$, at the point $(4, 0)$. Substituting $x = 2, 3, 5,$ and 6, we get the following graph:

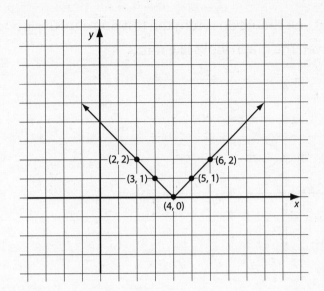

Example 7:   Let's graph $y = -|x + 3| + 1$.

Solution: The vertex occurs at $x = -3$; $y = 1$; $(-3, 1)$. Substituting $x = -5, -4, -2,$ -1, we get the following graph:

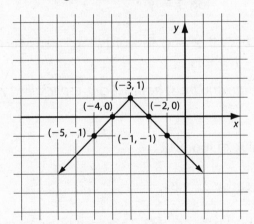

Example 7:   Given the graph $y = |x + 2|$ shown here, if we rotated it 90° clockwise, what would the figure look like?

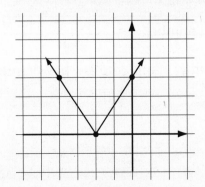

Solution: What you should do is turn the test booklet 90° clockwise to see the answer. The graph looks like this:

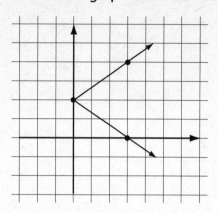

LOGARITHMS

Let us first define what is meant by logarithm. We write

$$\log_b x = y$$

(read as log(arithm) of x to the base b is y if $b^y = x$). In words, $\log_{\text{base}}$ answer = exponent, because base^{exponent} = answer.

Note   *This is a very strange definition and must be practiced, especially if you haven't had much experience with it.*

Example 8:   What is the value of $\log_3 81$?

Solution: $\log_3 81 = 4$ because $3^4 = 81$.

The **base** may be only positive numbers other than 1. There are two common bases. If we write "log," it means $\log_{10}$. The reason we use 10 as the base is because we have 10 fingers (really!). If we write "ln," it means log e, where e is a number like pi; $e \approx$ (approximately equals) 2.7. Although it doesn't stand for it, anything to do with e is easy!

The y values, the logarithms, can be any real number.

The x values must be positive because a positive number to any power **must** be positive!

Example 9: Find x:

Problem	Solution
a. $\log_5 125 = x$	$5^x = 125$, so $x = 3$
b. $\log_4 x = 3$	$x = 4^3 = 64$
c. $\log_x 81 = 2$	$x^2 = 81$, so $x = 9$ (only), because bases can't be negative

Because logarithms are exponents, the laws of logarithms are the laws of exponents.

Law | Example

1. When you multiply, you add exponents; the same is true for logs.

$\log_b cd = \log_b c + \log_b d$

$\log 6 = \log (2)(3) = \log 2 + \log 3$;
$\ln dry = \ln d + \ln r + \ln y$

2. When you divide, you subtract exponents; the same is true for logs.

$\log_b \dfrac{c}{d} = \log_b c - \log_b d$

$\log_7 \dfrac{3}{5} = \log_7 3 - \log_7 5$

3. A power to a power? You multiply exponents; the same is true for logs.

$\log_b c^d = d \log_b c$

$\log 128 = \log 2^7 = 7 \log 2$

4. Any number to the first power is that number.

$\log_b b = 1$, because $b^1 = b$.

$\log_3 3 = 1$, because $3^1 = 3$; $\log 10 = 1$ because $10^1 = 10$; $\ln e = 1$, because $e^1 = e$.

5. Any nonzero number to the zero power is 1.

$\log_b 1 = 0$, because $b^0 = 1$, where b is any base.

$\log_2 1 = 0$, because $2^0 = 1$; $\ln 1 = 0$ because $e^0 = 1$

In calculus if you can do the next example and absolutely no other, it is more than 50 percent of what you need to know about logs.

Example 10: Write as simpler logs with no (or fewer) exponents: $\log_b \dfrac{p^4 q^9}{v^3 \sqrt{u}}$

Solution: We add the logs that are products on the top, subtract the products on the bottom; exponents come down as coefficients:

$$4 \log_b p + 9 \log_b q - 3 \log_b v - \frac{1}{2} \log_b u.$$

Unfortunately, in Algebra 2 or Precalc, this type of problem is a very small part of the topic.

Here are two examples of problems you need to be able to solve.

Example 11: Solve for x: $\log_3 x + \log_3 (x + 6) = 3$

Solution: By the first law of logs, we get $\log_3 x(x + 6) = 3$. By the definition of logs, $x(x + 6) = 3^3$; $x^2 + 6x - 27 = (x + 9)(x - 3) = 0$. x can't be -9 because we can take the log of positive numbers only. The answer is $x = 3$. For fun, let's check: $\log_3 3 + \log_3 9 = 1 + \log_3 3^2 = 1 + 2 \log_3 3 = 1 + 2(1) = 3$.

Example 12: Solve for x: $\log_4 x - \log_4 (x - 2) = 2$.

Solution: By the second law of logarithms, we get $\log_4 \dfrac{x}{x - 2} = 2$. And by the definition of logs, $4^2 = \dfrac{16}{1} = \dfrac{x}{x - 2}$. By cross-multiplying, we get $16x - 32 = x$; so $x = \dfrac{32}{15}$. As long as this answer does not give the log of a negative number (it doesn't), this is the answer. Otherwise, this problem would have no answer.

Ⓠ   **Let's try some exercises.**

Exercise 5: $\log_4 x = -2$. $x =$

      A. -16 D. $\dfrac{1}{16}$

      B. -8 E. $\dfrac{1}{8}$

      C. $-\dfrac{1}{16}$

Exercise 6: $\log_{16} x = \dfrac{-3}{4}. x =$

A. 12

D. $-\dfrac{1}{8}$

B. 8

E. $-\dfrac{1}{12}$

C. $\dfrac{1}{8}$

Exercise 7: $\log_x 81 = 4. x =$

A. $\sqrt{3}$

D. $\dfrac{81}{4}$

B. 3

E. There is more than one answer.

C. 9

Exercise 8: $\log_{32} 64 = 5x. x =$

A. $\dfrac{1}{10}$

D. $\dfrac{1}{2}$

B. $\dfrac{6}{25}$

E. $\dfrac{6}{5}$

C. $\dfrac{2}{5}$

Exercise 9: $\log_2 x = 5 - \log_2 (x + 14). x =$

A. 2 only

D. no real number

B. 2 and -16

E. all real numbers

C. -16 only

 Let's look at the answers.

Answer 5:   D: $4^{-2} = \left(\dfrac{1}{4}\right)^2 = \dfrac{1}{16}$.

Answer 6:   C: $16^{-3/4} = \dfrac{1}{16^{3/4}} = \dfrac{1}{\left(\sqrt[4]{16}\right)^3} = \dfrac{1}{2^3} = \dfrac{1}{8}$.

Answer 7:   B: $x^4 = 81; x = 3$; only positive answers are allowed.

Answer 8:   B: $32^{5x} = 64; (2^5)^{5x} = 2^6$. When the bases are the same, the exponents must also be equal, so $25x = 6; x = \dfrac{6}{25}$.

Answer 9:   **A:** This is an incredibly tricky problem until you see the trick. You must put both logs on the same side! $\log_2 x + \log_2 (x + 14) = \log_2 x(x + 14) = 5$; so $x(x + 14) = 2^5 = 32$. Then $x^2 + 14x - 32 = (x + 16)(x - 2) = 0$; so $x = 2$, and $x = -16$, which is not allowed. Every once in a while the ACT gives choices for which you can see that only one can possibly be correct, even without doing the problem. From the expression $\log_2 x$ given in the exercise, we know that x must be greater than 0. Immediately, choices B, C, and E must be wrong. Substituting 2 in the problem, we see that it checks. If it didn't check, then the answer had to be no solution, the only one left.

Logarithms and their inverse, exponentiation (they are inverses, or opposites, similar to adding and subtracting), are the most interesting math-related topics below the level of calculus. Let me tell you the two stories I always tell at this point.

The first involves the Richter scale for earthquakes, which is roughly a logarithmic scale. Did you ever notice that a 3 causes a little shaking, a 5 causes minor damage, and at a 7, all #@$$#& breaks loose. On the Richter scale to go between two numbers, the power of the earthquake is multiplied by 1,000! A Richter scale 7 is a million times as strong as a Richter scale 3. Hopefully, it won't happen, but an earthquake of magnitude 9 is supposed to hit California before 2030. If it does, the chances are that San Francisco will be gone, Oakland will be gone, the Golden Gate Bridge will be gone. Like in a Superman movie, Nevada might become the West Coast.

Another story: This is one of the few stories for which I tell the punch line first. This is when the little guy wins. In 1905, some guy—I don't remember his name—invented a photographic process of some kind and brought it to a large company. The company said it couldn't use it, and six years later came out with the product. The little guy took the big company to court for stealing his process. Now, normally the little guy loses automatically. Not this time!!! The little guy had taken a picture of San Francisco. As you may know, in 1906 a huge earthquake destroyed San Francisco, and the little guy had a picture of the pre-earthquake city. That is when the little guy wins—when all of San Francisco gets destroyed.

Okay, okay. Enough stories for now. Let's look at trig.

CHAPTER 15: *Trigonometry*

"All math begins with whole numbers. Master them and you will begin to speak the language of math."

The secret of making trigonometry (trig) easy—yes, I mean easy—is to draw triangles. One topic, identities, is impossible to relate to triangles and is the only difficult topic in trig. It is treated very, very mildly by the ACT.

Let's start with angles. For trig purposes, we will have two measures of angles. The first one you know. There are 360 degrees in a circle. You may notice that there are many multiples of 60 in our measurements. More than 7,000 years ago, the Babylonians counted in 60s mainly because they thought there were 360 days in a year; 360 is a great number because it has many factors: 1, 2, 3, 4, 5, 6, 8, 9, 10, 12, 15, 18, 20, 24, 30, 36, 40, 45, 60, 72, 90, 120, 180, and 360. Whew!!!

Any intelligent life coming from another world would not have heard of degrees (they would quickly learn, of course!). However, all would have heard of **radians**.

Lay a radius on the circumference of a circle. The angle formed is said to be one radian.

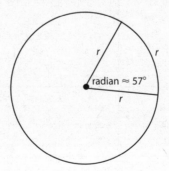

There are a little over 6, or exactly 2π radians in a circle. So $2\pi = 360°$. This means $1° = \dfrac{\pi}{180}$ radians, and a radian is $\approx 57°$. However, we usually express radian in terms of π, so we should be concerned with only two conversions:

1. To change from degrees to radians, multiply by $\dfrac{\pi}{180}$.

2. To change from radians to degrees, multiply by $\dfrac{180}{\pi}$.

   Example 1:   Change 45° to radians.

   Solution: $45 \times \dfrac{\pi}{180} = \dfrac{\pi}{4}$ radians.

   Example 2:   Change from $\dfrac{\pi}{6}$ radians to degrees.

   Solution: $\dfrac{\pi}{6} \times \dfrac{180}{\pi} = 30°$.

So we see that $\dfrac{\pi}{6}$ radians = 30°, and $\dfrac{\pi}{4}$ radians = 45°.

It also is a good idea to learn the most important multiples of 30° and 45°:

$$\dfrac{\pi}{6} = 30°, \dfrac{\pi}{4} = 45°, \dfrac{\pi}{3} = 60°, \dfrac{\pi}{2} = 90°, \pi = 180°, \dfrac{3\pi}{2} = 270°, \text{ and } 2\pi = 360°.$$

If you know more, that is better, but this is enough.

TRIG RATIOS

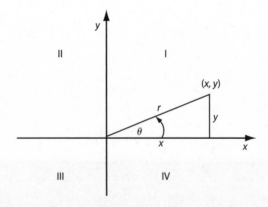

Angles, represented here by the Greek letter theta, θ, are positive if measured counterclockwise from the positive x-axis. The plane is divided into 4 quadrants, as indicated.

Locate the point (x, y) at a distance r from the origin, where $r = \sqrt{x^2 + y^2}$ is always positive.

Note *Always draw the triangle up or down to the x-axis.*

Referring to this triangle, which is a right triangle, we can define the six basic trigonometric ratios:

Function	Abbreviation	Ratio	Function	Abbreviation	Ratio
sine θ	sin θ	$\dfrac{y}{r}$	cotangent θ	cot θ	$\dfrac{x}{y}$
cosine θ	cos θ	$\dfrac{x}{r}$	secant θ	sec θ	$\dfrac{r}{x}$
tangent θ	tan θ	$\dfrac{y}{x}$	cosecant θ	csc θ	$\dfrac{r}{y}$

You must know these definitions!

Example 3: Let $\sin A = \dfrac{7}{10}$ in quadrant II. Find sec A.

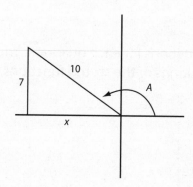

Solution: $\sin A = \dfrac{7}{10} = \dfrac{y}{r}$. Then, to find x, we can let $y = 7$ and $r = 10$, and we can use the Pythagorean Theorem: $x = \pm \sqrt{10^2 - 7^2} = \pm \sqrt{51}$. Because x is to the left, it is a negative x value. Then $\sec A = \dfrac{r}{x} = \dfrac{10}{-\sqrt{51}} = \dfrac{-10\sqrt{51}}{51}$.

Note *Once you get x, you have all six of the trig functions!*

Example 4:   Let $\tan B = \dfrac{5}{9}$ in quadrant III. Find $\cos B$.

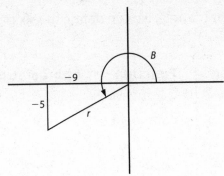

Solution: $\tan B = \dfrac{5}{9} = \dfrac{y}{x}$. In quadrant III, both x and y are negative. We let $y = -5$

and $x = -9$.

Then $r = \sqrt{9^2 + 5^2} = \sqrt{106}$. Then $\cos B = \dfrac{x}{r} = \dfrac{-9}{\sqrt{106}} = \dfrac{-9\sqrt{106}}{106}$.

Note   *Remember, r is always positive.*

It is necessary to know the signs of the trig functions for each quadrant. You should know the following sign diagram. If you know the definitions of the six trig functions, you should be able to figure this out yourself.

II	I
$x < 0$	$x > 0$
$y > 0$	$y > 0$
$r > 0$	$r > 0$
only sin, csc positive	all positive
$x < 0$	$x > 0$
$y < 0$	$y < 0$
$r > 0$	$r > 0$
only tan, cot positive	only cos, sec positive
III	IV

FINDING TRIG VALUES FOR MULTIPLES OF 30°, 45°, 60°, AND 90°

For this section, we have to recall the 45°-45°-90° and 30°-60°-90° triangles we discussed in Chapter 10. Let's give specific values for the sides of these triangles.

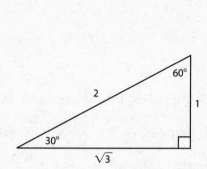

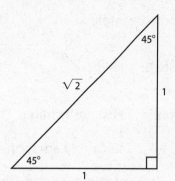

In the 30°-60°-90° triangle, if we let 1 = side opposite the 30° angle, then we know the hypotenuse is twice that, or 2, and we can find the side opposite the 60° angle, $\sqrt{3}$, by using the Pythagorean Theorem.

In the 45°-45°-90° triangle, if we let the sides opposite both 45° angles = 1, the Pythagorean Theorem tells us the side opposite the right angle = $\sqrt{2}$.

Example 5:　Find cos 150°.

Solution:

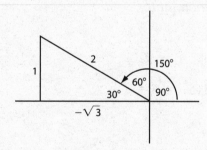

We draw the angle counterclockwise from the positive axis: 90° + 60° = 150°. The angle with the *x*-axis is 30°, giving us a 30°-60°-90° right triangle. The side opposite the 30° angle is 1, and it is +1 because it is "up." The side opposite the 60° angle is $-\sqrt{3}$. It is to the left, so it is negative. The hypotenuse is 2; as we have already seen, it is always positive. So $\cos 120° = \dfrac{x}{r} = \dfrac{-\sqrt{3}}{2}$.

 We always draw the triangle to the x-axis.

Let's do two more examples.

Example 6:   Find $\cot \dfrac{4\pi}{3}$.

Solution: First, let's change the angle to degrees. I do this wherever possible because I am more familiar with degrees. $\dfrac{4\pi}{3} \times \dfrac{180}{\pi} = 240°$. When we draw the picture (below), we see that $\cot 240° = \dfrac{-1}{-\sqrt{3}} \times \dfrac{\sqrt{3}}{\sqrt{3}} = \dfrac{\sqrt{3}}{3}$.

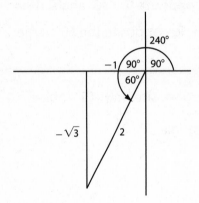

Note   *The ACT always rationalizes the denominator.*

Example 7:   Find $\csc 315°$.

Solution: Draw the figure. $\csc 315° = \dfrac{r}{y} = \dfrac{\sqrt{2}}{-1} = -\sqrt{2}$.

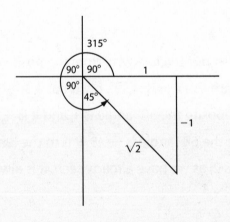

MULTIPLES OF 90°

To find the values of x, y, and r for angles on the axes, assume r is along the axis and equals 1. Then determine whether x and y are 0, $+1$, or -1 along that axis, and proceed as above.

Example 8:   Find all six trig functions for 180°.

Solution:

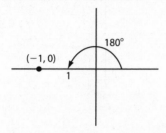

When we draw an angle of 180°, we wind up on the negative x-axis. Let $r = 1$, and then the point on the x-axis would be $(-1, 0)$ or $x = -1$ and $y = 0$. Once we know x, y, and r, we know all six trig functions. The ACT would ask for only one, but let's do all six in this case.

$$\sin 180° = y/r = 0/1 = 0 \qquad \cos 180° = x/r = -1/1 = -1$$
$$\tan 180° = y/x = 0/1 = 0 \qquad \cot 180° = x/y = -1/0, \text{ undefined}$$
$$\sec 180° = r/x = 1/-1 = -1 \qquad \csc 180° = r/y = 1/0, \text{ undefined}$$

 For all multiples of 90°, two of the trig functions will always be 0, two will always be undefined (0 is the denominator), and two will both be either 1 or -1.

SKETCHING SINES AND COSINES

The ACT will not ask you to sketch sines and cosines, but the questions the ACT asks can be answered only if you know what the sketches look like. We will do most everything in degrees, but we will refer to radians when appropriate.

All trig functions are **periodic**. That means they repeat. The **period** is the smallest interval in which the trig functions repeat. For sine and cosine (and secant and cosecant), the period is 360° or 2π. The period for tangent and cotangent is 180° or π.

If we were to graph $y = \sin x$ and $y = \cos x$, the pictures would look like these:

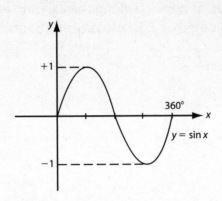

Example 9:   Sketch $y = 4 \sin x$.

Solution:

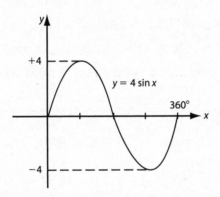

If you draw the figure, it goes four times as high as $y = \sin x$.

Note   *The height is called the **amplitude**. The definition of amplitude is* $\dfrac{\text{max} - \text{min}}{2}$.

Example 10:   Sketch $y = -6 \cos x$.

Solution:

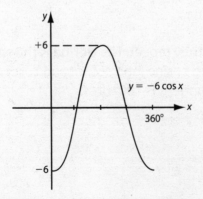

This graph is 6 times as high as $y = \cos x$. The minus sign means the curve is upside down. What is the amplitude? The amplitude is

$$\frac{\text{max} - \text{min}}{2} = \frac{6 - (-6)}{2} = \frac{12}{2} = 6.$$

Rule 1: If $y = A \sin x$ or $y = A \cos x$, the amplitude is $|A|$.

Example 11: Sketch $y = 10 \sin 4x$, in degrees.

Solution:

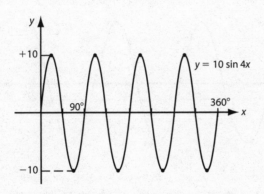

The amplitude is 10, and the graph is not upside down. The graph reaches 360° four times faster, so the period is $\dfrac{360°}{4} = 90°$.

Example 12: Sketch $y = -7 \sin \dfrac{x}{5}$.

Solution:

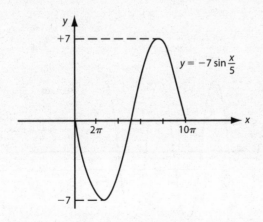

The amplitude is 7, and the graph is upside down. The period is

$\dfrac{2\pi}{\frac{1}{5}} = 10\pi$, meaning the graph is "stretched out" five times more than

$y = \sin x$.

So we can add to Rule 1:

Rules 1 and 2: If $y = A \sin Bx$ or $y = A \cos Bx$, the amplitude is $|A|$, and the period $= \dfrac{360°}{B}$ or $\dfrac{2\pi}{B}$ radians.

Example 13: Sketch $y = -2 \sin (3x - 120°)$.

Solution:

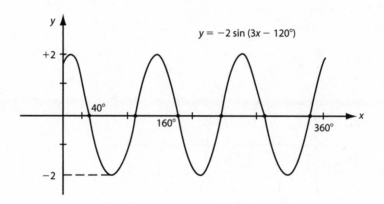

The amplitude is 2, the graph is upside down, and the period is $\dfrac{360°}{3} = 120°$. We know the beginning of our curve is at $0°$. If we set $3x - 120° = 0$, we get $x = 40°$. This means a **left-right shift** of $40°$ to the right.

Example 14: Sketch $y = 9 \cos (6x + \dfrac{\pi}{5})$.

Solution:

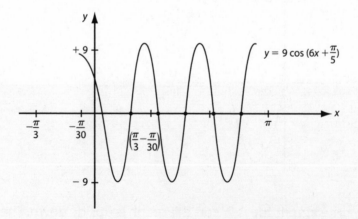

The amplitude is 9, the graph is not upside down, and the period is $\dfrac{2\pi}{6} = \dfrac{\pi}{3}$. If we set $6x + \dfrac{\pi}{5} = 0, x = -\dfrac{\pi}{30}$, so there is a $\dfrac{\pi}{30}$ shift to the left.

So we can add another rule:

Rules 1, 2, and 3: If $y = A \sin (Bx + C)$ or $y = A \cos (Bx + C)$, the amplitude is $|A|$, the period is $\dfrac{360°}{B}$ or $\dfrac{2\pi}{B}$, and the left-right shift is $-\dfrac{C}{B}$.

Example 15: Sketch $y = 2 \sin (5x - 30°) + 7$.

Solution:

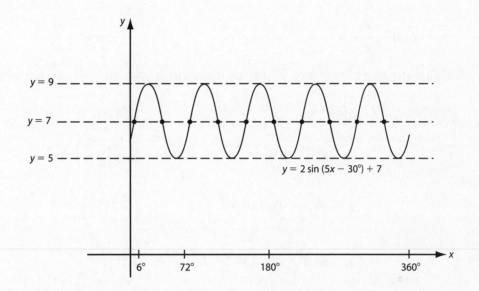

$$y = 2 \sin (5x - 30°) + 7$$

The amplitude is 2, the graph is not upside down, the period is $\dfrac{360°}{5} = 72°$, the left-right shift is $-\dfrac{(-30°)}{5} = 6°$ to the right, and the up-down shift is 7 up (sounds like a good name for a soft drink!).

So finally, we can put all the rules together:

Rules 1, 2, 3, and 4: If $y = A \sin (Bx + C) + D$ or $y = A \cos (Bx + C) + D$, then

- $|A|$ is the amplitude. If $A > 0$, the graph not upside-down; if $A < 0$, the graph is upside down.

- Period is $\dfrac{360°}{B}$ or $\dfrac{2\pi}{B}$.

- Left-right shift is $-\dfrac{C}{B}$.

- Up-down shift is D: if $D > 0$, it is up; if $D < 0$, it is down.

That's it for sketching sines and cosines.

TRIGONOMETRIC IDENTITIES

An **identity** is an equation that is always true as long as it is defined. For example, $2x + 3x = 5x$ is an identity because no matter what number is used for x, $2x + 3x = 5x$.

The ACT requires you to know some trigonometric identities. Fortunately, they are the most basic ones. Let's rewrite the basic six ratios again:

$$\sin \theta = \frac{y}{r} \qquad \cos \theta = \frac{x}{r} \qquad \tan \theta = \frac{y}{x}$$

$$\cot \theta = \frac{x}{y} \qquad \sec \theta = \frac{r}{x} \qquad \csc \theta = \frac{r}{y}$$

Now let's list the eight identities you absolutely, positively must know perfectly!

Identity	Reason
1. $\sin A \times \csc A = 1$	$\left(\dfrac{y}{r}\right)\left(\dfrac{r}{y}\right) = 1$
2. $\cos A \times \sec A = 1$	$\left(\dfrac{x}{r}\right)\left(\dfrac{r}{x}\right) = 1$
3. $\tan A \times \cot A = 1$	$\left(\dfrac{y}{x}\right)\left(\dfrac{x}{y}\right) = 1$
4. $\tan A = \dfrac{\sin A}{\cos A}$	$\dfrac{y}{r} \div \dfrac{x}{r} = \dfrac{y}{r} \times \dfrac{r}{x} = \dfrac{y}{x}$
5. $\cot A = \dfrac{\cos A}{\sin A}$	$\dfrac{x}{r} \div \dfrac{y}{r} = \dfrac{x}{r} \times \dfrac{r}{y} = \dfrac{x}{y}$
6. $\sin^2 A + \cos^2 A = 1$	Divide each term of $x^2 + y^2 = r^2$ by r^2.
7. $1 + \tan^2 A = \sec^2 A$	Divide each term of $x^2 + y^2 = r^2$ by x^2.
8. $1 + \cot^2 A = \csc^2 A$	Divide each term of $x^2 + y^2 = r^2$ by y^2.

Q **Let's do a few exercises.**

Exercise 1: $\sin G \times \cot G =$

A. $\sin G$ D. $\cot G$

B. $\cos G$ E. $\sec G$

C. $\tan G$

Exercise 2: Given $\sin (A + B) = \sin A \cos B + \cos A \sin B$, and given $\dfrac{5\pi}{12} = \dfrac{\pi}{4} + \dfrac{\pi}{6}$, then $\sin \left(\dfrac{5\pi}{12}\right) =$

A. $\dfrac{1}{2}$ D. $\dfrac{\sqrt{6} + \sqrt{2}}{4}$

B. $\dfrac{\sqrt{3}}{2}$ E. 1

C. $\dfrac{\sqrt{6} - \sqrt{2}}{4}$

A **Let's look at the answers.**

Answer 1: B: $\cot G = \dfrac{\cos G}{\sin G}$, so $\sin G \times \dfrac{\cos G}{\sin G} = \cos G$.

Answer 2: D: First change each of the radians to degrees. We get $75° = 45° + 30°$. So $\sin 75° = \sin 45° \cos 30° + \cos 45° \sin 30°$. Then $\sin(45° + 30°) =$

$$\frac{1}{\sqrt{2}} \times \frac{\sqrt{3}}{2} + \frac{1}{\sqrt{2}} \times \frac{1}{2} = \frac{\sqrt{3} + 1}{2\sqrt{2}} \times \frac{\sqrt{2}}{\sqrt{2}} = \frac{\sqrt{6} + \sqrt{2}}{4}.$$

TRIGONOMETRIC EQUATIONS

Trig equations are like regular equations except we must find the angles. The following three examples will give answers in both degrees and radians, with all answers between 0° and 360° (0 and 2π) including 0°.

Example 16: Solve for x: $\cos x + 2 \sin x \cos x = 0$.

Solution: Take out the common factor: $\cos x (2 \sin x + 1) = 0$. This means either $\cos x = 0$ or $\sin x = -\dfrac{1}{2}$. We know sine is negative in quadrants III and IV.

We then draw the appropriate triangles and we see that $x = 210°$ and $330°$, or in radians, $\frac{7}{6}\pi$ and $\frac{11}{6}\pi$.

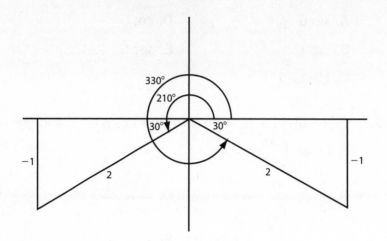

A little trick: Draw the $y = \cos x$ curve. From this curve, we see that $\cos x = 0$ at $90°$ or $270°$, or in radians, $\frac{\pi}{2}$ or $\frac{3\pi}{2}$.

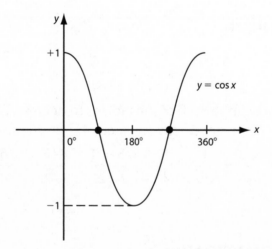

Note   *Also note that $\cos 0° = \cos 360° = 1$ and $\cos 180° = -1$.*

Example 17: Solve for x: $4 \sin^3 x - 3 \sin x = 0$.

Solution: We get $\sin x (4 \sin^2 x - 3) = 0$. Thus, $\sin x = 0$ or $4 \sin^2 x = 3$; $\sin^2 x = \frac{3}{4}$; $\sin x = \pm \frac{\sqrt{3}}{2}$. $\sin x = 0$ for $x = 0°$ and $180°$ (see the sine curve below), or in radians 0 and π. We don't include $360°$ or 2π because it is the same as 0.

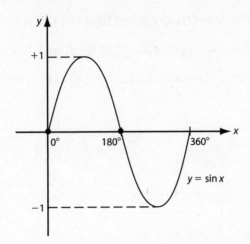

Next, we see $\sin x = +\dfrac{\sqrt{3}}{2}$ in quadrants I and II, and $x = -\dfrac{\sqrt{3}}{2}$ in quadrants III and IV. From the graph below, we can see that $x = 60°, 120°, 240°$, and $300°$, or in radians, $x = \dfrac{\pi}{3}, \dfrac{2\pi}{3}, \dfrac{4\pi}{3}$, and $\dfrac{5\pi}{3}$.

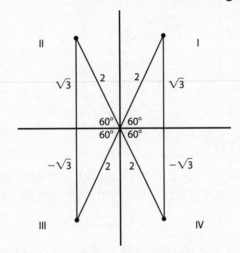

There are six solutions to this problem.

Note $\sin 90° \ (or \sin \dfrac{\pi}{2}) = 1; \ \sin 270° \ (or \sin \dfrac{3\pi}{2}) = -1.$

Example 18:   Solve for x: $\tan^2 x + \sec x - 1 = 0$.

Solution: We let $\tan^2 x = \sec^2 x - 1$. The equation becomes $\sec^2 x - 1 + \sec x - 1$

$= \sec^2 x + \sec x - 2 = (\sec x + 2)(\sec x - 1) = 0$. So the roots of the

equation are $\sec x = -2$ or $\sec x = 1$. But $\cos x = \dfrac{1}{\sec x}$, so we can

rewrite the roots as $\dfrac{1}{\cos x} = -2$, or $\cos x = -\dfrac{1}{2}$ and $\cos x = 1$.

From the graph of $y = \cos x$, we see that $\cos x = 1$ means $x = 0°$, or 0 radians. For $\cos x = -\dfrac{1}{2}$, $\cos x$ is negative in quadrants II and III, as seen in the graph below. Then $x = 120°$ and $240°$, or in radians, $\dfrac{2}{3}\pi$ and $\dfrac{4}{3}\pi$.

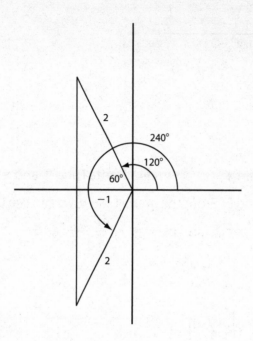

RIGHT-ANGLE TRIGONOMETRY

I believe that if you do non-right-angle trig first and then do right-angle trig last, right-angle trig seems very easy. If you do right-angle trig first, then non-right-angle trig is not so easy. That is why I'm following this order.

Take the definitions we have been using. Put the triangle in the first quadrant. Then remove the triangle from the x and y axes. You get the following right triangle:

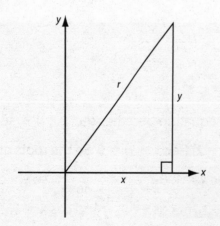
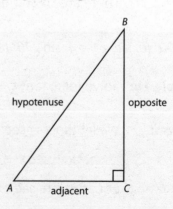

Notice: $\sin A = \dfrac{y}{r} = \dfrac{BC}{AB} = \dfrac{\text{opposite}}{\text{hypotenuse}}$ $\cos A = \dfrac{x}{r} = \dfrac{AC}{AB} = \dfrac{\text{adjacent}}{\text{hypotenuse}}$

  $\tan A = \dfrac{y}{x} = \dfrac{BC}{AC} = \dfrac{\text{opposite}}{\text{adjacent}}$ $\cot A = \dfrac{x}{y} = \dfrac{AC}{BC} = \dfrac{\text{adjacent}}{\text{opposite}}$

Note Notice $\sin A = \cos B$, $\cos A = \sin B$, $\tan A = \cot B$, and $\cot A = \tan B$.

Note We don't bother with secant and cosecant with right triangles because no one has A.C. (After Calculator). Sometimes we don't even bother with cotangent.

Q **Let's try an ACT-type exercise.**

Exercise 3:

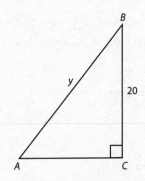

For triangle *ABC*, in terms of angle *A*, *y* =

A. 20 cos *A*   **D.** $\dfrac{20}{\sin A}$

B. $\dfrac{20}{\cos A}$ **E.** $\dfrac{20}{\tan A}$

C. 20 sin *A*

A **Let's look at the answer.**

Answer 3:   D: $\sin A = \dfrac{\text{opposite}}{\text{hypotenuse}} = \dfrac{20}{y}$; $y \sin A = 20$; so $y = \dfrac{20}{\sin A}$.

LAW OF SINES AND LAW OF COSINES

This is not a required topic on the ACT. However, the ACT may ask questions on these topics. If you have not seen them, you are at a disadvantage.

In geometry we learned that the largest side of a triangle lies opposite the largest angle (see triangle *ABC*).

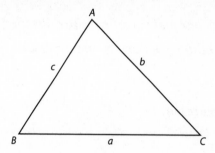

In fact, for any triangle (not just right triangles), the ratios of any side to the sine of the angle opposite that side are always the same. This is represented mathematically by the **law of sines**:

$$\frac{a}{\sin A} = \frac{b}{\sin B} = \frac{c}{\sin C}$$

The **law of cosines** states that for any triangle *ABC*:

$$c^2 = a^2 + b^2 - 2ab \cos C$$

In general, (side 1)^2 = (side 2)^2 + (side 3)^2 − 2(side 2)(side3)(cos of the angle opposite side 1).

Those of you who have had trig know that these two laws are not quite enough, but it is more than enough for the ACT.

Example 19:   In a triangle *ABC*, let $c = 5$, $b = 6$ and $\angle A = 52°$. Find the length of side *a*.

Solution: We do not have a side and an angle opposite, so we need the law of cosines. We have $a^2 = b^2 + c^2 - 2bc \cos A$, or $6^2 + 5^2 - 2(6)(5) \cos 52°$. Then $a = \sqrt{61 - 60 \cos 52°}$, which we would do by calculator.

Note   *Once you get four parts of a triangle, you could always use the law of sines for the other parts. If you know two angles, to get the third angle you would subtract the sum of the other two from 180°.*

Example 20: In a triangle DEF, let $d = 7$, $e = 8$, and $f = 9$. Find the middle angle.

Solution: We have no angles, so we must use the law of cosines, which can be written as $e^2 = f^2 + d^2 - 2fd \cos E$, or $8^2 = 9^2 + 7^2 - 2(9)(7) \cos E$; $64 = 130 - 126 \cos E$; $\cos E = \dfrac{66}{126}$.

Note *E is the middle angle because e is the middle side (in size).*

Note *To find angle E, you would hit $\cos^{-1}$ (inverse cosine) on the calculator. It is not part of the ACT.*

Example 21: In a triangle MNP, let $\angle M = 40°$, $\angle N = 85°$, and $m = 10$ meters. Find side p.

Solution: $\angle P = 180° - (40° + 85°) = 55°$. We have a side and an angle opposite. We can use the law of sines, $\dfrac{m}{\sin M} = \dfrac{p}{\sin P}$, or $\dfrac{10}{\sin 40°} = \dfrac{p}{\sin 55°}$. By cross-multiplying and solving, we get $p = 10\left(\dfrac{\sin 55°}{\sin 40°}\right)$.

That's all for the trig. Let's get to the chapter on the topics that didn't seem to fit well into any other chapter.

"*At this point, your probability of success has greatly increased.*"

This chapter is a combination of the remaining topics.

COUNTING

The **basic law of counting** says: "If you can do something in p ways, and a second thing in q ways, and a third thing in r ways, and so on, the total number of ways you can do the first thing, then the second thing, then the third thing , etc., is $p \times q \times r \times \ldots$.

Example 1: If we have a lunch choice of 5 sandwiches, 4 desserts, and 3 drinks, and we can have one of each, how many different meals could we choose?

Solution: We can choose from $(5)(4)(3) = 60$ different meals

Arrangements

Let $n(A)$ be the number of elements in set A. In how many ways can these elements be arranged? The answer is that the first has n choices, the second has $(n - 1)$ choices (because one is already used), the third has $(n - 2)$ choices, all the way down to the last element, which has only one choice. In general, if there are n choices, the number of ways to choose is $n!$ (read as "**n factorial**") $= n(n - 1)(n - 2) \times \ldots (3)(2)(1)$.

Example 2: How many ways can five people line up?

Solution: This is just $5 \times 4 \times 3 \times 2 \times 1 = 120$.

Example 3: How many ways can 5 people sit in a circle?

Solution: It would appear to be the same question as Example 2, but it's not. If we draw the picture, each of the five positions would be the same. The answer is $(5)(4)(3)(2)(1) \div 5 = (4)(3)(2)(1) = 24$. So n people can sit in a circle in $(n - 1)!$ ways.

Permutations

Permutations are essentially the law of counting without repeating, but order is important.

Example 4: How many ways can 7 people occupy 3 seats on a bench?

Solution: Any one of 7 people can be in the first seat, then any one of 6 people can be in the second seat, and any one of 5 people can be in the third seat. The total number would be $(7)(6)(5) = 210$ ways. There are many notations for permutations. One notation for this example would be $P(7, 3)$.

Combinations

Combinations are essentially the law of counting, with no repetition, and order doesn't matter.

Example 5: How many sets of three different letters can be made from eight different letters?

Solution: Because order doesn't matter, unlike the case for permutations, AB is the same as BA. So we can take the number of permutations, but we have to divide by the number of duplicates. It turns out that the duplicates for 3 letters is $3 \times 2 \times 1 = 6$. So we would have $\dfrac{8 \times 7 \times 6}{3 \times 2 \times 1} = 56$.

Again, there are many notations for combinations. One notation for this example is $C(8, 3)$.

Avoiding Duplicates

When we count how many ways to do A or B, we should be careful not to count any item twice. We must subtract any items that include both A and B:

$$N(A \text{ or } B) = N(A) + N(B) - N(A \text{ and } B)$$

Example 6:   Thirty students take French or German. If 20 took French and 18 took German, and if each student took at least one language, how many took both French and German?

Solution: $N(A \text{ or } B) = N(A) + N(B) - N(A \text{ and } B)$ or $30 = 20 + 18 - x$, so $x = 8$ took both languages.

Example 7:   Forty students take Chinese or Japanese. If 9 take both and 20 take Japanese, how many students take Chinese?

Solution: $N(C \text{ or } J) = N(C) + N(J) - N(\text{both})$, or $40 = x + 20 - 9$, so $x = 29$ take Chinese.

(Q)   **Let's do some exercises.**

For Exercises 1–5, use the set {e, f, g, h, i}. A word is considered to be any group of letters together; for example, hhg is a three-letter word.

Exercise 1:   From this set, the number of three-letter words is:

A. 6   D. 60

B. 27   E. 125

C. 30

Exercise 2:   How many three-letter permutations are there in this set?

A. 6   D. 60

B. 27   E. 125

C. 30

Exercise 3:   How many three-letter words starting with a vowel and ending in a consonant can be made from this set?

A. 6   D. 60

B. 27   E. 125

C. 30

Exercise 4:   How many three-letter words with the second and third letters the same can be made from this set?

A. 5   D. 60

B. 20   E. 125

C. 25

Exercise 5:   How many three-letter permutations with the first and last letters *not* vowels can be made from this set?

A. 18   D. 45

B. 27   E. 125

C. 30

Exercise 6:   Fifty students take Spanish or Portuguese. If 20 take both and 40 take Spanish, the number of students taking Portuguese *only* is

A. 0   D. 20

B. 5   E. 30

C. 10

 Let's look at the answers.

Answer 1:   E: (5)(5)(5) = 125.

Answer 2:   D: (5)(4)(3) = 60.

Answer 3:   C: The first letter has 2 choices, the second can be any 5, and the third has 3 choices, so (2)(5)(3) = 30.

Answer 4:   C: There are 5 choices for the first two letters, but there is only 1 choice for the third letter because it must be the same as the second, so (5)(5)(1) = 25.

Answer 5:   A: There are 3 choices for the first letter, but only 2 choices for the last letter because it can't be a vowel and must be different than the first letter. There are three choices for the middle letter because two letters have already been used, so the answer is (3)(3)(2) = 18. These questions must be read very carefully!

Answer 6: **C:** This is not quite the same as the previous exercise. $N(S \text{ or } P) = N(S) + N(P) - N(\text{both})$; $50 = 40 + x - 20$; $x = 30$. But that is not the answer. If 30 take Portuguese and 20 take both, then 10 take Portuguese only.

PROBABILITY

The probability of an event is the number of "good" outcomes divided by the total number of outcomes possible, or $Pr(\text{success}) = \dfrac{\text{good outcomes}}{\text{total outcomes}}$.

Example 8: Consider the following sets: {26-letter English alphabet}; vowels = {a, e, i, o, u}; consonants = {the rest of the letters}. What are the probabilities of choosing a vowel? a consonant? any letter? π?

Solutions: $Pr(\text{vowel}) = \dfrac{5}{26}$; $Pr(\text{consonant}) = \dfrac{21}{26}$; $Pr(\text{letter}) = \dfrac{26}{26} = 1$; $Pr(\pi) = \dfrac{0}{26} = 0$.

Probability follows the same rule about avoiding duplicates as discussed in the previous section.

$$Pr(A \text{ or } B) = Pr(A) + Pr(B) - Pr(A \text{ and } B)$$

Example 9: What is the probability that a spade or an ace is pulled from a 52-card deck?

Solution: $Pr(\text{Spade or ace}) = Pr(\text{Spade}) + Pr(\text{Ace}) - Pr(\text{Spade ace}) =$

$$\dfrac{13}{52} + \dfrac{4}{52} - \dfrac{1}{52} = \dfrac{16}{52} = \dfrac{4}{13}.$$

As weird as it sounds, whenever I taught this in a class, I never failed to have at least two students who didn't know what a deck of cards was, and I taught in New York City!

Use this figure for Examples 10 and 11. In the jar are five red balls and three yellow balls.

Example 10: What is the probability that two yellow balls are picked, with replacement?

Solution: $Pr(2 \text{ yellow balls, with replacement}) = \left(\dfrac{3}{8}\right)\left(\dfrac{3}{8}\right) = \dfrac{9}{64}$

Example 11: What is the probability of picking two yellow balls, without replacement?

Solution: $Pr(2 \text{ yellow balls, no replacement}) = \left(\dfrac{3}{8}\right)\left(\dfrac{2}{7}\right) = \dfrac{3}{28}$

CHARTS AND GRAPHS

The arithmetic on the actual ACT could be less or more, nicer or messier, than the following exercises.

(Q)   **Let's do some exercises.**

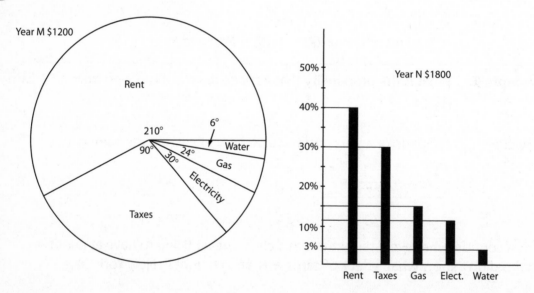

Some of the major expenses of the apartment of Mr. and Mrs. Smith in Smallville, USA, are shown in this pie chart and bar graph. The pie chart is for year *M* with a $1200 budget, and the bar graph is for year *N*, some years later, with an $1800 budget. Use these data for Exercises 7 through 11.

Exercise 7:   The smallest percentage increase from year *M* to year *N* is for

A. rent

B. taxes

C. electricity

D. gas

E. water

Exercise 8:　The largest percentage increase from year *M* to year *N* is for

    A. rent　　　　　　　　　**D.** gas

    B. taxes　　　　　　　　　**E.** water

    C. electricity

Exercise 9:　The change in rent from year *M* to year *N* was

    A. −$80　　　　　　　　　**D.** +$100

    B. none　　　　　　　　　**E.** +$190

    C. +$20

Exercise 10:　The two closest monetary amounts are

    A. rent in year *M* and　　　　**D.** taxes in year *M* and gas in year *N*
       rent in year *N*

    B. electricity in year *M* and　　**E.** electricity in year *M* and electricity
       gas in year *N*　　　　　　　　in year *N*

    C. water in year *M* and
       water in year *N*

Exercise 11:　Which expenses exceeded the percentage increase in the total budget?

    A. All the expenses　　　　　**D.** All except water and rent

    B. All except rent　　　　　　**E.** All except rent and taxes

    C. All except rater

These exercises are easier to answer if we exactly calculate all of the money answers and put the items next to each other in a table:

	Year *M*	Year *N*
Rent	$\frac{210}{360} \times \$1200 = \frac{7}{12} \times \$1200 = \$700$	$.40 \times \$1800 = \$720$
Taxes	$300	$540
Electricity	$100	$216
Gas	$80	$270
Water	$20	$54

Let's look at the answers.

Answer 7:   **A:** Rent increased by only $20 (due perhaps to rent control or family member owner); the percentage increase is the smallest increase $\left(= \dfrac{20}{700} \times 100\right)$. We don't actually have to calculate the exact percentage. We only have to note the percentage increase is obviously much smaller than the percentage increase of any other item.

Answer 8:   **D:** The percentage increase for gas is $\dfrac{190}{80} \times 100\%$, or more than a 200% increase.

Answer 9:   **C:** $720 - $700 = $20.

Answer 10:   **A:** The rents in year M and year N are only $20 apart. No other choices are this close.

Answer 11:   **B:** The total increase from year M to year N is 50%, taxes almost doubled, electricity more than doubled: gas more than tripled, and water almost tripled.

The ACT doesn't usually ask more than one question on graphs or charts.

SETS

We have mentioned the topic of sets informally. Now let's be a little more formal.

Sets are denoted by braces $\{a, b, c\}$. This set has three elements: a, b, and c.

Example 12: $A = \{a, b\}$, $B = \{b, a\}$, $C = \{a, b, b, b, a, b, b, a, a\}$. How is set A related to set B? To set C?

Solutions: $A = B$ because the order does not matter in sets. $A = C$ because repeated elements are counted only once; C has only two elements in it: a and b.

We write $A \cup B$, read "A **union** B," as the set of elements in A or in B or in both.

We write $A \cap B$, read "A **intersect(ion)** B," as the set of elements common to A and B.

The **null set**, written $\{\}$ or ϕ (the Greek letter phi), is the set with nothing in it.

Example 13: Let $D = \{a, b, c, d, e, f\}, E = \{c, d, f, g\}, F = \{a, b, e\}$. Find $D \cup E, D \cap E$, and $E \cap F$.

Solution: $D \cup E = \{a, b, c, d, e, f, g\}; D \cap E = \{c, d, f\}; E \cap F = \phi$. Sets with no common elements are called **disjoint**.

We say A is a subset of B, written $A \subseteq B$ if every element in A is also in B. If a set has n elements, it has 2^n subsets.

Example 14: Write all the subsets of $G = \{a, b, c\}$.

Solution: Because G has 3 elements, there are $2^3 = 8$ subsets. They are: ϕ, $\{a\}$, $\{b\}$, $\{c\}$, $\{a, b\}$, $\{a, c\}$, $\{b, c\}$, $\{a, b, c\}$

Two other terms relating to sets that we need to know are:

- The **universe**, which is the set of everything we are talking about.

  Example 15: The universe U could be {all animals}, or it could be $A = $ {all mammals.} It depends on what our topic of interest is. Note that $A \subseteq U$.

- A **complement** is the set of elements in the universe not in a specific set. The complement is denoted by a superscript letter c, so A^c is the complement of A. There are many other symbols in math for the complement.

  Example 16: If $U = $ {all animals} and $M = $ {all mammals}, then $M^c = $ {reptiles, insects, fish, etc.}

  Example 17: If the alphabet is the universe, and $A = $ {vowels}, then $A^c = $ {consonants}.

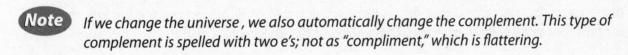 *If we change the universe, we also automatically change the complement. This type of complement is spelled with two e's; not as "compliment," which is flattering.*

MATRICES

The topic of matrices (singular is matrix) is my least favorite. It is not because it is hard; it actually is pretty easy. It is because it is unnecessary. Other topics are a lot more important but have less time spent on them because of the topic of matrices. However, the ACT says you need it; so we'll do it.

A matrix is an array of numbers. We will use letters to stand for numbers. $\begin{bmatrix} a & b & c \\ d & e & f \end{bmatrix}$ is a 2 by 3 matrix, written 2 × 3. It has 2 rows: row 1, $\begin{bmatrix} a & b & c \end{bmatrix}$; and row 2, $\begin{bmatrix} d & e & f \end{bmatrix}$. It has 3 columns: column 1, $\begin{bmatrix} a \\ d \end{bmatrix}$; column 2, $\begin{bmatrix} b \\ e \end{bmatrix}$; and column 3, $\begin{bmatrix} c \\ f \end{bmatrix}$.

To add two matrices, they must have the same number of rows and columns. You then add the corresponding entries.

Example 18: $\begin{bmatrix} a & b & c \\ d & e & f \end{bmatrix} + \begin{bmatrix} r & s & t \\ u & v & w \end{bmatrix} =$

Solution: $\begin{bmatrix} a+r & b+s & c+t \\ d+u & e+v & f+w \end{bmatrix}$

To multiply two matrices, the number of columns of the first matrix must be the same as the number of rows of the second. If we have a 2 × 5 matrix multiplied by a 5 × 3 matrix, we would get a 2 × 3 matrix. However, multiplying a 5 × 3 matrix by a 2 × 5 matrix is impossible because 3 (columns in the first matrix) is not equal to 2 (rows in the second matrix).

The next example shows the procedure for multiplying matrices.

Example 19: Let $A = \begin{bmatrix} b & c & d \\ f & g & h \end{bmatrix}$ and $B = \begin{bmatrix} j & m \\ k & n \\ l & p \end{bmatrix}$. Find AB and BA.

Solution: A is a 2 × 3 matrix, and B is a 3 × 2 matrix. AB would be a 2 × 2 matrix.

The first entry is found by multiplying the first row of A by the first column of B. The entry would be the element in the first row, first column of AB. We get $bj + ck + dl$. The first row of A multiplied by the second column of B gives the first row, second column of AB. We get $bm + cn + dp$. The second row, first column of AB is $fj + gk + hl$, and the second column, second row of AB is $fm + gn + hp$. The matrix AB would look like this:

$$AB = \begin{bmatrix} bj + ck + dl & bm + cn + dp \\ fj + gk + hl & fm + gn + hp \end{bmatrix}$$

Similarly, to get BA, we are multiplying a 3 × 2 matrix by a 2 × 3 matrix, so we get a 3 × 3 matrix:

$$BA = \begin{bmatrix} jb + mf & jc + mg & jd + mh \\ kb + nf & kc + ng & kd + nh \\ lb + pf & lc + pg & ld + ph \end{bmatrix}$$

TRANSLATIONS

Let's look at the graph of $y = x^2$:

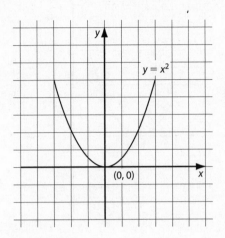

Translations of this graph include the following:

- The same graph 3 units down would be $y = x^2 - 3$.

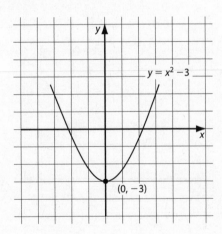

- Or the same graph 5 units up would be $y = x^2 + 5$.

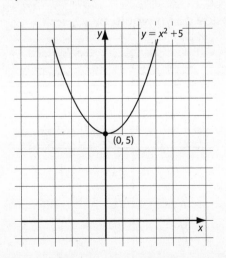

- Or the same graph 4 units to the left would be $y = (x + 4)^2$.

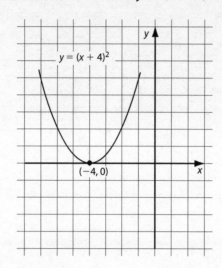

- Or the same graph 9 units to the right would be $y = (x - 9)^2$.

Note *Each box represents 2 units.*

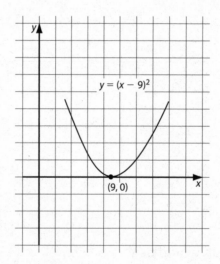

- Finally, the same graph upside down would be $y = -x^2$.

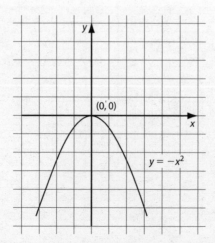

Example 20: What would the curve look like if it were 4 units to the left, 3 units down, and upside down?

Solution: The equation would be $y = -(x + 4)^2 - 3$.

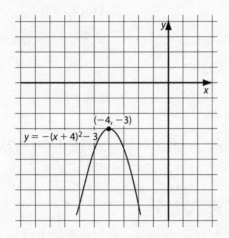

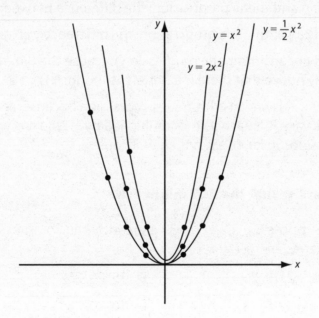

Note The higher the positive coefficient in front of the x^2 term, the quicker the curve goes up. (Conversely, the higher the absolute value of the negative coefficient in front of the x^2 term, the quicker the curve goes down.)

Note Notice that with trig functions, we did the same thing.

Let's try an exercise with translations.

Exercise 12: After moving 4 units to the left and down 6 units, a point on a graph ended up at (3, 3). The original point was

    A. (7, 9)   **D.** (7, −3)

    B. (−1, 9)   **E.** none of these

    C. (−1, −3)

A **Let's look at the answer.**

Answer 12: **A:** If the original point was (x, y), the new point would be $(x − 4, y − 6)$. So $(x − 4, y − 6) = (3, 3)$, and $x = 7$, $y = 9$.

ARITHMETIC PROGRESSIONS

This particular topic is usually done informally, so we will also do it that way.

An arithmetic progression is a series of numbers for which the differences between them are the same. For example,

- 9, 13, 17, 21, . . . is an arithmetic progression; the difference between the terms is 4.

- 4, 3.5, 3, 2.5, 2, . . . is an arithmetic progression; the difference between the terms is −.5.

- 1, 4, 9, 16, 25, . . . is *not* an arithmetic progression because the differences between the terms vary. You may notice that there is a pattern, though; it is $1^2, 2^2, 3^2, \ldots$

- 5, −10, 20, −40, 80, . . . is *not* an arithmetic progression because, again, the differences between the terms vary. But each term is multiplied by −2, so it is what is called a geometric progression. So far, this is not an ACT topic.

Q **Let's do an exercise that the ACT might ask.**

Exercise 13: Suppose 8, __, __, __, 32 is an arithmetic progression. The three missing terms are

    A. 12, 19, 26   **D.** 15, 20, 25

    B. 13, 18, 23   **E.** 10, 20, 30

    C. 14, 20, 26

 Let's look at the answer.

Answer 13: **C:** Here is the thought process to solve this one. There are 5 numbers. So there are 4 (one less than 5) differences, d, between the numbers. Then the total number of differences, $4d = 32 − 8 = 24$, so $d = 6$. The missing numbers are $8 + 6 = 14$, $14 + 6 = 20$, $20 + 6 = 26$.

IMAGINARY (COMPLEX) NUMBERS

Let's start with a fractured fairy tale history of numbers.

Once upon a time, we had the counting numbers (natural numbers) 1, 2, 3, 4, ... But mathematicians wanted an answer to the equation $x + 6 = 6$. So 0 was invented. (Actually, 0 was invented in India around the seventh or eighth century. At that time, the Indians were the great mathematicians of the world. Today, India is still pretty darn good!) Then mathematicians wanted even more. They wanted the answer to the equation $x + 5 = 3$. So negative integers were invented. This was still not enough. Mathematicians wanted an answer to the equations $3x = 7$ and $5x = -2$. So rational numbers were invented. Still, they wanted an answer to the equation $x^2 = 41$. So irrational numbers, such as $\pm\sqrt{41}$, were invented. Finally, mathematicians wanted an answer to the equation $x^2 = -1$. Alas! There is no real number such that $x^2 = -1$. So they invented i to stand for the "imaginary" number $\sqrt{-1}$. This was almost complete, but not quite enough. **Complex numbers** were invented. A **complex number** is of the form $a + bi$, where a and b are real numbers, and $i = \sqrt{-1}$.

Two complex numbers are equal if their real parts are equal and their imaginary parts are equal.

$$a + bi = c + di \text{ if } a = c \text{ and } b = d$$

Complex numbers cannot be graphed on a real graph. So instead of x and y axes, there is an x and a yi axis. On the axes below, we have graphed the point $-8 + 6i$.

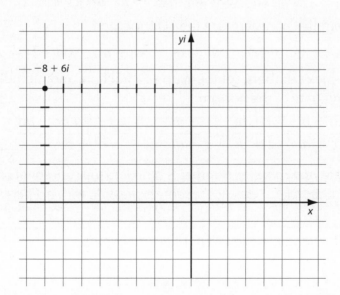

There are only a few things we need to know about complex numbers.

The distance of the number $a + bi$ from the origin $(0 + 0i)$ is $|a + bi| = \sqrt{a^2 + b^2}$. This is similar to what we get for real numbers by using the distance formula.

Example 21: What is the distance of the point $(6 - 8i)$ from the origin?

Solution: $|6 - 8i| = \sqrt{6^2 + (-8)^2} = 10$.

Note *The distance is always a positive real number and i is not involved in the square root.*

We also need to know how to raise *i* to any power. We see that $i = \sqrt{-1}$, so $i^2 = -1$. $i^3 = i^2 i = -i$; $i^4 = i^2 i^2 = (-1)(-1) = 1$; $i^5 = i^4 i = i$, etc. So *i* is cyclic, and the cycle is 4.

Example 22: Simplify i^{1359}.

Solution: To find what part of the i^n cycle this is, we divide 1359 by 4. We are not interested in the answer—only the remainder. The answer is 339 R 3. Because the remainder is 3, the answer is $-i$.

To summarize, to find the value of *i* raised to any power, we divide the exponent by 4. If the remainder is 1, the answer is *i*. If the remainder is 2, the answer is -1. If the remainder is 3, the answer is $-i$. If the remainder is 0, the answer is 1.

To add, subtract, multiply and divide complex numbers, follow these rules:

1. To add (subtract) complex numbers, add (subtract) the real parts and add (subtract) the imaginary parts.

$$(a + bi) \pm (c + di) = (a + c) \pm (b + d)i.$$

2. To multiply two complex numbers, use the FOIL method.

$$(a + bi)(c + di) = ac + adi + bci + bdi^2 = ac + adi + bci + bd(-1) = ac - bd + (ad + bc)i$$

3. To divide two complex numbers, set them up as a fraction, and multiply the top and bottom by the conjugate of the bottom.

$$\frac{a + bi}{c + di} = \frac{a + bi}{c + di} \times \frac{c - di}{c - di} = \frac{ac + bd + i(bc - ad)}{c^2 + d^2}$$

Note *The **conjugate of a complex number** is similar to the concept of conjugates with radicals (see Chapter 4), namely, the same expression with a different sign between the terms.*

Note *The final denominator is always a positive real number.*

Example 23: Let $Y = 8 + 2i$ and $Z = 6 + 5i$. Find **a.** $Y + Z$; **b.** $Y - Z$; **c.** YZ; **d.** $\dfrac{Y}{Z}$.

Solution:

a. $Y + Z = 14 + 7i$

b. $Y - Z = 2 - 3i$

c. $YZ = 48 + 40i + 12i + 10i^2 = 38 + 52i$

d. $\dfrac{Y}{Z} = \dfrac{8 + 2i}{6 + 5i} \times \dfrac{6 - 5i}{6 - 5i} = \dfrac{48 - 40i + 12i - 10i^2}{36 - 30i + 30i - 25i^2} = \dfrac{58 - 28i}{61}$

$\quad\ = \dfrac{58}{61} - \dfrac{28}{61}i$

EXPONENTIAL GROWTH AND DECAY

This last topic in the book is perhaps the most fascinating to discuss in a nonmathematical way. This topic relates to population growth, earthquakes, the age of dinosaurs, and the real destructive properties of an atomic bomb.

Let's mention a little about the first one. Assume human beings first appeared on Earth 40,000 years ago. If we counted every human being who lived from that time until the year 1900 (probably 1920 by now), there are still more people alive today than that total number. That is an example of exponential growth.

Let's see how we do such problems.

Example 24: Deb started with $10,000. If her net worth triples every five years, how much will she have in 30 years?

Solution: In 5 years, the $10,000 will be $30,000; in 10 years, $90,000; in 15 years $270,000; in 20 years, $810,000; in 25 years, $2,430,000; and in 30 years, $7,290,000!

Example 25: A half-life is the time required for half of a radioactive substance to disintegrate. Suppose radioactive goo has a half-life of 15 minutes. If there are 240 pounds of radioactive goo, how much radioactive goo is left in an hour?

Solution: In 15 minutes, the 240 pounds will be 120 pounds; in 30 minutes, that 120 pounds will be 60 pounds; in 45 minutes, there will be 30 pounds; and in one hour, only 15 pounds will be left.

Now that you have finished the book, let's practice what you've learned.

CHAPTER 17: *Four Sample ACT Math Exams with Answers*

"*For total success, you must practice your skills.*"

Now that we've finished the material, it is necessary to practice. Included are some fun problems because most books are so serious you want to run away from them. Most of the fun problems, as well as all the rest, are problems the ACT could ask or ask similar ones. All the problems will help you learn or think or both. Although there are 60 questions in each ACT-like practice test, you should not try to do them in 60 minutes—the actual test time. That's because instead of watching the clock, I want you to work on applying what you've learned in this book. The more problems you do, the better your timing will get! After doing the tests you should check the answers. It is essential not only to do and understand the questions, but also to be able to do the questions in as little time as possible. This will at least enable you to finish the test comfortably and do as well as you possibly can. Good luck!

Answers are at the end of each test.

Practice Test A

A1: If $x - 4 = 4 - x$, then $4x =$

    A. 0

    B. 4

    C. 8

    D. 16

    E. 256

A2: If $x = \sqrt[3]{-111}$, we know that x is

    F. $-11 < x < -10$

    G. $-10 < x < -9$

    H. $-5 < x < -4$

    J. $-4 < x < -3$

    K. undefined

A3: If $y = \dfrac{a^5}{b^3}$, then $\dfrac{ay}{b} =$

$$\dfrac{a^5 \cdot \dfrac{a^5}{b^3}}{b^3}$$

- A. $\dfrac{a^6}{b^4}$
- B. $\dfrac{a^4}{b^2}$
- C. $\dfrac{a}{b}$
- D. $\dfrac{a^{10}}{b^6}$
- E. $\dfrac{a^5}{b^3}$

A4: If $(x - 6)\left(6 - \dfrac{2}{x}\right) = 0$ and $x \neq 6$, then $x =$

- F. 0
- G. $\dfrac{1}{3}$
- H. $\dfrac{1}{2}$
- J. 2
- K. 3

A5: The sum of two numbers is 22 and their difference is 4. The smaller number is

- A. 9
- B. 10
- C. 11
- D. 12
- E. 13

12

13

9
13

A6:   *m* years ago *Cy* was *n* years old; how old was *Cy* *p* years ago?

    F. $m + n - p$

    G. $m - n - p$

    H. $n - m - p$

    J. $m - n - p$

    K. $m + n + p$

A7:   Which pairs are inverses of each other?

    I: 3 and -3

    II: 7 and $\dfrac{1}{7}$

    III: $\sqrt{7}$ and $\dfrac{\sqrt{7}}{7}$

    A.   II only

    B.   II and III only

    C.   I and III only

    D.   I and II only

    E.   All of them

Questions A8–A10 refer to the line *L*: $3x - 4y = 7$.

A8:   The slope of *L* is

    F. $\dfrac{7}{4}$

    G. $\dfrac{3}{4}$

    H. $\dfrac{4}{3}$

    J. $-\dfrac{3}{4}$

    K. $-\dfrac{4}{3}$

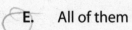

$3x = 7$

A9: The x-intercept of L is:

A. $\left(\dfrac{7}{3}, 0\right)$

B. $\left(0, \dfrac{7}{3}\right)$

C. $\left(-\dfrac{7}{4}, 0\right)$

D. $\left(0, -\dfrac{7}{4}\right)$

E. $\left(\dfrac{3}{7}, 0\right)$

A10: The y-intercept of L is:

F. $\left(\dfrac{7}{3}, 0\right)$

G. $\left(0, \dfrac{7}{3}\right)$

H. $\left(-\dfrac{7}{4}, 0\right)$

J. $\left(0, -\dfrac{7}{4}\right)$

K. $\left(0, -\dfrac{3}{4}\right)$

A11: $.9375 =$

A. $\dfrac{7}{8}$

B. $\dfrac{10}{11}$

C. $\dfrac{11}{12}$

D. $\dfrac{15}{16}$

E. $\dfrac{17}{18}$

A12: If x and y are integers, and at least one is odd, which of these expressions can never be odd?

    F. $x^2 + y^2$

    G. $2x^2 + y^2$

    H. $2xy + 1$

    J. $xy + 1$

    K. $x^2 + x + y^2 + y$

A13: $\dfrac{(6)(0.0048)}{0.72} =$

    A. 6

    B. 0.6

    C. .4

    D. 0.06

    E. 0.04

A14: $\dfrac{4 + 4\sqrt{7}}{4} =$

    F. $\sqrt{7}$

    G. $1 + 4\sqrt{7}$

    H. $1 + \sqrt{7}$

    J. $4 + \sqrt{7}$

    K. $4\sqrt{7}$

A15: The arithmetic mean of five numbers is 17. If one of the numbers is thrown away, the arithmetic mean is 18. The number thrown away is

    A. 16

    B. 15

    C. 14

    D. 13

    E. 12

$\dfrac{85}{5} = 17 \quad\longrightarrow\quad \dfrac{x}{4} = 18$

A16: 7% of 48 is x% of 12; $x =$

F.   14

G.   21

H.   28

J.   42

K.   56

A17: The area and the circumference of a circle have the same numerical value. The diameter of the circle is

A.   1

B.   2

C.   3

D.   4

E.   5

A18: A fraction is equivalent to $\frac{2}{3}$; if 5 is added to the numerator, the fraction is equivalent to $\frac{5}{6}$. The original fraction was

F. $\frac{54}{72}$

G. $\frac{28}{42}$

H. $\frac{20}{30}$

J. $\frac{18}{27}$

K. $\frac{16}{24}$

A19: What is the minimum number of sides you need to color a cube so that no two sides touching have the same color?

A.   2

B.   3

C.   4

D.   5

E.   6

A20: If $\dfrac{y-x}{xy} = 2$, $y =$

F. $\dfrac{x}{1-x}$

G. $\dfrac{x}{1-2x}$

H. $\dfrac{x}{2-x}$

J. $\dfrac{2x}{1-2x}$

K. $3x$

$2 = \dfrac{y-x}{xy}$

$2xy = y - x$

$\dfrac{2xy}{2x} + y$

$2y = 2x - x$

$\dfrac{2y}{2} = x$

A21: Don has 30 coins in dimes and nickels that total $2.10. How many are dimes?

A. 10

B. 12

C. 14

D. 16

E. 18

$10x + 5(30-x) = 2.10$

A22: $4^{2x} = 8^{x+5}$; $x =$

F. 2

G. 4

H. 5

J. 8

(K.) 15

$(2^2)^{2x} = 2^{3(x+5)}$

$4x = 3x + 15$

$-3x \qquad -3x$

$y = 15$

A23: $x^2 - y^2 = 28$ and $x + y = 2$; $x - y =$

A. 4

B. 7

C. 14

D. 21

E. Cannot be determined

A24: In an arithmetic progression, $a_1 = 15$, $a_2 = 9$, and $a_3 = 3$. Then $a_6 =$

    F. -3

    G. -9

    H. -15

    J. -21

    K. $\dfrac{1}{9}$

A25: Mel starts to read on the top of page 222 and ends reading at the bottom of page 358. The number of pages read is

    A.   136

    B.   137

    C.   138

    D.   139

    E.   580

A26: $x^2 - y^2 = 56$ and $x - y = 4$; $y =$

    F.   1

    G.   3

    H.   5

    J.   7

    K.   9

A27: $a \nabla b = ab^2 - b$. Then $-5 \nabla 3 =$

    A.   222

    B. -5

    C. -10

    D. -35

    E. -48

A28: $\sqrt{x-3} = 5; x =$

    F.   5

    G.   25

    H.   28

    J.   64

    K.   628

A29: $3x + 5$ is odd; the sum of the next two consecutive odd integers is

    A. $6x + 13$

    B. $6x + 14$

    C. $6x + 15$

    D. $6x + 16$

    E. $6x + 20$

A30: If x pounds of fruit cost c cents, how many pounds of fruit can you buy for d dollars?

    F. $\dfrac{100dx}{c}$

    G. $100cdx$

    H. $\dfrac{100c}{xd}$

    J. $\dfrac{cx}{100d}$

    K. $\dfrac{1}{100cdx}$

A31: $x + y = 12; x + \dfrac{x}{3} + y + \dfrac{y}{3} =$

    A.   4

    B.   8

    C.   12

    D.   16

    E.   20

A32: A jar has 5 yellow balls and 2 green balls; if two balls are picked one at a time, with replacement, the probability that both balls are green is

F. $\dfrac{4}{7}$

G. $\dfrac{4}{49}$

H. $\dfrac{2}{21}$

J. $\dfrac{1}{21}$

K. $\dfrac{2}{49}$

A33: $3(2x - 1) + 4 = 2x;\ x =$

A. $-\dfrac{1}{8}$

B. $-\dfrac{1}{4}$

C. $-\dfrac{1}{2}$

D. $\dfrac{1}{4}$

E. $\dfrac{1}{2}$

A34: In a small class, every girl sees that there is an equal number of girls and boys, while every boy sees there are twice as many girls as boys, not counting himself or herself. How many boys and how many girls are in the class?

F.   3 boys and 3 girls

G.   3 boys and 4 girls

H.   4 boys and 3 girls

J.   4 boys and 6 girls

K.   2 boys and 3 girls

A35: Meg is 16 and her mother is 50. In how many years will Meg be half as old as her mother?

    A. 10

    B. 12

    C. 16

    D. 18

    E. It can't happen

A36: If 3 bligs = 5 bloogs, and 7 bloogs = 8 blugs, the ratio of bligs to blugs is

    F. $\dfrac{21}{40}$

    G. $\dfrac{40}{21}$

    H. $\dfrac{105}{8}$

    J. $\dfrac{8}{105}$

    K. $\dfrac{21}{13}$

A37: Given the numbers 2, 2, 5, 7, 9, 17, the sum of the median, mean, and mode is

    A. 13

    B. 14

    C. 15

    D. 16

    E. greater than 16

A38: $f(x) = x^2 + 5x; f(x + h) =$

    F. $x^2 + 5x + h$

    G. $x^2 + h^2 + 5x$

    H. $x^2 + 2hx + h^2 + 5x$

    J. $x^2 + 2hx + h^2 + 5x + h$

    K. $x^2 + 2hx + h^2 + 5x + 5h$

A39: An arithmetic sequence is 8, __, __, −28. The two terms that are missing are

    A. 0 and −20

    B. −2 and −18

    C. −4 and −16

    D. −6 and −14

    E. −8 and −12

A40: The volume V of a box with a square base is $V = s^2h$. If the side of the square s is multiplied by 5, then to have the same volume, the height h must be multiplied by

    F. $\dfrac{1}{25}$

    G. $\dfrac{1}{5}$

    H. 1

    J. 5

    K. 25

Questions A41 and A42 refer to the following matrices: $X = [c \quad 0 \quad 2c]$ and $Y = \begin{bmatrix} 3 \\ 2 \\ 0 \end{bmatrix}$.

A41: $XY =$

    A. $3c$

    B. $[3c]$

    C. $\begin{bmatrix} 3c & 0 & 6c \\ 2c & 0 & 4c \\ 0 & 0 & 0 \end{bmatrix}$

    D. $15c$

    E. $[3c + 5]$

A42: $YX =$

    F. $3c$

    G. $[3c]$

    H. $\begin{bmatrix} 3c & 0 & 6c \\ 2c & 0 & 4c \\ 0 & 0 & 0 \end{bmatrix}$

    J. $15c$

    K. $[3c + 5]$

A43: $\dfrac{3 + \sqrt{3}}{1 + \sqrt{3}} =$

    A. $\sqrt{3} - 1$

    B. $\dfrac{\sqrt{3}}{3}$

    C. $\dfrac{\sqrt{3}}{2}$

    D. $\sqrt{3}$

    E. $\sqrt{3} + 1$

A44: $f(x) = 2x + 3$ and $g(x) = 4x + 1$; then $f(g(5)) =$

    F.   273

    G.   53

    H.   45

    J.   34

    K.   8

A45: $i^{11} + i^{12} + i^{13} + i^{14} =$

    A.   0

    B.   1

    C. -1

    D. i

    E. $-i$

A46: $\sin^2 x + \cos^2 x + \tan^2 x =$

    F.   0

    G.   1

    H. $\cot^2 x$

    J. $\csc^2 x$

    K. $\sec^2 x$

For questions A47 and A48, let the positive geometric means $m = \sqrt{xy}$.

A47: If $x = 21$ and $y = 3$, $m =$

    A. $2\sqrt{6}$

    B. $3\sqrt{7}$

    C. $7\sqrt{3}$

    D.   21

    E.   63

A48: If $x = 1.5$ and $m = 6$, $y =$

    F.   3

    G.   9

    H.   24

    J.   36

    K.   54

A49: $\dfrac{1}{x+2} - \dfrac{1}{x+3} =$

    A. $\dfrac{1}{x+6}$

    B. $\dfrac{1}{(x+2)(x+3)}$

    C. $\dfrac{-1}{2x+5}$

    D. 1

    E. −1

A50: 1 hour, 1 minute, plus 1 second is how many seconds?

    F. 10,001

    G. 3,661

    H. 3,601

    J. 1,001

    K. 901

A51: The distance from the center of a circle to a chord is 24 inches. If the chord is 20 inches, the diameter of the circle is

    A. 26

    B. 36

    C. 48

    D. 52

    E. 72

A52: The number of diagonals of a hexagon is

    F. 2

    G. 5

    H. 9

    J. 20

    K. 35

A53: Two triangles are similar, with a ratio of similarity of $\frac{2}{3}$. If the area of the smaller triangle is 12, the area of the larger triangle is

A. 18

B. 21

C. 24

D. 27

E. 54

A54: Cy had a choice of 6 sandwiches, 3 desserts, and 5 drinks. If a meal consists of one of each, the total number of different meal choices is

F. 13

G. 23

H. 45

J. 90

K. 6^{15}

Questions A55 and A56 refer to triangle *MNP*.

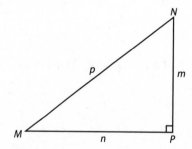

A55: $\sin M \tan N =$

    A. $\dfrac{m^2}{np}$

    B. $\dfrac{n}{p}$

    C. $\dfrac{np}{m^2}$

    D. $\dfrac{mp}{n^2}$

    E. $\dfrac{p}{m}$

A56: $\sin^2 M + \sin^2 N =$

    F. $\dfrac{2m^2}{p^2}$

    G. $\dfrac{2n^2}{p^2}$

    H. $\dfrac{mn}{p^2}$

    J. 0

    K. 1

A57: $\dfrac{4x^2 + 2x}{2x} =$

    A. $4x^2$

    B. $4x^2 + 1$

    C. $2x$

    D. $2x + 1$

    E. $4x$

A58: If $y = \dfrac{x+3}{x-5}$, $x =$

   F. $\dfrac{5y+3}{y-1}$

   G. $\dfrac{5y-3}{y+1}$

   H. $\dfrac{5y+3}{y+1}$

   J. $\dfrac{5y-3}{y-1}$

   K. $\dfrac{y+1}{5y-3}$

For questions A59 and A60, let $f(x) = \dfrac{x^2 - 4x - 5}{x^2 - 4x}$.

A59: $f(x) = 0$ if $x =$

   A. $0, 4$ only

   B. $5, -1$ only

   C. $-1, 4, 5$ only

   D. 0 only

   E. $-2, 2$ only

A60: $f(x)$ is undefined if $x =$

   F. $0, 4$ only

   G. $5, -1$ only

   H. $-1, 4, 5$ only

   J. 0 only

   K. $2, -2$ only

Let's look at the answers.

A1: D: $2x = 8$; $x = 4$; $4x = 16$.

A2: H: $(-4)^3 = -64$; $(-5)^3 = -125$.

A3: A: $y = \dfrac{a^5}{b^3}$, $\dfrac{ay}{b} = \dfrac{aa^5}{bb^3} = \dfrac{a^6}{b^4}$.

A4: G: $6 - \dfrac{2}{x} = 0$; $\dfrac{2}{x} = 6$; $6x = 2$; $x = \dfrac{1}{3}$.

A5: A: We can do this problem three ways:

- $x - (22 - x) = 4$; $2x = 26$; $x = 13$; $22 - x = 9$, the answer

- or $x + y = 22$ and $x - y = 4$; adding $2x = 26$; $x = 13$; so $y = 9$, the answer

- or trial and error

A6: F: The age now is the key; it is $m + n$; p years ago, it was $m + n - p$.

A7: E: I is an additive inverse; II is a multiplicative inverse; III is a multiplicative inverse.

A8: G: The slope-intercept form of the equation is $y = \left(\dfrac{3}{4}\right)x - \dfrac{7}{4}$. The slope is the coefficient of x.

A9: A: $y = 0$ at the x-intercept, so $3x = 7$, and $x = \dfrac{7}{3}$ and the intercept is the point $\left(\dfrac{7}{3}, 0\right)$.

A10: J: From the slope-intercept form of the equation, $y = \left(\dfrac{3}{4}\right)x - \dfrac{7}{4}$, the y-intercept is $-\dfrac{7}{4}$.

At the y-intercept, $x = 0$, so the intercept is the point $\left(0, -\dfrac{7}{4}\right)$.

A11: D: Write $.9375$ as $\dfrac{9375}{10,000}$. Divide the numerator and denominator by 25 to get $\dfrac{375}{400}$, then reduce this fraction to $\dfrac{15}{16}$ by dividing the numerator and denominator by 25 again. Or perhaps you answered this from memorizing the fractions in Chapter 2.

A12: K: If x is odd, then x^2 is odd and the sum $(x + x^2)$ is even; if y is even, then y^2 is even and the sum $(y + y^2)$ is even. The sum of evens is even. If you let x be even and y odd, all the others are odd. If both x, y are odd, then each of the four terms is odd and their sum is even.

A13: E: Divide first! 6 into $.72$ is $.12$ and $.12$ into $.0048 = 0.04$.

A14: **H:** $\dfrac{a+b}{c} = \dfrac{a}{c} + \dfrac{b}{c}$; so $\dfrac{4+4\sqrt{7}}{4} = \dfrac{4}{4} + \dfrac{4\sqrt{7}}{4} = 1 + \sqrt{7}$.

A15: **D:** Total is $5(17) = 85$; $4(18) = 72$; $85 - 72 = 13$.

A16: **H:** Ignore the %; $7(48) = 12x$; $x = \dfrac{7(48)}{12} = 7(4) = 28$.

A17: **D:** $\pi r^2 = 2\pi r$; so $r = 2$; and $d = 4$.

A18: **H:** $\dfrac{2x+5}{3x} = \dfrac{5}{6}$; so $12x + 30 = 15x$; $3x = 30$, $x = 10$; thus $\dfrac{2x}{3x} = \dfrac{20}{30}$.

A19: **B:** Top and bottom can be one color; left and right can be another color; front and back can be another color.

A20: **G:** $y - x = 2xy$; $y - 2xy = x$; $y(1 - 2x) = x$; so $y = \dfrac{x}{1 - 2x}$.

A21: **B:** The easiest way to do this problem is to substitute each of the answer choices. If there are 10 dimes (answer choice A), then there would be 20 nickels, and the value would be $1.00 + 1.00 = 2.00$. If there are 12 dimes (answer choice B), then there would be 18 nickels, and the value would be $1.20 + .90 = 2.10$. That's the answer. Incidentally, the equation for solving this problem is $10x + 5(30 - x) = 210$, where x is the number of dimes.

A22: **K:** $(2^2)^{2x} = (2^3)^{(x+5)}$, so exponents are equal; $2(2x) = 3(x + 5)$, or $4x = 3x + 15$; $x = 15$.

A23: **C:** $x^2 - y^2 = (x - y)(x + y)$; $28 = (x - y)(2)$; $x - y = 14$.

A24: **H:** The difference is -6. So the terms of the progression are $15, 9, 3, -3, -9, -15$.

A25: **B:** $358 - 222 + 1 = 137$; note that you have to include the first page.

A26: **H:** Similar to problem A23, we now have $x + y = 14$; $x - y = 4$. By adding, we get $2x = 18$; $x = 9$; $y = 5$.

A27: **E:** $(-5)(3^2) - 3 = -48$.

A28: **H:** Use trial and error with each of the answer choices. Alternatively, by squaring, $x - 3 = 25$, and $x = 28$.

A29: **D:** $(3x + 7) + (3x + 9) = 6x + 16$. Note that even if the integers are odd, you must add 2 to get the next consecutive odd integer.

A30: **F:** $\dfrac{x}{c} = \dfrac{?}{100d}$, or $? = \dfrac{100dx}{c}$.

A31: **D:** $x + \dfrac{x}{3} + y + \dfrac{y}{3} = x + y + \dfrac{x}{3} + \dfrac{y}{3} = (x + y) + \dfrac{x + y}{3} = 12 + \dfrac{12}{3} = 16.$

A32: **G:** $\left(\dfrac{2}{7}\right)\left(\dfrac{2}{7}\right) = \dfrac{4}{49}$; note that if there is no replacement, this changes to
$\left(\dfrac{2}{7}\right)\left(\dfrac{1}{6}\right) = \dfrac{1}{21}.$

A33: **B:** $6x - 3 + 4 = 2x$; $4x = -1$; $x = -\dfrac{1}{4}.$

A34: **G:** Each girl sees 3 girls and 3 boys; each boy sees 4 girls and 2 boys. So there are 3 boys and 4 girls in the class.

A35: **D:** $\dfrac{(x + 16)}{(x + 50)} = \dfrac{1}{2}$; so $2x + 32 = x + 50$; $x = 18.$

A36: **G:** $\dfrac{\text{bligs}}{\text{bloogs}} = \dfrac{5}{3}$ and $\dfrac{\text{bloogs}}{\text{blugs}} = \dfrac{8}{7}$; therefore, $\dfrac{\text{bligs}}{\text{blugs}} = \dfrac{5}{3} \times \dfrac{8}{7} = \dfrac{40}{21}.$

A37: **C:** The median is 6; the mode is 2; the mean is $\dfrac{42}{6} = 7$; the sum is 15.

A38: **K:** $f(x) = x^2 + 5x$; $f(x + h) = (x + h)^2 + 5(x + h) = (x + h)(x + h) + 5x + 5h = x^2 + 2hx + h^2 + 5x + 5h.$

A39: **C:** There are three differences d between 8 and -28; the difference between 8 and -28 is -36. So $3d = -36$; $d = -12$. The numbers are 8, $8 - 12$, $8 - 24$, and $8 - 36$, or 8, -4, -16, and -28. The missing terms are -4 and -16.

A40: **F:** Let $s = 1$ and $h = 1$ mean $V = 1$. If $s = 5$, then $s^2 = 25$; so $h = \dfrac{1}{25}$, to give $V = 1.$

A41: **B:** If you multiply a 1×3 matrix by a 3×1 matrix, you get a 1×1 matrix, $[c(3) + 0(2) + 2c(0)] = [3c].$

A42: **H:** A 3×1 matrix times a 1×3 matrix is a 3×3 matrix.

A43: **D:** You can try the conjugate; however, if you multiply the bottom by $\sqrt{3}$, you get the top.

A44: **H:** You go inside out; $g(5) = 21$ and $f(21) = 45$. This is called the composite; it is not multiplication.

A45: **A:** These are four consecutive powers of i: one must be 1; one must be i; one must be -1; one must be $-i$; they must add to 0.

A46: **K:** $(\sin^2 x + \cos^2 x) + \tan^2 x = 1 + \tan^2 x = \sec^2 x.$

A47: **B:** $\sqrt{63} = \sqrt{(3)(3)(7)} = 3\sqrt{7}$.

A48: **H:** $6 = \sqrt{1.5y}$; $36 = \dfrac{3y}{2}$; $3y = 72$; $y = 24$.

A49: **B:** $\dfrac{x+3}{(x+2)(x+3)} - \dfrac{x+2}{(x+2)(x+3)} = \dfrac{1}{(x+2)(x+3)}$

A50: **G:** $3600 + 60 + 1 = 3661$.

A51: **D:** The distance to the center is both perpendicular and bisects the chord; we have a 10 (half of 20)-24-26 Pythagorean triple, where 26 is the radius, so 52 is the diameter.

A52: **H:** The formula is $\dfrac{n(n-3)}{2} = \dfrac{(6)(6-3)}{2} = 9$. If you don't remember the formula, sketch the six-sided figure.

A53: **D:** The ratio of the areas is $\dfrac{4}{9}$, the square of $\dfrac{2}{3}$; we have $\dfrac{4}{9} = \dfrac{12}{x}$, so $x = 27$.

A54: **J:** The product of the three is the answer.

A55: **B:** $\left(\dfrac{m}{p}\right)\left(\dfrac{n}{m}\right) = \dfrac{n}{p}$.

A56: **K:** $\left(\dfrac{m}{p}\right)^2 + \left(\dfrac{n}{p}\right)^2 = \dfrac{m^2 + n^2}{p^2} = \dfrac{p^2}{p^2} = 1$.

A57: **D:** $\dfrac{4x^2}{2x} + \dfrac{2x}{2x} = 2x + 1$.

A58: **F:** $xy - 5y = x + 3$; $xy - x = 5y + 3$; $x(y-1) = 5y + 3$; so $x = \dfrac{5y+3}{y-1}$.

A59: **B:** The fraction $= 0$ if the numerator $= 0$; $(x-5)(x+1) = 0$.

A60: **F:** The fraction is undefined if the denominator $= 0$; $x(x-4) = 0$.

Practice Test B

B1: If m and n are odd integers, which are always odd?

I: m^{n+1}

II: $mn + m + n$

III: $(m - 2)^{n-4}$

A.   None

B.   I and II only

C.   I and III only

D.   II and III only

E.   I, II, and III

B2: If y is four less than the square root of x, and $x > 100$, then

F. $x = 4 + y^2$

G. $x = 4 - y^2$

H. $x = y^2 - 4$

J. $x = (y - 4)^2$

K. $x = (y + 4)^2$

B3: .3% of .3% of .3 $=$

A.   .027

B.   .0027

C.   .00027

D.   .000027

E.   .0000027

B4: If $-1 < x < 0$, which of the following is arranged in order, largest to smallest?

F. $x^5 > x^4 > x^3$

G. $x^3 > x^4 > x^5$

H. $x^5 > x^3 > x^4$

J. $x^4 > x^3 > x^5$

K. $x^4 > x^5 > x^3$

B5:   At 60° F, you need 15 SPF sunscreen. For each 5-degree increase, the SPF must increase by 3. At 95° F, the required SPF is

A.   30

B.   35

C.   36

D.   40

E.   50

B6:   In a large lecture hall, the ratio of men to women is 2 : 3. If there are 365 people in the lecture hall, the number of women is

F.   73

G.   105

H.   126

J.   155

K.   219

B7:   If circle has area 1, its diameter is

A. $\dfrac{1}{\pi}$

B. $\dfrac{2}{\pi}$

C. $\dfrac{1}{\sqrt{\pi}}$

D. $\dfrac{2}{\sqrt{\pi}}$

E. π

B8:   The volume of a cube whose surface area is 6 is

F.   1

G.   6

H.   36

J.   216

K.   1996

B9: $\dfrac{x}{2} + \dfrac{x}{3} = 1; x =$

    A. $\dfrac{2}{3}$

    B. $\dfrac{3}{2}$

    C. $\dfrac{6}{5}$

    D. $\dfrac{9}{4}$

    E. $\dfrac{11}{10}$

B10: $2^n + 2^n + 2^n + 2^n =$

    F. 2^{n+1}

    G. 2^{n+2}

    H. 2^{n+4}

    J. 4^n

    K. 2^{n^4}

B11: $\dfrac{\left(5x^4\right)^2 x^3}{5x^4} =$

    A. x^3

    B. $5x^3$

    C. x^7

    D. $5x^7$

    E. x^{15}

B12: $x^6 = m$; $x^5 = \dfrac{n}{3}$; in terms of m and n, $x =$

F. $3mn$

G. $\dfrac{3}{mn}$

H. $\dfrac{mn}{3}$

J. $\dfrac{3m}{n}$

K. $\dfrac{3n}{m}$

B13: A $60 radio is discounted 25%, then another 10%; with a 4% sales tax, the final cost is

A. $41.06

B. $42.12

C. $43.18

D. $44.24

E. $45.30

B14: a is a positive integer; a^2 ends in a 9; $(a + 1)^2$ ends in a 4; $(a + 2)^2$ ends in

F.   1

G.   4

H.   5

J.   6

K.   9

B15: Set $R = \{1, 3, 5, 7\}$ and $R \cup S = \{1, 2, 3, 4, 5, 6, 7\}$. S can be which one of the following sets?

A. $\{1, 4, 6\}$

B. $\{2, 4, 6\}$

C. $\{1, 2, 3, 4, 5, 6, 7, 8\}$

D. $\{1, 3, 5, 7\}$

E. $\{1, 2, 3, 4\}$

B16: Two sides of a right triangle are $13\sqrt{2}$ and 13. The third side could be

    F. only 13

    G. only $13\sqrt{2}$

    H. only $13\sqrt{3}$

    J. either 13 or $13\sqrt{3}$

    K. need to know the angles to answer the problem

B17: $\sqrt{.000036}$ is exactly

    A. .00006

    B. .0006

    C. .006

    D. .06

    E. Not an exact number

Problems B18 and B19 refer to a Norman window, which is a rectangle surmounted by a semicircle. The height of the rectangular part is x and the width of the rectangular part is $4y$.

B18: The perimeter is

    F. $2x + 8y + 4\pi y$

    G. $2x + 4y + 4\pi y$

    H. $2x + 4y + 2\pi y$

    J. $2x + 4y + \pi y$

    K. $2x + y + \dfrac{\pi y}{2}$

B19: The area is

    A. $xy + \dfrac{\pi y^2}{2}$

    B. $4xy + 4\pi y^2$

    C. $4xy + 2\pi y^2$

    D. $4xy + \pi y^2$

    E. $4xy + \dfrac{\pi y^2}{4}$

B20: If $\dfrac{x - 6}{y + 4} = 0$, then

    F. $x = 0, y \neq 0$

    G. $x = 6, y = -4$

    H. $x = 6, y \neq -4$

    J. $x \neq 6, y \neq -4$

    K. $x \neq 6, y \neq -4$

B21: If $\dfrac{2}{5}$ of n is $\dfrac{7}{3}$; $\dfrac{2}{7}$ of n is

    A. $\dfrac{3}{5}$

    B. $\dfrac{5}{3}$

    C.   6

    D.   35

    E.   210

B22: An item cost $600 after a 25% discount. Originally the cost was

    F. $150

    G. $200

    H. $700

    J. $750

    K. $800

B23: A and B are on opposite sides of point P on a line and $3AP = 4PB$. M is the midpoint of AP. $AM : MB =$

    A. $1 : 4$

    B. $2 : 7$

    C. $1 : 3$

    D. $2 : 5$

    E. $4 : 9$

B24: Simplified, $\dfrac{\frac{1}{m^2} - \frac{1}{n^2}}{\frac{1}{m} - \frac{1}{n}} =$

　　F.　1

　　G.　$\dfrac{1}{mn}$

　　H.　$\dfrac{m+n}{mn}$

　　J.　$mn + 1$

　　K.　$\dfrac{1}{mn + 1}$

B25: $100^M = 10^{100}$; $M =$

　　A.　10

　　B.　20

　　C.　25

　　D.　50

　　E.　75

B26: $(x - 7)^2 = (x - 19)^2$; $x =$

　　F.　9

　　G.　11

　　H.　13

　　J.　15

　　K.　17

B27: If $c + d - 6 = 8g$, which is the mean of c, d, and g?

　　A.　$3g - 2$

　　B.　$3g$

　　C.　$3g + 2$

　　D.　$2g + 1$

　　E.　$2g - 1$

B28: $abc = bcde > 0$, and a, b, c, d, e are all integers > 1. Which of the following *must* be true?

F. $a > d$

G. $b > c$

H. $c > e$

J. $d > b$

K. $e > a$

B29: Given the sequence $-1, 0, 1, -1, 0, 1, \ldots$, the sum of the 82nd term and 112th term is

A. -2

B. -1

C. 0

D. 1

E. 2

B30: $a \# b = b + a^3$; $2 \# x^2 = 9x$ has solutions

F. $x = 0$ and 1 only

G. $x = 0$ and 8 only

H. $x = 1$ and 8 only

J. $x = 0, 1,$ and 8 only

K. It involves a 6th-degree equation, which is unsolvable

B31: The sum of seven consecutive odd integers is -105. The product of the two largest is

A. 99

B. 182

C. 225

D. 206

E. 399

B32: Max goes 80 km/hr in one direction and 100 km/hr on the return trip on the same road. The average speed to the nearest tenth of a km is

    F.   85.3

    G.   86.7

    H.   88.9

    J.   90.0

    K.   92.3

B33: $M = 2^r$; $8M =$

    A. 16^r

    B. 64^r

    C. 2^{r^3}

    D. 2^{r+3}

    E. 2^{3r}

B34: The maximum value of $\dfrac{m + n}{m - n}$ with $8 \leq m \leq 10$ and $2 \leq n \leq 4$ is

    F. $\dfrac{3}{2}$

    G. $\dfrac{5}{3}$

    H. $\dfrac{7}{3}$

    J.   3

    K.   6

B35: $0 < m < 1$

I: $m < \dfrac{1}{\sqrt{m}}$

II: $\dfrac{1}{m} < \dfrac{1}{m^2}$

III: $1 - m \le m.$

Which statement(s) is (are) always true?

A.   None

B.   I and II only

C.   I and III only

D.   II and III only

E.   All are always true

B36: $\dfrac{x + 1}{x - 1} = \dfrac{x - 1}{x + 1}$; the solution(s) for x is (are)

F. $x = 0$ only

G. $x = 0, 1$ only

H. $x = 0, -1$ only

J. $x = 0, 1, -1$ only

K.   There are no solutions

B37: $\dfrac{3\frac{2}{3} - 1\frac{2}{3}}{\frac{5}{3} - \frac{1}{3}} =$

A.   1

B. $\dfrac{3}{2}$

C.   2

D. $\dfrac{5}{2}$

E. $\dfrac{8}{3}$

B38: Ben goes 40 mph for 2 hours, 50 mph for 3 hours, and 60 miles per hour for 5 hours. His average speed is

F.   48 mph

G.   50 mph

H.   53 mph

J.   55 mph

K.   58 mph

B39: $g(x) = x^2 + 4x - 7; g(x + h) - g(x) =$

A. h

B. $2xh$

C. $2xh + 4h$

D. $2xh + h^2 + 4h$

E. 1

B40: $\log_8 x = -\dfrac{2}{3}; x =$

F.   4

G.   4

H. $\dfrac{1}{4}$

J. $\dfrac{16}{3}$

K. $-\dfrac{16}{3}$

B41: A circle whose center is at the point $(-3, -4)$ and is tangent to the y-axis has a radius of

A.   3

B.   4

C.   5

D.   8

E.   10

B42:   The parabola $y = 2x^2 - 5x + 3$ has intercepts

F. $(0, 3), (\frac{3}{2}, 0), (1, 0)$

G. $(0, 3), (-\frac{3}{2}, 0), (-1, 0)$

H. $(0, -3), (\frac{3}{2}, 0), (1, 0)$

J. $(0, -3) (-\frac{3}{2}, 0), (-2, 0)$

K. $(0, 3)$ only

B43:   Given the formula $\sin (X + Y) = \sin X \cos Y + \cos X \sin Y$, $\sin X = \frac{3}{5}$ in quadrant I, and $\cos Y = \frac{12}{13}$ in quadrant I. Then $\sin (X + Y) =$

A. $\frac{36}{65}$

B. $\frac{43}{65}$

C. $\frac{46}{65}$

D. $\frac{53}{65}$

E. $\frac{56}{65}$

B44:   Let $\sin P = .3456$. To the nearest ten thousandth, $\sin^2 P + \cos^2 P =$

F.   0

G.   .4573

H.   .5210

J.   .7761

K.   1

B45: If $3s + 4y = 21$ and $7s + 6y = 89$, then the mean of s and y is

A. 5.5

B. 6

C. .5

D. 11

E. 12

B46: If x is a positive real number and $\dfrac{1}{x} = \dfrac{37}{x} + x$, then $x =$

F. 5.5

G. 6

H. 6.5

J. 7

K. none of these

B47: $3\dfrac{3}{4} + x = 4\dfrac{1}{6}; x =$

A. $-\dfrac{2}{5}$

B. $\dfrac{2}{5}$

C. $\dfrac{5}{12}$

D. $1\dfrac{5}{12}$

E. $7\dfrac{11}{12}$

B48: $\log_2 x + \log_2 (x + 6) = 4; x =$

F. -8 only

G. 2 only

H. -8 and 2 only

J. $-\dfrac{96}{15}$ only

K.   all real numbers

B49:   Let $y = |x + 4|$; rotated 90° clockwise; the picture looks like

A.

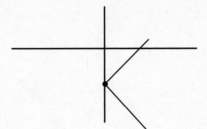

B.

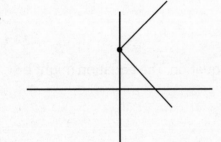

C.

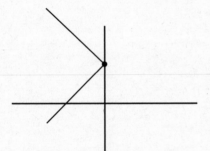

D.

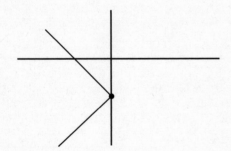

E.

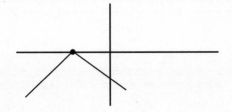

B50: If $f(x) = \begin{cases} 4x - 1, & -3 \leq x \leq 2 \\ x^2 + 6, & 2 < x < 4 \\ 4x - 1, & 4 \leq x \leq 7 \end{cases}$, then $f(2) =$

- **F.** −9 only

- **G.** 7 only

- **H.** 10 only

- **J.** 7 and 10 only

- **K.** −9, 7, and 10

B51: $\dfrac{2}{3}$ and $-\dfrac{3}{2}$ are two solutions to a quadratic equation. The equation might be

- **A.** $6x^2 - 5x - 6 = 0$

- **B.** $6x^2 + 5x - 6 = 0$

- **C.** $x^2 - 5x - 6 = 0$

- **D.** $x^2 + 5x - 6 = 0$

- **E.** $4x^2 - 9 = 0$

B52: In the figure below, $\sin A = \dfrac{5}{13}$; $BC =$

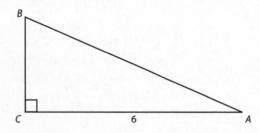

- **F.** 2.5

- **G.** 6.5

- **H.** $\dfrac{30}{13}$

- **J.** $\dfrac{17}{5}$

- **K.** 12

B53: In the figure below, the largest square has a side of length 10. The length of each successively smaller square is two units less than its predecessor. What is the percentage that throwing a dart randomly at the target will score at least a 3?

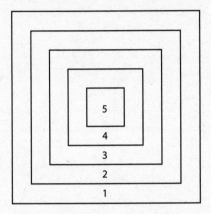

A. 25%

B. 32%

C. 36%

D. 40%

E. 60%

B54: Given the law of cosines: $c^2 = a^2 + b^2 - 2ab \cos C$. The missing side in the figure below is

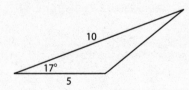

F. 5

G. $5\sqrt{5}$

H. $\sqrt{125 + 50 \cos 17°}$

J. $\sqrt{125 - 50 \cos 17°}$

K. $\sqrt{125 - 100 \cos 17°}$

B55: If $\dfrac{x}{7} = \dfrac{3}{4}$, then $\dfrac{x}{3} =$

    A. $\dfrac{7}{4}$

    B. $\dfrac{4}{7}$

    C.   28

    D. $\dfrac{1}{28}$

    E. $\dfrac{21}{4}$

B56: The distance from point $P(1, 3)$ to the midpoint of the line segment joining $A(5, 7)$ and $B(9, 15)$ is

    F. $\sqrt{32}$

    G. $\sqrt{80}$

    H.   10

    J. $\sqrt{128}$

    K. $\sqrt{208}$

For questions B57 and B58, let $f(x) = \dfrac{(x - 4)^2}{x^2 + 16x}$.

B57: $f(x) = 0$ if

    A. $x = 4$ only

    B. $x = 4$ and -4 only

    C. $x = -16$ only

    D. $x = 0$ and -16 only

    E. $x = 4, -4, -16,$ and 0

B58: $f(x)$ is undefined if

 F. $x = 4$ only

 G. $x = 4$ and -4 only

 H. $x = -16$ only

 J. $x = 0$ and -16 only

 K. $x = 4, -4, -16$, and 0

B59: The area of a triangle is equal to the area of a rectangle. The ratio of the base of the triangle to the base of the rectangle is

 A. $\dfrac{4}{1}$

 B. $\dfrac{2}{1}$

 C. $\dfrac{\sqrt{2}}{1}$

 D. $\dfrac{1}{1}$

 E. impossible to tell

B60: Four less than the square root of the difference between x and 4 is $y, x > 4$. This may be written as

 F. $\sqrt{x-4} - 4 = y$

 G. $4 - \sqrt{x-4} = y$

 H. $\sqrt{4-x} - 4 = y$

 J. $4 - \sqrt{4-x} = y$

 K. $(y+4)^2 = 4 + x$

(A)   **Let's look at the answers.**

B1:   **B:** I is always odd; an odd integer to an even power is odd. II is odd because the sum of 3 odd integers is always odd. III is not always odd; for example, let $m = 5$ and $n = 1$.

B2:   **K:** The equation is $y = \sqrt{x} - 4$, or $y + 4 = \sqrt{x}$, which is $(y + 4)^2 = x$. The fact that $x > 100$ is superfluous to the solution.

B3:   **E:** $(.003)(.003)(.3) = .0000027$.

B4:   **K:** x^4 is largest because it is the only positive. $\left(-\dfrac{1}{2}\right)^5 > \left(-\dfrac{1}{2}\right)^3$ because it is closer to 0.

B5:   **C:** $95 - 60 = 35$, Thus, there are 7 groups of 5; $7(3) = 21$ increase in SPF; $21 + 15 = 36$.

B6:   **K:** $2x + 3x = 365$; $x = \dfrac{365}{5} = 73$; $3x = 219$.

B7:   **D:** Area $= 1 = \pi r^2$; $r = \dfrac{1}{\sqrt{\pi}}$; $d = 2r = \dfrac{2}{\sqrt{\pi}}$.

B8:   **F:** $6e^2 = 6$; $e^2 = 1$; $e^3 = 1$.

B9:   **C:** Multiply the equation by 6 to get $5x = 6$. Then $x = \dfrac{6}{5}$.

B10:   **G:** This is a tough one! $2(2^n + 2^n) = 2(2)(2^n) = (2^2)(2^n) = 2^{n+2}$.

B11:   **D:** $\dfrac{25x^8(x^3)}{5x^4} = 5x^7$, or cancel $5x^4$ from the top and bottom, to get $(5x^4)(x^3) = 5x^7$.

B12:   **J:** $\dfrac{x^6}{x^5} = \dfrac{m}{\left(\frac{n}{3}\right)} = \dfrac{3m}{n}$.

B13:   **B:** $60 discounted 25% = $45 discounted 10% ($.90 \times 45$) = $40.50 \times .04 = $1.62 + $40.50 = 42.12.

B14:   **F:** The cycle of the last digits of the squares, starting at 0, is 0, 1, 4, 9, 6, 5, 6, 9, 4, 1, 0, . . . ($0^2 = 0$; $1^2 = 1$; $2^2 = 4$; $3^2 = 9$; $4^2 = 16$; $5^2 = 25$; $6^2 = 36$; $7^2 = 49$; $8^2 = 64$; $9^2 = 81$; $10^2 = 100$). Because a^2 ends in a 9, a must end in a 3 or 7, but $(a + 1)^2$ ends in a 4, so a must end in a 7. Thus, $a + 2$ ends in a 9, which means $(a + 2)^2$ must end in a 1.

B15:   **B:** Each element in the union of two sets is an element in one or the other or both sets, and all elements in either set must be included in the union.

B16:   **J:** Use the Pythagorean Theorem. The missing side could be the hypotenuse ($13\sqrt{3}$) or one of the legs (13).

B17: **C:** The square root has half the decimal places as the radicand (quantity under the root sign).

B18: **H:** $p = \left(\dfrac{1}{2} \times 2\pi r\right) + x + x + 4y$; $r = 2y$; $p = 2\pi y + 2x + 4y$.

B19: **C:** Rectangle is $bh = 4xy$; semicircle $\left(\dfrac{1}{2}\right)\pi(2y)^2 = 2\pi y^2$. $A = \dfrac{1}{2}\pi r^2 + bh = \dfrac{1}{2}\pi(2y)^2 + 4y(x) = 4xy + 2\pi y^2$.

B20: **H:** A fraction equals 0 if the top equals 0 and the bottom does not equal 0.

B21: **B:** $\dfrac{2}{5}n = \dfrac{7}{3}$; so $\dfrac{2}{7}n = \dfrac{5}{3}$. Exchange the 5 and 7 (just another pattern of fractions).

B22: **K:** Plug numbers into the answer choices, or use $x - .25x = 600$, so $\dfrac{3}{4}x = 600$, and $x = 800$.

B23: **D:** This is hard to picture in your mind, so draw a sketch. Let $AB = AP + PB$, where $AP = 4$ (equal intervals) and $PB = 3$. Thus, AP is divided into 7 equal parts. Because M is the midpoint of AP, $AM = 2$, and $MB = 7 - 2 = 5$; so the ratio $AM : MB = 2 : 5$.

B24: **H:** Multiplying by m^2n^2 and factoring, we get $\dfrac{(m+n)(m-n)}{mn(m-n)} = \dfrac{m+n}{mn}$.

B25: **D:** $10^{2M} = 10^{100}$; $2M = 100$, so $M = 50$.

B26: **H:** Trial and error with each answer choice gives $(13 - 7)^2 = (13 - 19)^2$, or $(6)^2 = (-6)^2$. Note that 13 is the mean of 7 and 19. In this problem, trial and error is easier and quicker than multiplying out the binomials and solving for x.

B27: **C:** The mean of c, d, and g is $\dfrac{c + d + g}{3}$. If $c + d - 6 = 8g$, then $c + d = 8g + 6$. Substituting, we get the mean $= \dfrac{8g + 6 + g}{3} = 3g + 2$.

B28: **F:** b and c are unknown, but $a = de$; because a, d, and e are positive integers, a is larger than either d or e.

B29: **A:** Divide each number by 3; they each have a remainder of 1. Therefore, the 82nd and 112th numbers are both the first number of the three-number repeating sequence $-1, 0, 1$. They both end in -1, and therefore their sum is -2.

B30: **H:** $x^2 + 8 = 9x$, or $x^2 - 9x + 8 = 0$, or $(x - 8)(x - 1) = 0$.

B31: **A:** The middle term is the average, or $\dfrac{-105}{7} = -15$; The integers are $-21, -19, -17,$ $-15, -13, -11, -9,$ and the product of the two largest is $(-11)(-9) = 99$.

B32: **H:** Suppose the trip was 400 km each way. Then the times of travel $(t = \dfrac{d}{r})$ are $\dfrac{400}{80} = 5$ hours in one direction and $\dfrac{400}{100} = 4$ hours in the other direction. The rate for the entire trip is the total distance divided by total time, or $\dfrac{800}{9} = 88.9$.

B33: **D:** $8M = 8(2^r) = 2^3 2^r = 2^{r+3}$.

B34: **J:** In this case $m = 8$ and $n = 4$ works. Substituting only the end numbers, $\dfrac{8+4}{8-4} = 3$.

B35: **B:** Statement I is true because $m < 1$ and $\dfrac{1}{\sqrt{m}} > 1$; Statement II is true because $m^2 < m$; so $\dfrac{1}{m^2} > \dfrac{1}{m}$; Statement III is false (try $m = \dfrac{1}{4}$, for example.)

B36: **F:** By cross multiplying, we get $4x = 0$, so $x = 0$ only.

B37: **B:** $\dfrac{\frac{6}{3}}{\frac{4}{3}} = \dfrac{6}{4} = \dfrac{3}{2}$

B38: **H:** $\dfrac{(40 \times 2) + (50 \times 3) + (60 \times 5)}{10} = \dfrac{530}{10} = 53$; notice the answer had to be more than 50; 58 was unlikely; 53 was the most likely guess if you were short of time.

B39: **D:** $(x + h)(x + h) + 4(x + h) - 7 - (x^2 + 4x - 7) = x^2 + 2xh + h^2 + 4x + 4h - 7 - x^2 - 4x + 7 = 2xh + h^2 + 4h$.

B40: **H:** $x = 8^{-2/3} = \dfrac{1}{8^{2/3}} = \dfrac{1}{(\sqrt[3]{8})^2} = \dfrac{1}{2^2} = \dfrac{1}{4}$.

B41: **A:** By drawing the picture, you would see the radius is 3. You should get used to drawing pictures to help you. It is the way mathematicians work!

B42: **F:** For the y-intercept, $x = 0$, so $y = 3$ and the point is $(0, 3)$. For the x-intercept, $y = 0$, so $2x^2 - 5x + 3 = (2x - 3)(x - 1) = 0$, and the points are $\left(\dfrac{3}{2}, 0\right)$ and $(1, 0)$.

B43: **E:** Draw the two triangles; with angle X, we have a 3-4-5 right triangle, so $\cos X = \dfrac{4}{5}$. With angle Y, we have a 5-12-13 right triangle, so $\sin Y = \dfrac{5}{13}$. So $\sin X \cos Y + \cos X$ $\sin Y = \left(\dfrac{3}{5}\right)\left(\dfrac{12}{13}\right) + \left(\dfrac{4}{5}\right)\left(\dfrac{5}{13}\right) = \dfrac{56}{65}$. In a problem like this, you never reduce any fraction until the end, if possible.

B44: **K:** No matter what the angle is, sine square plus cosine square of the same angle is 1. That's what an identity is!

B45: **A:** Adding, we get $10s + 10y = 110$; dividing by 10, we get $s + y = 11$; the mean is $\dfrac{s + y}{2} = 5.5$.

B46: **K:** Multiplying by x and simplifying, we get $x^2 = -36$, which has no real solution.

B47: **C:** $x = 4\dfrac{2}{12} - 3\dfrac{9}{12} = 3\dfrac{14}{12} - 3\dfrac{9}{12} = \dfrac{5}{12}$.

B48: **G:** $\log_2 x(x + 6) = 4$ or $x^2 + 6x = 2^4 = 16$; $x^2 + 6x - 16 = (x + 8)(x - 2) = 0$. Only $x = 2$ is okay because you cannot have the log of a negative number.

B49: **B:** Sketch the figure and turn your paper 90° clockwise.

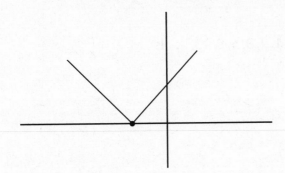

B50: **G:** You can use only the first part of the map, $4x - 1$, for $x = 2$.

B51: **B:** $\dfrac{2}{3}$ is a solution, so $x - \dfrac{2}{3}$, or $(3x - 2)$ is a factor. $-\dfrac{3}{2}$ is a solution, so $x + \dfrac{3}{2}$, or $(2x + 3)$ is a factor. Multiplying $(3x - 2)(2x + 3)$, we get $6x^2 + 5x - 6$.

B52: **F:** If $\sin A = \dfrac{5}{13}$, then triangle ABC is a 5-12-13 triangle, similar to a triangle with $AC = 12$. But $AC = \dfrac{1}{2}(12)$, so $BC = \dfrac{1}{2}(5) = 2.5$

B53: **C:** The squares worth 3, 4, or 5 are contained within the third square, with side 6. Probability $= \dfrac{\text{area of desired square}}{\text{area of all squares}} = \dfrac{36}{100} = 36\%$.

B54: **K:** $c^2 = 5^2 + 10^2 - 2(5)(10)\cos 17°$, so $c^2 = 125 - 100 \cos 17°$.

B55: **A:** Interchange the 7 and 3.

B56: **H:** Midpoint, $M = \left(\dfrac{5+9}{2}, \dfrac{7+15}{2}\right) = (7, 11)$; the distance between M and

$P = \sqrt{(7-1)^2 + (11-3)^2}$.

B57: **A:** $f(x) = 0$ if the top of the fraction $= 0$. $(x-4)^2 = (x-4)(x-4) = 0$; 4 is a double answer, so only 4.

B58: **J:** $f(x)$ is undefined if the bottom of the fraction $= 0$. $x(x+16) = 0$.

B59: **E:** The bases and heights could be anything!

B60: **F:** "Four less than" something means subtract 4 from that something.

Practice Test C

C1: The next term in the sequence 0, 1, 1, 2, 3, 5, 8, 13, . . . is

    A. 18

    B. 19

    C. 21

    D. 23

    E. 25

C2: $(-3)^{2m} = 3^{9-m}$, m an integer; $m =$

    F. 1

    G. 2

    H. 3

    J. 4

    K. 5

C3: $x^2 + kx - 24 = (x+3)(x+m)$; $k =$

    A. 8

    B. 5

    C. -5

    D. -8

    E. -13

C4: $\dfrac{m}{n} = \dfrac{3}{4}$. Which is NOT true?

    F. $\dfrac{3m}{4n} = \dfrac{9}{16}$

    G. $\dfrac{(m + n)}{n} = \dfrac{7}{4}$

    H. $\dfrac{(n - m)}{m} = \dfrac{1}{3}$

    J. $\dfrac{n^2}{m^2} = \dfrac{16}{9}$

    K. $\dfrac{(m - n)}{n} = \dfrac{1}{4}$

C5: All 35 students take at least French or Russian. If 25 take Russian and 10 take both, how many students take only French?

    A.   5

    B.   10

    C.   15

    D.   20

    E.   25

Problems C6 and C7 refer to the following figure, in which AB $\parallel$ CD.

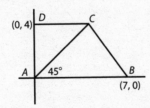

C6: The area of ABCD =

    F.   11

    G.   16

    H.   22

    J.   32

    K.   56

C7:   The perimeter of *ABCD* =

    A.   20

    B.   22

    C.   25

    D.   40

    E.   140

C8: $0 < x < 1$. Which must be true?

    I: $x^9 < x^7$

    II: $x^7 + x^5 < x^6 + x^4$

    III: $x^7 - x^5 < x^6 - x^4$

    F.   I only

    G.   II only

    H.   III only

    J.   I and II only

    K.   I, II, and II

C9:   In the figure below, twice the area of $\triangle XYZ$ =

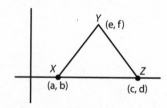

    A. $(d - b)e$

    B. $(c - a)f$

    C. $(c - a)e$

    D. $\frac{1}{2}(c - a)f$

    E. $\frac{1}{2}(d - b)e$

C10: The closest approximation to $\sqrt{\dfrac{(8.97)(902.1)}{35.97}}$ is

    F.   5

    G.   15

    H.   30

    J.   225

    K.   900

C11: A football team averaged x points (the mean) in the first n games, scored y points in the next game, and z points in the one after that. The mean of the $n + 2$ games is

    A. $\dfrac{x + y + z}{n + 2}$

    B. $\dfrac{nxyz}{n + 2}$

    C. $\dfrac{nx + y + z}{n + 2}$

    D. $x + \dfrac{y + z}{2}$

    E. $\dfrac{nx + yz}{n + 2}$

C12: The postage in country X is 50 gruff for the first ounce and 22 gruff for each additional ounce. A half-pound letter mailed in country X cost how many gruff?

    F.   204

    G.   226

    H.   248

    J.   270

    K.   292

C13: Three business partners, U, V, and W, divided the profits, respectively, in a ratio of $5 : 7 : 8$. If W's share was \$200,000, the total profit of the business was

    A.   \$100,000

    B.   \$200,000

    C.   \$250,000

    D.   \$500,000

    E.   \$1,000,000

C14: In the figure below, the largest side is

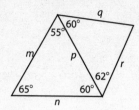

F.   *m*

G.   *n*

H.   *p*

J.   *q*

K.   *r*

C15: Two sides of a triangle are 4 and 7. If the sides are integers, the product of the smallest possible perimeter and largest possible perimeter is

A.   17

B.   36

C.   40

D.   210

E.   315

C16: *j*, *k*, and *m* are three consecutive odd integers, with $j < k < m$. Which is true?

I: $m - j = 4$

II: $jk + jm + km + 1$ is even

III: $\dfrac{(j + k + m)}{3}$ is an integer

F.   I only

G.   I and II only

H.   I and III only

J.   II and III only

K.   I, II, and III

C17: The sum of the three smallest primes greater than 30 is

    A. 99

    B. 109

    C. 111

    D. 115

    E. 131

C18: If the following were written as decimals, which would have the longest repeating sequence of different digits?

    F. $\dfrac{1}{3}$

    G. $\dfrac{1}{6}$

    H. $\dfrac{1}{7}$

    J. $\dfrac{1}{9}$

    K. $\dfrac{1}{99}$

C19: The perimeter of a sector of $40°$ in a circle whose circumference is 36π is

    A. $2\pi + 18$

    B. $2\pi + 36$

    C. $4\pi + 18$

    D. $4\pi + 36$

    E. $4\pi + 72$

C20: Which is not equivalent to $36a^2 = b^2 - 25$?

    F. $(b + 6a)(b - 6a) = 25$

    G. $b^2 = (6a + 5)(6a - 5)$

    H. $\dfrac{(b^2 - 25)}{36a^2} = 1$

    J. $-a^2 = \dfrac{(5 - b)(5 + b)}{36}$

    K. $36a^2 + 25 - b^2 = 0$

C21: Which of the following equations has a root in common with $x^2 - 7x + 6 = 0$?

   A. $x^2 + 36 = 0$

   B. $x^2 + 1 = 0$

   C. $x^2 + 7x + 6 = 0$

   D. $x^2 - 5x - 6 = 0$

   E. $x^2 + 8x + 12 = 0$

C22: The largest factor of 3,000,000,036 listed here is

   F.   2

   G.   6

   H.   12

   J.   132

   K.   396

C23: $\sqrt{6561}$ is exactly

   A.   81

   B.   83

   C.   89

   D.   91

   E.   99

C24: $\dfrac{x}{4} + \dfrac{x}{8}$ is what percent of x?

   F. $33\dfrac{1}{3}$

   G. $37\dfrac{1}{2}$

   H.   40

   J. $43\dfrac{3}{4}$

   K.   45

C25: If $x > 10,000$, $\dfrac{2x}{3x + 5}$ is approximately

A. $\dfrac{2}{3}$

B. $\dfrac{2}{5}$

C. $\dfrac{1}{4}$

D. $\dfrac{1}{5}$

E. $\dfrac{1}{15}$

C26: According to the chart below, the median grade was

Number of Students	Grade
10	60
64	70
35	80
25	90
15	100

F.   70

G.   75

H.   80

J.   85

K.   Cannot be determined

C27: $\dfrac{6}{x} = 2$ and $\dfrac{12}{y} = 24$; $\dfrac{3x + 1}{y + 2} =$

A. $\dfrac{5}{2}$

B.   3

C. $\dfrac{7}{2}$

D.   4

E.   6

C28: Which fraction has the greatest value?

F. $\dfrac{6}{2^2 5^2}$

G. $\dfrac{8}{2^3 5^2}$

H. $\dfrac{12}{2^3 5^3}$

J. $\dfrac{18}{2^4 5^3}$

K. $\dfrac{112}{2^4 5^4}$

C29: If c and d are different integers and $c^2 = cd$, which must be true?

I. $c = -d$

II. $c = 0$

III. $d = 0$

A.   I only

B.   II only

C.   III only

D.   II and III only

E.   I, II, and III

C30: How many square inches of wrapping paper will Kara need to just cover a gift box that measures 3 inches by 5 inches by one foot?

F.   15 square inches

G.   36 square inches

H.   60 square inches

J.   111 square inches

K.   222 square inches

C31: How many nonnegative integers x are there such that $x^4 < 1{,}000$?

    A.   2

    B.   3

    C.   4

    D.   5

    E.   More than 5

C32: In the figure below, which line is not part of the boundary?

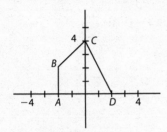

    F. $x = -2$

    G. $y = 0$

    H. $y - x = 4$

    J. $2x + y = 4$

    K. $x + 2y = 4$

C33: $(\sqrt{2} - 1)(\sqrt{2} + 1)(\sqrt{3} + 1)(\sqrt{3} - 1)(\sqrt{5} - 1)(\sqrt{5} + 1) =$

    A. $\sqrt{30}$

    B.   7

    C.   8

    D.   16

    E.   30

C34: A certain virus triples every 15 minutes. Originally there are 10,000 viruses. How many viruses are there in one hour?

    F. 30^4

    G. 10^8

    H. 30^8

    J. $3^4 10^8$

    K. 30^{16}

C35: The perimeter of a small garden is 24 feet and its area is 20 square feet. The length of the shorter side is

A.   2 ft

B.   4 ft

C.   6 ft

D.   8 ft

E.   10 ft

C36: How many total ounces are there in $\frac{1}{2}$ gallon, 1 quart, plus $1\frac{1}{2}$ pints?

F.   100 ounces

G.   110 ounces

H.   120 ounces

J.   128 ounces

K.   132 ounces

C37: To convert from Fahrenheit (F) temperature to Celsius (C), the formula is $F = \frac{9}{5}C + 32$. Where do the two scales have the same temperature?

A.   20°

B.   −20°

C.   −40°

D.   −100°

E.   −273°

C38: If $\log_b c = \log_b d$ means that $c = d$, and $2\log_7 x = \log_7 16$; $x =$

F.   2 only

G.   4 only

H.   4 and −4 only

J.   7 only

K.   −7 and 7 only

For questions C39 and C40, use this figure of a box with a square base.

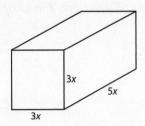

C39: The surface area of the box is

    A. $14x^2$

    B. $44x^2$

    C. $45x^2$

    D. $69x^2$

    E. $78x^2$

C40: The volume of the box is

    F. $14x^3$

    G. $44x^3$

    H. $45x^3$

    J. $69x^3$

    K. $78x^3$

C41: A rectangle has sides 54 inches and 72 inches. The diagonal, in inches, is

    A. 18

    B. 63

    C. 90

    D. 126

    E. 3888

C42: The amount of element X in a water sample A is 1.5×10^{-8} ounces per gallon of water. This is 10,000 times the amount of element X in water sample B. The amount of element X in water sample B is

F. 10^4

G. 1.5×10^{-4}

H. 1.5×10^{-12}

J. 1.5×10^{-16}

K. 1.5×10^{-64}

C43: $\sec^2 x - \csc^2 x =$

A. 0

B. $\sin^2 x - \cos^2 x$

C. $\cos^2 x - \sin^2 x$

D. $\tan^2 x - \cot^2 x$

E. $\cot^2 x - \tan^2 x$

C44: $\left(\dfrac{1}{2}x - \dfrac{1}{3}y\right)^2 =$

F. $\dfrac{1}{4}x^2 + \dfrac{1}{9}y^2$

G. $\dfrac{1}{4}x^2 - \dfrac{1}{9}y^2$

H. $\dfrac{1}{4}x^2 + \dfrac{1}{3}xy + \dfrac{1}{9}y^2$

J. $\dfrac{1}{4}x^2 - \dfrac{1}{3}xy + \dfrac{1}{9}y^2$

K. $\dfrac{1}{4}x^2 - xy + \dfrac{1}{9}y^2$

C45: Which are equal to $|x|$?

    I: $\sqrt{(-x)^2}$

    II: $|-x|$

    III: $-|-x|$

    A.   I only

    B.   II only

    C.   III only

    D.   I and II only

    E.   I, II, and III

C46: Avogadro's Number is $6.0^{23} \times 10^{23}$ molecules per mole. If there are 166,770 moles, approximately how many molecules are there?

    F. 10^{28}

    G. 10^{29}

    H. 10^{30}

    J. 10^{31}

    K. 10^{115}

C47: Given $\log_b m = c$, $\log_b n = d$, and $\log_b p = g$; in terms of c, d, and g, what is $\log_b \dfrac{m^4}{n^6 p^8}$?

    A. $4c - 6d + 8g$

    B. $2(2c - 3d - 4g)$

    C. $c^4 - d^6 + g^8$

    D. $c^4 - d^6 - g^8$

    E. $2(c^2 - d^3 + g^4)$

C48: The total amount of money in an interest-bearing account is given by $A = p + prt$, where p = principal, r = the rate of interest, and t = time. Then $p =$

F. $A - rt$

G. $\dfrac{A}{rt}$

H. $\dfrac{A}{(1 + rt)}$

J. $\dfrac{A}{(1 - rt)}$

K. $A + rt$

For questions C49 and C50, $F(x) = x^2 - x - 7$.

C49: $F(-7) =$

A.   1 only

B.   0, 1 only

C.   0, 1, 49 only

D.   49 only

E.   −49 only

C50: $F(x) = -7; x =$

F.   1 only

G.   0, 1 only

H.   0, 1, 49 only

J.   49 only

K.   −49 only

C51: $a + bi = (3 + 5i)(4 + i); a + b =$

    A.　-30

    B.　-16

    C.　16

    D.　30

    E.　-161

C52: $i^{2346} =$

    F.　i

    G.　$-i$

    H.　-1

    J.　1

    K.　0

C53: Simplify: $\dfrac{3 + 2x - x^2}{x^2 - 9} =$

    A.　$\dfrac{2x}{3}$

    B.　$\dfrac{2x - 3}{9}$

    C.　$\dfrac{1}{3}$

    D.　$\dfrac{x + 1}{x + 3}$

    E.　$\dfrac{-x - 1}{x + 3}$

C54: $\sqrt{12} \times \sqrt{8} =$

    F. $\sqrt{20}$

    G. $3\sqrt{10}$

    H. $2\sqrt{48}$

    J. $4\sqrt{6}$

    K. 12

C55: If m is even and n is odd, which statement must *always* be even?

    I. $(m + n)^2$

    II. $mn + n + 3$

    III. $nm + 1$

    A.   None of them

    B.   I only

    C.   II only

    D.   III only

    E.   All of them

C56: The graph of the solution to $|x - 4| \geqslant 3$ is

    F.

    G.

    H.

    J.

    K.

Questions C57, C58, C59, and C60 refer to the line $5x - 7y = 30$.

C57:   The *x*-intercept is

    A. $(6, 0)$

    B. $(30, 0)$

    C. $(0, 30)$

    D. $(0, -\dfrac{30}{7})$

    E. 35

C58:   The *y*-intercept is

    F. $(6, 0)$

    G. $(30, 0)$

    H. $(0, 30)$

    J. $(0, -\dfrac{30}{7})$

    K. 35

C59:   The slope is

    A. $-\dfrac{30}{7}$

    B. $\dfrac{7}{5}$

    C. $-\dfrac{7}{5}$

    D. $\dfrac{5}{7}$

    E. $-\dfrac{5}{7}$

C60:   Which points are on the line $5x - 7y = 30$?

I $(13, 5)$

II $(-1, -5)$

III $(4, -1\frac{3}{7})$

F.   None of them

G.   I and II only

H.   I and III only

J.   II and III only

K.   All of them

Ⓐ   **Let's look at the answers.**

C1:   **C:** Add the last two terms to get the next one: $0 + 1 = 1$; $1 + 1 = 2$; $1 + 2 = 3$; $2 + 3 = 5$; $3 + 5 = 8$; $5 + 8 = 13$; $8 + 13 = 21$.

C2:   **H:** The minus sign doesn't matter because both sides are positive; $2m = 9 - m$; $m = 3$.

C3:   **C:** $3m = -24$; $m = -8$; $3x + mx = 3x + -8x = -5x$; so $k = -5$.

C4:   **K:** $\dfrac{(m - n)}{n} = \dfrac{m}{n} - \dfrac{n}{n} = \dfrac{m}{n} - 1 = \dfrac{3}{4} - 1 = -\dfrac{1}{4}$.

C5:   **B:** $N(F) + N(R) - N(\text{both}) = N(F \text{ or } R)$; $N(F) + 25 - 10 = 35$; $N(F) = 20$; but $N(F) = 20$ and $N(\text{both}) = 10$; so $N(F \text{ only}) = 20 - 10 = 10$.

C6:   **H:** Point $C = (4, 4)$; Area $= \left(\dfrac{1}{2}\right)h(b_1 + b_2) = \left(\dfrac{1}{2}\right)AD(AB + CD) = \left(\dfrac{1}{2}\right)(4)(7 + 4) = 22$.

C7:   **A:** $p = AD + CD + AB + BC = 4 + 4 + 7 + \sqrt{(4 - 7)^2 + (4 - 0)^2} = 15 + 5 = 20$.

C8:   **J:** I is true; II is true because $x^5(1 + x^2) < x^4(1 + x^2)$ and because $x^5 < x^4$; III is false. $x^7 - x^5 = x^5(x^2 - 1)$ and $x^6 - x^4 = x^4(x^2 - 1)$. We know that $x^5 < x^4$ when $0 < x < 1$. However, $x^2 - 1$ is a negative number for $0 < x < 1$. Thus, $x^5(x^2 - 1)$ is actually greater than $x^4(x^2 - 1)$. Using $x = .5$, $x^7 - x^5 \approx -.023$ and $x^6 - x^4 \approx -.047$.

C9:   **B:** Remember, it asks for twice the area: only on a test like this one! You must read carefully. Notice that $b = d = 0$, because points x and z lie on the x axis.

C10:   **G:** The given square root is approximately $\sqrt{\dfrac{9(900)}{36}} = \dfrac{3(30)}{6} = \dfrac{30}{2} = 15$.

C11: **C:** In the first n games, an average of x means nx total points. Then add the next two games. Mean $= \dfrac{\text{total points}}{\text{total games}} = \dfrac{nx + y + z}{n + 2}$.

C12: **F:** 16 ounces to a pound, and 8 ounces to a half pound. The first ounce cost 50 gruff, and the remaining 7 cost 22 gruff each: $50 + 7(22) = 204$ gruff.

C13: **D:** $5x + 7x + 8x = 20x$, the total; $8x = \$200{,}000$; $4x = \$100{,}000$; $20x = 5(4x) = \$500{,}000$.

C14: **J:** In the left triangle, p is the largest side; in the right triangle, q is the largest side; but p and q are in the same triangle, so q is the largest side.

C15: **E:** The missing side s: $7 - 4 < s < 7 + 4$. Because they are all integers, s could be 4 through 10. The smallest perimeter is $4 + 4 + 7 = 15$. The largest is $10 + 4 + 7 = 21$. The product is $15 \times 21 = 315$. In this case, use approximation to see that the answer must be larger than $15 \times 20 = 300$, and the only answer choice is 315.

C16: **K:** The three consecutive odd numbers can be represented as j, $j + 2$, and $j + 4$. Statement I is true, because $j + 4 - j = 4$. Statement II is true, because (odd)(odd) + (odd)(odd) + (odd)(odd) + 1 = odd + odd + odd + 1 = even. Statement III is true, because $\dfrac{j + (j + 2) + (j + 4)}{3} = \dfrac{3j + 6}{3} = j + 2$, which is the middle integer K.

C17: **B:** $31 + 37 + 41 = 109$.

C18: **H:** $\dfrac{1}{7}$ repeats every 6 places; all the others repeat a single digit, except $\dfrac{1}{99}$ which repeats 2 digits.

C19: **D:** $p = 2r + s$; $c = 36\pi = 2\pi r$; $r = 18$; $s = \dfrac{40}{360}(2\pi r) = \dfrac{1}{9}(36\pi) = 4\pi$; $p = 36 + 4\pi$.

C20: **G:** $b^2 = 36a^2 + 25$, which does not factor.

C21: **D:** Both have root $x = 6$. $x^2 - 7x + 6 = 0$ factors as $(x - 6)(x - 1) = 0$ and $x^2 - 5x - 6 = 0$ factors as $(x - 6)(x + 1) = 0$.

C22: **J:** The sum of the digits is 12, which is divisible by 3 (but not 9); The sum of the odd digits = the sum of the even digits ($6 = 6$), so the number is divisible by 11. The number ends in 36, which is divisible by 4; $4(11)(3) = 132$. 396 is not okay because 9 is one of its factors.

C23: **A:** $\sqrt{6400} = 80$; the number ends in 1. So the answer must be 81 or 89. The number is closer to 6400 than 8100.

C24: **G:** $\dfrac{x}{4} + \dfrac{x}{8} = \dfrac{3}{8}x$; and $\dfrac{3}{8} = 37\dfrac{1}{2}\%$.

C25: **A:** For very big x's or very small x's ($x = -1000, -2000$, etc.). We can throw away all terms that do not involve the highest power of x; here, we throw away the 5: $\dfrac{2x}{3x} = \dfrac{2}{3}$.

C26: **H:** 149 total; the median is the grade of the 75th student, or 80.

C27: **D:** $x = 3$ and $y = \dfrac{1}{2}$, so $\dfrac{3x + 1}{y + 2} = \dfrac{10}{2.5} = 4$.

C28: **F:** Notice $2(5) = 10$; with manipulations, all denominators are powers of 10! $F = .06$, $G = .04$, $H = .012$, $J = .009$, $K = .0112$.

C29: **B:** The others would imply $c = d = 0$. Also, we can rewrite as $c^2 - cd = 0$, which factors as $c(c-d) = 0$. Because $c \ne d$, c must equal 0.

C30: **K:** Kara will need 222 square inches. $SA = 2(\ell \times w) + 2(h \times w) + 2(\ell \times h)$. Don't forget to change 1 foot to 12 inches.

C31: **E:** There are six: 1, 2, 3, 4, 5, and 0. Don't forget the 0!

C32: **K:** Each of the other answer choices is a side of the polygon. Answer choice F corresponds to AB, answer choice G corresponds to AD, answer choice H correponds to BC, and answer choice J corresponds to CD.

C33: **C:** $(1)(2)(4) = 8$.

C34: **F:** $3^4 10^4 = 30^4$.

C35: **A:** The sides are 10 and 2; trial and error works best for a quick answer. Algebraically, $L + W = 12$ and $LW = 20$. By substitution, $(W)(12 - W) = 20$ or $W^2 - 12W + 20 = 0$. Then $(W - 10)(W - 2) = 0$, which means $W = 10$ or $W = 2$. Select $W = 2$, the smaller number.

C36: **H:** $\dfrac{1}{2}$ gallon $= 64$ ounces; 1 quart $= 32$ ounces; $1\dfrac{1}{2}$ pints $= (16 + 8)$ ounces, so the total is $(64 + 32 + 16 + 8) = 120$ ounces.

C37: **C:** $F = C = \left(\dfrac{9}{5}\right)C + 32$; $\left(-\dfrac{4}{5}\right)C = 32$; $C = 32\left(-\dfrac{5}{4}\right) = 8(-5) = -40$.

C38: **G:** $2\log_7 x = \log_7 x^2 = \log_7 16$: so $x^2 = 16$; only positive answers are okay, so $x = 4$.

C39: **E:** $2(9x^2) + 4(15x^2) = 78x^2$.

C40: **H:** $V = l \times w \times h = (3x)(3x)(5x) = 45x^3$.

C41: **C:** This example is really instructive. There are many ways to do this problem. First, you can use the Pythagorean Theorem (messy!). Second, you can notice that it is a 3-4-5 triangle: 3(18) = 54, 4(18) = 72, 5(18) = 90. However, just by looking at the answers you can tell. Answer choices A and B are wrong: the diagonal is the largest side. Answer choices D and E are wrong: two sides of a triangle have to be greater than the third side. Sometimes you can choose an answer without doing the problem.

C42: **H:** $\dfrac{1.5 \times 10^{-8}}{10^4} = 1.5 \times 10^{-8} \times 10^{-4} = 1.5 \times 10^{-12}$.

C43: **D:** Use identities: $(\tan^2 x + 1) - (\cot^2 x + 1)$.

C44: **J:** $\left(\dfrac{1}{2}x - \dfrac{1}{3}y\right)\left(\dfrac{1}{2}x - \dfrac{1}{3}y\right) = \dfrac{1}{4}x^2 - \dfrac{2}{6}xy + \dfrac{1}{9}y^2$.

C45: **D:** III is a negative absolute value.

C46: **G:** $(6.023 \times 10^{23})(1.667 \times 10^5) \approx 10^1 \times 10^{28} = 10^{29}$

C47: **B:** Simplifying, we get $4\log_b m - 6\log_b n - 8\log_b p = 4c - 6d - 8g = 2(2c - 3d - 4g)$

C48: **H:** $p(1 + rt) = A$, so $p = \dfrac{A}{(1 + rt)}$.

C49: **D:** $(-7)(-7) - (-7) - 7 = 49$.

C50: **G:** $x^2 - x - 7 = -7; x^2 - x = x(x - 1) = 0$.

C51: **D:** $a + bi = 12 + 23i + 5i^2 = 7 + 23i; a = 7$ and $b = 23$, so $a + b = 30$.

C52: **H:** Dividing the exponent by 4, the remainder is 2; $i^2 = -1$.

C53: **E:** $\dfrac{-1(x^2 - 2x - 3)}{x^2 - 9} = \dfrac{-1(x - 3)(x + 1)}{(x - 3)(x + 3)} = \dfrac{-1(x + 1)}{x + 3}$

C54: **J:** $\sqrt{(2)(2)(2)(2)(3)(2)} = 4\sqrt{6}$.

C55: **C:** The other two are always odd.

C56: **J:** $|x - 4| \geqslant 3$ means $x - 4 \geqslant 3$ or $x - 4 \leqslant -3$.

C57: **A:** $y = 0; x = 6$.

C58: **J:** $x = 0; y = -\dfrac{30}{7}$.

C59: **D:** Solving for y, $y = \left(\dfrac{5}{7}\right)x - \left(\dfrac{30}{7}\right)$.

C60: **K:** If you substitute each x and y value, all three pairs make the right side $= 30$; if it did not equal 30, a point wouldn't be on the line.

Practice Test D

D1:   In a parallel circuit in electricity, the total resistance R of resistors X and Y is given by the formula $\dfrac{1}{X} + \dfrac{1}{Y} = \dfrac{1}{R}$, where the resistance is in ohms. If $X = 12$ ohms and $Y = 6$ ohms, $R =$

A.   3

B.   4

C.   8

D.   18

E.   24

D2:   If $a = -2$ and $b = -3$, the value of $ab^2 - (ab)^2$ is

F.   0

G. -36

H. -54

J. -72

K. -324

D3: $x^{12} =$

A. $x^6 + x^6$

B. $(x^6)^6$

C. $\dfrac{x^3}{x^{15}}$

D. $x^{17} - x^5$

E. $x^3 x^9$

D4:   If $\dfrac{x^2 - 3x - 18}{x + 4} = 0$, then $x =$

F.   6 only

G. -3 only

H. -3 and 6 only

J. $6, 0, -3$ only

K. $-4, -3, 6$ only

D5: $\left(\sqrt{6} + \sqrt{6}\right)^2$

   A.   6

   B.   12

   C.   24

   D.   72

   E.   576

D6: $\dfrac{\frac{1}{3} + \frac{1}{4}}{\frac{1}{6}}$

   F. $\dfrac{1}{2}$

   G. $\dfrac{6}{7}$

   H. $\dfrac{12}{7}$

   J.   2.5

   K.   3.5

D7: If the area of a square is p. In terms of p what is the diagonal?

   A. $p\sqrt{2}$

   B. $\sqrt{p}$

   C. $\sqrt{2p}$

   D. $2\sqrt{p}$

   E. $\dfrac{p\sqrt{2}}{2}$

D8: A monkey is trying to climb out of a 40-foot hole. Each morning he climbs up 4 feet. At night he gets so tired he falls back 3 feet. Every day this is repeated. On what day does he climb out of the hole?

   F.   37

   G.   38

   H.   40

   J.   41

   K.   42

D9:   A 40-foot fence is in front of my house (not true), and it has a fence post every 4 feet. The number of fence posts is

A.   9

B.   10

C.   11

D.   12

E.   24

D10:   A 40-foot ribbon is cut into 4-foot pieces. The number of cuts is

F.   9

G.   10

H.   11

J.   12

K.   24

D11:   Sue starts at the top of page 484 and finishes at the bottom of page 524. Sue has read how many pages?

A.   38

B.   39

C.   40

D.   41

E.   42

D12:   Jim has a 40-inch, 40-pound metal bar to be cut into integer multiples. That is, a piece or pieces can be 1 pound or 2 pounds or 3 pounds or whatever. If he is to measure on a balance scale every integer between 1 and 40 inclusive, what is the fewest number of pieces into which the bar can be cut? (See the hint on the next page.)

F.   4

G.   6

H.   8

J.   39

K.   40

Hint about a balance scale: You can put weights on either side. For example, if you had weights of 2 pounds, 4 pounds, and 10 pounds, you could weigh 6 pounds by putting the 4-pound weight on the same side and the 10-pound weight on the other. Or you could weigh 14 pounds: you would put a 10-pound weight and 4-pound weight on one side and the 14 pounds you want weighed on the other.

D13: 960 ounces of radioactive roast beef loses half its radioactivity every 4 hours. How many ounces of radioactive roast beef remain after one full day?

   A.   0

   B.   15

   C.   30

   D.   60

   E.   120

D14: If $n \neq 3$, then $\dfrac{2n^2(n-3) - n + 3}{n-3} =$

   F. $2n^2 - n + 3$

   G. $2n^2$

   H. $2n^2 - 1$

   J. $2n^2 + 1$

   K. $2n^2 + 3$

D15: $\dfrac{(.5)^8}{(.5)^4} =$

   A.   .25

   B.   .125

   C.   .0625

   D.   .03125

   E.   .015625

D16:   A circle fits inside a square, touching all the sides of the square. If a side of the square is 6, what is the area of the circle?

   F. 3π

   G. 6π

   H. 9π

   J. $\sqrt{6\pi}$

   K.   Not enough information is given

D17:   If $4x + 3y = 11$ and $6x + 5y = 27$, the average (mean) of x and y is

   A.   2

   B.   4

   C.   8

   D.   9.5

   E.   19

D18:   A cube and a rectangular solid have the same volume. If the dimensions of the rectangular solid are 1, 3, and 9, how long is one side of the cube?

   F.   1

   G.   3

   H.   13

   J. $\sqrt[3]{13}$

   K.   27

D19:   If $M = \{$all even numbers$\}$ and $N = \{$all prime numbers$\}$, what is $M \cap N$?

   A. $\{1, 3, 5, \ldots\}$

   B. $\{2, 4, 6, \ldots\}$

   C. $\{$all prime numbers$\}$

   D.   2

   E. ϕ

D20: If n is divided by 7, the remainder is 5. If $2n$ is divided by 7, the remainder is

    F. 2

    G. 3

    H. 4

    J. 5

    K. 6

D21: If $(x - 2)^2 = 900$, the value of x could be

    A. 30

    B. 28

    C. -28

    D. -30

    E. -32

D22: A right triangle has sides 1 and $\sqrt{2}$. What can the third side be?

    I. 1

    II. $\sqrt{2}$

    III. $\sqrt{3}$

    F. I only

    G. II only

    H. III only

    J. I and II only

    K. I and III only

D23: If $(x + y)^2 = 100$ and $xy = -3$, then $x^2 + y^2 =$

    A. 4

    B. 7

    C. 94

    D. 100

    E. 106

D24: A bell rings 6 times every 5 minutes. If it rings at 1:00 PM, how many times does it ring between 1:00 PM and 1:30 PM, inclusive?

F.   30

G.   35

H.   36

J.   42

K.   48

D25: The number of boys is twice the number of girls in a group of 60 children. The pair of equations that best describes this is

A. $b - 2g = 0, b + g = 60$

B. $b + 2g = 0, b + g = 60$

C. $b - 2g = 0, b + 2g = 60$

D. $b + 2g = 0, 2b + g = 60$

E. $2b - g = 0, b + g = 60$

D26: If m and n are consecutive integers, which can never be even?

F. mn

G. $m + n$

H. $mn + 2$

J. $(mn)^2$

K. $m^2 + n^2 + 1$

D27: The price of a book is increased by 20%, and then the new price is discounted by 20%. Compared to the original price of the book, what is the final price?

A.   10% less

B.   4% less

C.   Same as the original price

D.   4% more

E.   10% more

D28: The price of a second book is discounted 20%, and then the new price is increased by 20%. Compared to the original price of the book, what is the final price?

F. 10% less

G. 4% less

H. Same as the original price

J. 4% more

K. 10% more

D29: A $400 item is taxed at 5%. Then the whole price is discounted by 10%. A second $400 item is discounted at 10% and then the 5% sales tax is added on. The difference in cost between the two methods is

A. nothing

B. $10

C. $20

D. $30

E. $40

D30: $\dfrac{31^2 + 31}{31} =$

F. 31

G. 32

H. 62

J. 941

K. 942

D31: $3^6 + 3^6 + 3^6 =$

A. 9^6

B. 27^6

C. 3^7

D. 3^{18}

E. 3^{216}

D32: If the diagonal of a square is 10, its area is

F. 25

G. 50

H. 75

J. 100

K. 200

D33: If $4^{\frac{4}{3}}4^{\frac{5}{3}} = x^2$; x could equal

A. 8

B. 6

C. 4

D. 2

E. -4

D34: If m books cost $4 apiece and n books cost $6 apiece, the mean cost per book is

F. $\dfrac{24mn}{m+n}$

G. $4m + \dfrac{6n}{mn}$

H. $\dfrac{4m+6n}{m+n}$

J. $\dfrac{4m+6n}{10}$

K. $\dfrac{4m-6n}{m-n}$

D35: A taxi ride costs $2.00 for the first quarter mile and 40 cents for each additional quarter of a mile. How much does a 3-mile trip cost?

A. $6.80

B. $6.40

C. $6.00

D. $5.60

E. $4.80

D36: $\dfrac{4}{1 + \frac{2}{x}} = 2;\ x =$

    F. 4

    G. 2

    H. 1

    J. $\dfrac{1}{2}$

    K. $\dfrac{1}{4}$

D37: A 6-sided die is tossed, then a coin is flipped. What is the probability that a head and a number greater than 4 will come up together?

    A. $\dfrac{1}{12}$

    B. $\dfrac{1}{6}$

    C. $\dfrac{1}{4}$

    D. $\dfrac{1}{3}$

    E. $\dfrac{5}{12}$

D38: What is the maximum number of $1\frac{1}{4}$-foot pieces that can be cut from a 32-foot board?

    F. 24

    G. 25

    H. 26

    J. 27

    K. 28

D39: If $f(x) = x^2 + 4x + 9$, then $\dfrac{f(x + h) - f(x)}{h} =$

    A.   1

    B. h

    C. $h + 4$

    D. $2x + h + 13$

    E. $2x + h + 4$

D40: The area of a circle with diameter 20 is equal to the area of a square. The side of the square is

    F. $\sqrt{10\pi}$

    G. $10\sqrt{\pi}$

    H. $\pi\sqrt{10}$

    J. $20\sqrt{\pi}$

    K. $\pi\sqrt{20}$

D41: $\log_3 x + \log_3 (x + 6) = 3; x =$

    A.   3 only

    B.   3, -9 only

    C. -9 only

    D. $\dfrac{246}{26}$ or $\dfrac{123}{13}$ only

    E.   no solution

D42:

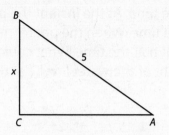

For the given figure, tan $A =$

F. $\dfrac{x}{5}$

G. $\dfrac{5}{x}$

H. $\dfrac{x\sqrt{25 - x^2}}{25 - x^2}$

J. $\dfrac{\sqrt{25 - x^2}}{x}$

K. $\dfrac{\sqrt{25 - x^2}}{5}$

D43: A swimming pool is filled. It empties as the square of the time. At the instant the pool is emptied, two hoses are opened and it fills at twice the time. When the pool is mostly filled, one hose shuts off, and the pool continues to fill at half the time. What could the graph of the water level versus time look like? (y = height of the water level, t = time)

A.

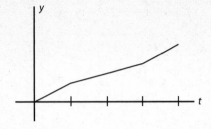

B.

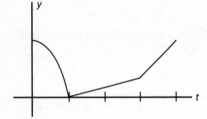

C.

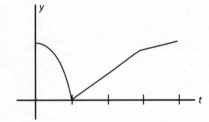

D.

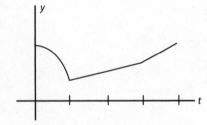

E.

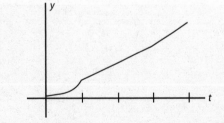

D44: $\sin^2 x + \sin x = 0$, where $0 \leqslant x < 2\pi$. Then $x =$

   F.   0 only

   G. $0, \pi$ only

   H. $0, \pi, \dfrac{3\pi}{2}$ only

   J. $\dfrac{3\pi}{2}$ only

   K. $0, \dfrac{3\pi}{2}$ only

For questions D45 through D49, $y = -3\sin\left(4x - \dfrac{\pi}{4}\right) + 10$.

D45: The amplitude is

   A.   3

   B. -3

   C.   4

   D.   10

   E.   13

D46: The left-right shift is

   F. π

   G. $\dfrac{\pi}{4}$

   H. $-\dfrac{\pi}{4}$

   J. $\dfrac{\pi}{16}$

   K. $-\dfrac{\pi}{16}$

D47:   The period is

    A.   1440°

    B.   360°

    C.   180°

    D.   90°

    E.   45°

D48:   The up-down shift is

    F.   up 3

    G.   down 3

    H.   up 10

    J.   down 10

    K.   up 13

D49:   If $x = 0$, the y value on this graph is

    A.   13

    B.   10

    C.   7

    D. $10 + \dfrac{3\sqrt{2}}{2}$

    E. $10 - \dfrac{3\sqrt{2}}{2}$

D50:   Meg goes north 6 miles, east 10 miles, north 2 miles, and west 16 miles. How many miles from the start is Meg?

    F.   34

    G.   14

    H.   12

    J.   10

    K. $\sqrt{86}$

D51: $2(2x - 4) + 10 > 4x + 6$ is true

    A. when $x > 4$

    B. when $x > -4$

    C. when $x > 0$

    D. for all real numbers

    E. for no real numbers

D52: $\dfrac{i}{i - 1} =$

    F. $\dfrac{-1 - i}{2}$

    G. $\dfrac{-1 + i}{2}$

    H. $\dfrac{i - 1}{2}$

    J. $\dfrac{1 - i}{2}$

    K. 0

D53: $g(x) = x^2 - 4x - 7$ and $f(x) = x^2 + 2x + 11$. Where does $f(x) = g(x)$?

    A. $(3, -6)$

    B. $(1, -10)$

    C. $(-1, -2)$

    D. $(-3, 14)$

    E. $(-5, 38)$

D54: $f(x) = x2^x$. If $f(x) = 150$, which answer is best?

    F. $3 < x < 4$, closer to 3

    G. $3 < x < 4$, closer to 4

    H. $4 < x < 5$, closer to 4

    J. $4 < x < 5$, closer to 5

    K. $x > 5$

D55: The graphs of $x + y < 2$ and $x > 4$ intersect in which quadrant(s)?

    A. I

    B. II

    C. III

    D. IV

    E. more than one quadrant

D56: A triangle and a trapezoid have equal areas and equal heights. Which statement must be true?

    F. The base of the triangle must be bigger than either of the bases of the trapezoid.

    G. The base of the triangle must be bigger than one of the bases and smaller than one of the bases.

    H. The base of the triangle must be smaller than both of the bases of the trapezoid.

    J. The perimeter of the triangle must be smaller than the perimeter of the trapezoid.

    K. None of these must be always true.

D57: $\dfrac{2^8 4^4}{16^4} =$

    A. 2^8

    B. 2^4

    C. 2^2

    D. 2^0

    E. $\dfrac{1}{2^8}$

D58: The graphs of $3x + 4y = 8$ and $2x + 5y = 3$ meet at the point

    F. $(3, -\tfrac{1}{4})$

    G. $(8, -4)$

    H. $(4, -1)$

    J. $(5, -\tfrac{7}{4})$

    K. $(9, -5)$

D59: $1 - 4x - 2(3x - 4) = 6; x =$

    A. $-.3$

    B. $.3$

    C. 1.4

    D. -1.4

    E. 1

D60: How many cubic feet of dirt are found in a rectangular hole that is 6 feet long, 4 feet wide, and 2 inches deep?

    F.   48

    G.   24

    H.   6

    J.   4

    K.   0

A **Let's look at the answers**

D1: **B:** $\dfrac{1}{12} + \dfrac{1}{6} = \dfrac{1}{12} + \dfrac{2}{12} = \dfrac{3}{12} = \dfrac{1}{4} = \dfrac{1}{R}$, so $R = 4$.

D2: **H:** $(-2)(-3)^2 - ((-2)(-3))^2 = -18 - 36 = -54$

D3: **E:** $x^3 x^9 = x^{(3 + 9)} = x^{12}$

D4: **H:** For a fraction to equal 0, the top $= 0$ and the bottom $\neq 0$. So $x^2 - 3x - 18 = (x - 6)(x + 3) = 0$; and $x = 6$ and -3.

D5: **C:** $(\sqrt{6} + \sqrt{6})^2 = (2\sqrt{6})^2 = 4(6) = 24$.

D6: **K:** Multiply the top and bottom by 12, and you get  $\dfrac{7}{2}$, or 3.5.

D7: **C:** Each side is $s = \sqrt{p}$. The diagonal is then $s\sqrt{2} = \sqrt{p}\sqrt{2} = \sqrt{2p}$.

D8: **F:** After 36 days, the monkey is 36 feet up. On the 37th day, the monkey climbs up 4 feet. It is now at 40 feet and out of the hole. It does not fall back.

D9: **C:** $\dfrac{40}{4} = 10$. Then add 1 for the post at the beginning.

D10: **F:** You need only 9 cuts to get 10 pieces.

D11:   **D:** $524 - 484 + 1 = 41$.

D12:   **F:** The pieces weigh 1, 3, 9, and 27. I included this one because it was another "40" problem (notice that a lot of the problems in this test have to do with the number 40). However, this one is just for fun, for those who think these puzzles are fun.

D13:   **B:** 480 left after 4 hours, 240 left after 8 hours, 120 left after 12 hours, 60 left after 16 hours, 30 left after 20 hours, and 15 left after 24 hours = 1 day.

D14:   **H:** $\dfrac{2n^2(n-3) - n + 3}{n - 3} = \dfrac{2n^2(n-3) - 1(n-3)}{(n-3)} = \dfrac{(n-3)(2n^2-1)}{(n-3)} = 2n^2 - 1$.

D15:   **C:** $(.5)^4 = \left(\dfrac{1}{2}\right)^4 = \dfrac{1}{16} = .0625$.

D16:   **H:** The diameter of the circle must be the same as the side of the square, which is 6. So $r = 3$, and the area is $\pi r^2 = \pi(3^2) = 9\pi$.

D17:   **B:** Subtracting the first equation from the second, we get $2x + 2y = 16$; $x + y = 8$, so $\dfrac{x+y}{2} = 4$.

D18:   **G:** The volume of the rectangular solid is $V = \ell wh = 27$; the volume of a cube is s^3. Then the length of a side of the cube is $\sqrt[3]{27} = 3$.

D19:   **D:** The only even prime number is 2.

D20:   **G:** Doubling the number doubles the remainder, so the remainder is 10, but $\dfrac{10}{7}$ has a remainder of 3.

D21:   **C:** $x - 2 = \pm 30$; so $x = 2 + 30 = 32$ or $2 - 30 = -28$.

D22:   **K:** 1 is okay because $(1)^2 + (1)^2 = \left(\sqrt{2}\right)^2$, and $\sqrt{3}$ is okay because $1^2 + \left(\sqrt{2}\right)^2 = \left(\sqrt{3}\right)^2$.

D23:   **E:** $x^2 + 2xy + y^2 = 100$; $x^2 + y^2 + 2(-3) = 100$; $x^2 + y^2 = 106$.

D24:   **J:** This is actually like the fence-post problem. There are 30 minutes between 1:00 PM and 1:30 PM. $30 \div 5 = 6$ five-minute intervals, so $(6)(6) = 36$ rings. But you must add in the 6 rings at 1:00 PM, for a total of 42 rings.

D25:   **A:** The number of boys is twice the number of girls can be expressed as $b = 2g$, which is equivalent to $b - 2g = 0$. Because there are 60 children, the number of boys added to the number of girls is 60. This is written algebraically as $b + g = 60$.

D26:   **G:** An odd plus an even always equals an odd.

D27:   **B:** $100 increased by 20% = $120; 20% off is $24; $120 − $24 = $96, which is 4% less than the original price.

D28:   **G:** 20% off $100 is $80; 20% of $80 is $16. $80 + $16 = $96, which is 4% less than the original price.

D29:   **A:** Each gives a final price of $378.

D30:   **G:** $\dfrac{31(31 + 1)}{31} = 31 + 1 = 32.$

D31:   **C:** The sum is $3(3^6) = 3^1 3^6 = 3^7.$

D32:   **G:** The easy formula to remember is $A = \left(\dfrac{1}{2}\right) d^2$; or $\left(\dfrac{10}{\sqrt{2}}\right)^2 = \dfrac{100}{2} = 50.$

D33:   **A:** $4^3 = x^2; x^2 = 64; x = \pm 8.$

D34:   **H:** Mean $= \dfrac{\text{Total cost of books}}{\text{Total number of books}} = \dfrac{4m + 6n}{m + n}.$

D35:   **B:** After the first quarter mile, there are 11 quarter miles left. The cost is 2.00 + 11(.40) = $6.40.

D36:   **G:** 2. Try to do it by sight; $\dfrac{2}{x}$ must equal 1. Another approach is to multiply each side of the equation by $1 + \dfrac{2}{x}$ to get $4 = 2\left(1 + \dfrac{2}{x}\right)$, which simplifies to $4 = 2 + \dfrac{4}{x}$. Then, $2 = \dfrac{4}{x}$, so $x = 2.$

D37:   **B:** Probability $= \dfrac{\text{Success}}{\text{Possibilities}}$. The probabilty of a 5 or 6 on a 6-sided die is $\dfrac{2}{6}$, and the probability is $\dfrac{1}{2}$ for a head on a coin. $\dfrac{2}{6} \times \dfrac{1}{2} = \dfrac{1}{6}.$

D38:   **G:** There will be 4 pieces every 5 feet, or 24 pieces for 30 feet, or 25 pieces for $31\dfrac{1}{4}$ feet. The next piece will be $1\dfrac{1}{4}$ feet; the answer is 25, because $31\dfrac{1}{4} + 1\dfrac{1}{4} > 32.$

D39:   **E:** $\dfrac{(x + h)^2 + 4(x + h) + 9 - (x^2 + 4x + 9)}{h} = \dfrac{2xh + h^2 + 4h}{h} = 2x + h + 4$. This question is a very important problem in math. It is called the difference quotient. If you let h approach 0 here, you would get the formula of the slope of the line tangent to $f(x) = x^2 + 4x + 9$. In other words, the slope at the point (1, 14), which is on the curve for $f(x)$, is $m = 2x + 4 = 6$, since $x = 1$. Congratulations! You just took the first step into calculus!

D40: **G:** Area $A = \pi 10^2 = 100\pi = s^2$, so $s = \sqrt{100\pi} = 10\sqrt{\pi}$.

D41: **A:** $\log_3 x(x + 6) = 3$; $x^2 + 6x = 3^3$; $x^2 + 6x - 27 = (x + 9)(x - 3) = 0$; only $x = 3$ is okay because you cannot have the log of a negative number.

D42: **H:** By the Pythagorean Theorem, the missing side $AC = \sqrt{25 - x^2}$;

$$\tan A = \frac{\text{opposite}}{\text{adjacent}} = \frac{x}{\sqrt{25 - x^2}} \times \frac{\sqrt{25 - x^2}}{\sqrt{25 - x^2}} = \frac{x\sqrt{25 - x^2}}{25 - x^2}.$$

D43: **C:** The first part of the graph is $y = h - t^2$, the second part is a straight line segment, and the third part is a straight line segment whose slope that is half the slope of the second part of the graph.

D44: **H:** $\sin x (\sin x + 1) = 0$; $\sin x = 0$ (at 0° and 180°) and $\sin x = -1$ at 270°. We get the answer by looking at the curve $y = \sin x$ and converting to radians.

D45: **A:** The amplitude is the absolute value of the coefficient of sin, or -3.

D46: **J:** $4x - \dfrac{\pi}{4} = 0$; $4x = \dfrac{\pi}{4}$; so $\dfrac{1}{4} \times \dfrac{\pi}{4} = \dfrac{\pi}{16}$, a shift to the right.

D47: **D:** Because we have $4x$, the period is $\dfrac{360°}{4} = 90°$.

D48: **H:** $+10$ means a shift up 10.

D49: **D:** Substituting $x = 0$ and changing to degrees, we get $y = -3 \sin (-45°) + 10$. We use the sketch here to find $\sin(-45°) = \dfrac{-1}{\sqrt{2}} = \dfrac{-\sqrt{2}}{2}$. Then $y = -3 \times \dfrac{-\sqrt{2}}{2} + 10$.

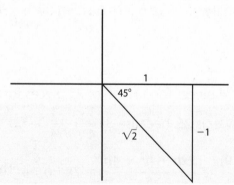

D50: **J:** We are 8 miles north and 6 miles west. This is a 6-8-10 Pythagorean triangle, so she is 10 miles from home.

D51: **E:** Solving, we get $4x + 2 > 4x + 6$, or $2 > 6$, which is never true.

D52: J: $\dfrac{i}{i-1} \times \dfrac{i+1}{i+1} = \dfrac{-1+i}{-2} = \dfrac{1-i}{2}$.

D53: D: Canceling the x^2 terms, we get, $-4x - 7 = 2x + 11$; solving, we get $x = -3$. Then, by substitution into either $f(x)$ or $g(x)$, $f(-3) = g(-3) = 14$.

D54: J: We get the answer by pure substitution; $5(2^5)$ is 160, very close to 150.

D55: D:

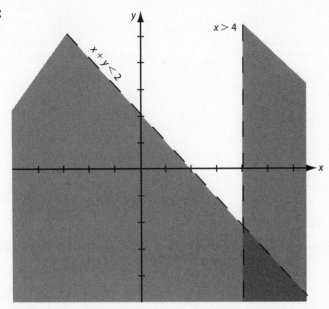

D56: F: The area for a triangle is $\left(\dfrac{1}{2}bh\right)$; the area of a trapezoid is $\dfrac{1}{2}h(b_1 + b_2)$. Because the heights are equal, $b = b_1 + b_2$. Because all bases are positive, both bases of the trapezoid must be smaller than the base of the triangle.

D57: D: $\dfrac{2^8 2^8}{2^{16}} = 2^0 = 1$.

D58: H: Multiplying the first equation by 2 and the second by -3 and adding each side, we get $6x + 8y - 6x - 15y = 16 - 9$; $-7y = 7$; $y = -1$; substituting, we get $x = 4$.

D59: B: $1 - 4x - 6x + 8 = 6$; $-10x + 9 = 6$; $-10x = -3$; so $x = .3$.

D60: K: The last question in the book is an old joke. The answer is there is no dirt in a hole. The point to this question, as with many questions on this test, is to read all questions very carefully and as quickly as possible. If you misread the question, no matter how good your math is, you will miss it.

CHAPTER 18: *What to Do Now*

"If you feel more is needed, then you may need a little more for your confidence. But if our journey together has been complete, you have all you need for success."

Congratulations on finishing the book. At this point, you should be really well prepared for the ACT. The question you might ask is, "What more can I do?"

1. Review any weak points you still may have.

2. Buy the ACT publication, *The Real ACT Prep Guide*. It has real ACT tests from the past. It has only three of them, but three is better than none. Try at least one of the tests for time.

3. If you take the ACT on Thursday (which is probably not true), do not study past Tuesday afternoon. I believe your subconscious has answers. If you study until the end, you will not be relaxed. Your subconscious will not give you answers that would raise your score.

4. If you have a few items that are still bothering you, those are the only things you should look at in the last two days.

5. The night before the ACT, you must have everything ready: pencils, permitted calculators, entrance cards, proper ID, etc.

6. Go to sleep at your normal time unless you normally go to bed very late (then try to go to bed earlier).

7. Eat a good breakfast! This is a long test, and you want to keep your energy level high. Wear comfortable clothes.

8. If you are a slow test starter, do a few of the easier problems at home to get your mind going. They should be easy to maintain your confidence.

9. Arrive at the test 20 minutes early. This will relax you before the test. Bring some food and drink to keep your energy level up.

10. It is okay to be nervous. I was always nervous before my tests. But once I started, I was okay. You will be, too.

11. If there is a question you don't know, guess and move on.

12. Don't spend too much time on a question. Guess and come back to it, if there is time.

13. Don't use your calculator unless you must.

14. Never change an answer unless you are 100 percent sure the new answer is correct or if you just guessed the first time around. The last real test I took, I changed an answer I wasn't 100 percent sure was right. Guess what? I changed the answer from right to wrong!

15. Have fun on the test.

Have lots of good luck on this test and for the rest of your life!

ANSWER SHEET: *Practice Test A*

1. Ⓐ Ⓑ Ⓒ Ⓓ Ⓔ

2. Ⓕ Ⓖ Ⓗ Ⓙ Ⓚ

3. Ⓐ Ⓑ Ⓒ Ⓓ Ⓔ

4. Ⓕ Ⓖ Ⓗ Ⓙ Ⓚ

5. Ⓐ Ⓑ Ⓒ Ⓓ Ⓔ

6. Ⓕ Ⓖ Ⓗ Ⓙ Ⓚ

7. Ⓐ Ⓑ Ⓒ Ⓓ Ⓔ

8. Ⓕ Ⓖ Ⓗ Ⓙ Ⓚ

9. Ⓐ Ⓑ Ⓒ Ⓓ Ⓔ

10. Ⓕ Ⓖ Ⓗ Ⓙ Ⓚ

11. Ⓐ Ⓑ Ⓒ Ⓓ Ⓔ

12. Ⓕ Ⓖ Ⓗ Ⓙ Ⓚ

13. Ⓐ Ⓑ Ⓒ Ⓓ Ⓔ

14. Ⓕ Ⓖ Ⓗ Ⓙ Ⓚ

15. Ⓐ Ⓑ Ⓒ Ⓓ Ⓔ

16. Ⓕ Ⓖ Ⓗ Ⓙ Ⓚ

17. Ⓐ Ⓑ Ⓒ Ⓓ Ⓔ

18. Ⓕ Ⓖ Ⓗ Ⓙ Ⓚ

19. Ⓐ Ⓑ Ⓒ Ⓓ Ⓔ

20. Ⓕ Ⓖ Ⓗ Ⓙ Ⓚ

21. Ⓐ Ⓑ Ⓒ Ⓓ Ⓔ

22. Ⓕ Ⓖ Ⓗ Ⓙ Ⓚ

23. Ⓐ Ⓑ Ⓒ Ⓓ Ⓔ

24. Ⓕ Ⓖ Ⓗ Ⓙ Ⓚ

25. Ⓐ Ⓑ Ⓒ Ⓓ Ⓔ

26. Ⓕ Ⓖ Ⓗ Ⓙ Ⓚ

27. Ⓐ Ⓑ Ⓒ Ⓓ Ⓔ

28. Ⓕ Ⓖ Ⓗ Ⓙ Ⓚ

29. Ⓐ Ⓑ Ⓒ Ⓓ Ⓔ

30. Ⓕ Ⓖ Ⓗ Ⓙ Ⓚ

31. Ⓐ Ⓑ Ⓒ Ⓓ Ⓔ

32. Ⓕ Ⓖ Ⓗ Ⓙ Ⓚ

33. Ⓐ Ⓑ Ⓒ Ⓓ Ⓔ

34. Ⓕ Ⓖ Ⓗ Ⓙ Ⓚ

35. Ⓐ Ⓑ Ⓒ Ⓓ Ⓔ

36. Ⓕ Ⓖ Ⓗ Ⓙ Ⓚ

37. Ⓐ Ⓑ Ⓒ Ⓓ Ⓔ

38. Ⓕ Ⓖ Ⓗ Ⓙ Ⓚ

39. Ⓐ Ⓑ Ⓒ Ⓓ Ⓔ

40. Ⓕ Ⓖ Ⓗ Ⓙ Ⓚ

41. Ⓐ Ⓑ Ⓒ Ⓓ Ⓔ

42. Ⓕ Ⓖ Ⓗ Ⓙ Ⓚ

43. Ⓐ Ⓑ Ⓒ Ⓓ Ⓔ

44. Ⓕ Ⓖ Ⓗ Ⓙ Ⓚ

45. Ⓐ Ⓑ Ⓒ Ⓓ Ⓔ

46. Ⓕ Ⓖ Ⓗ Ⓙ Ⓚ

47. Ⓐ Ⓑ Ⓒ Ⓓ Ⓔ

48. Ⓕ Ⓖ Ⓗ Ⓙ Ⓚ

49. Ⓐ Ⓑ Ⓒ Ⓓ Ⓔ

50. Ⓕ Ⓖ Ⓗ Ⓙ Ⓚ

51. Ⓐ Ⓑ Ⓒ Ⓓ Ⓔ

52. Ⓕ Ⓖ Ⓗ Ⓙ Ⓚ

53. Ⓐ Ⓑ Ⓒ Ⓓ Ⓔ

54. Ⓕ Ⓖ Ⓗ Ⓙ Ⓚ

55. Ⓐ Ⓑ Ⓒ Ⓓ Ⓔ

56. Ⓕ Ⓖ Ⓗ Ⓙ Ⓚ

57. Ⓐ Ⓑ Ⓒ Ⓓ Ⓔ

58. Ⓕ Ⓖ Ⓗ Ⓙ Ⓚ

59. Ⓐ Ⓑ Ⓒ Ⓓ Ⓔ

60. Ⓕ Ⓖ Ⓗ Ⓙ Ⓚ

ANSWER SHEET: *Practice Test B*

1. Ⓐ Ⓑ Ⓒ Ⓓ Ⓔ
2. Ⓕ Ⓖ Ⓗ Ⓙ Ⓚ
3. Ⓐ Ⓑ Ⓒ Ⓓ Ⓔ
4. Ⓕ Ⓖ Ⓗ Ⓙ Ⓚ
5. Ⓐ Ⓑ Ⓒ Ⓓ Ⓔ
6. Ⓕ Ⓖ Ⓗ Ⓙ Ⓚ
7. Ⓐ Ⓑ Ⓒ Ⓓ Ⓔ
8. Ⓕ Ⓖ Ⓗ Ⓙ Ⓚ
9. Ⓐ Ⓑ Ⓒ Ⓓ Ⓔ
10. Ⓕ Ⓖ Ⓗ Ⓙ Ⓚ
11. Ⓐ Ⓑ Ⓒ Ⓓ Ⓔ
12. Ⓕ Ⓖ Ⓗ Ⓙ Ⓚ
13. Ⓐ Ⓑ Ⓒ Ⓓ Ⓔ
14. Ⓕ Ⓖ Ⓗ Ⓙ Ⓚ
15. Ⓐ Ⓑ Ⓒ Ⓓ Ⓔ
16. Ⓕ Ⓖ Ⓗ Ⓙ Ⓚ
17. Ⓐ Ⓑ Ⓒ Ⓓ Ⓔ
18. Ⓕ Ⓖ Ⓗ Ⓙ Ⓚ
19. Ⓐ Ⓑ Ⓒ Ⓓ Ⓔ
20. Ⓕ Ⓖ Ⓗ Ⓙ Ⓚ

21. Ⓐ Ⓑ Ⓒ Ⓓ Ⓔ
22. Ⓕ Ⓖ Ⓗ Ⓙ Ⓚ
23. Ⓐ Ⓑ Ⓒ Ⓓ Ⓔ
24. Ⓕ Ⓖ Ⓗ Ⓙ Ⓚ
25. Ⓐ Ⓑ Ⓒ Ⓓ Ⓔ
26. Ⓕ Ⓖ Ⓗ Ⓙ Ⓚ
27. Ⓐ Ⓑ Ⓒ Ⓓ Ⓔ
28. Ⓕ Ⓖ Ⓗ Ⓙ Ⓚ
29. Ⓐ Ⓑ Ⓒ Ⓓ Ⓔ
30. Ⓕ Ⓖ Ⓗ Ⓙ Ⓚ
31. Ⓐ Ⓑ Ⓒ Ⓓ Ⓔ
32. Ⓕ Ⓖ Ⓗ Ⓙ Ⓚ
33. Ⓐ Ⓑ Ⓒ Ⓓ Ⓔ
34. Ⓕ Ⓖ Ⓗ Ⓙ Ⓚ
35. Ⓐ Ⓑ Ⓒ Ⓓ Ⓔ
36. Ⓕ Ⓖ Ⓗ Ⓙ Ⓚ
37. Ⓐ Ⓑ Ⓒ Ⓓ Ⓔ
38. Ⓕ Ⓖ Ⓗ Ⓙ Ⓚ
39. Ⓐ Ⓑ Ⓒ Ⓓ Ⓔ
40. Ⓕ Ⓖ Ⓗ Ⓙ Ⓚ

41. Ⓐ Ⓑ Ⓒ Ⓓ Ⓔ
42. Ⓕ Ⓖ Ⓗ Ⓙ Ⓚ
43. Ⓐ Ⓑ Ⓒ Ⓓ Ⓔ
44. Ⓕ Ⓖ Ⓗ Ⓙ Ⓚ
45. Ⓐ Ⓑ Ⓒ Ⓓ Ⓔ
46. Ⓕ Ⓖ Ⓗ Ⓙ Ⓚ
47. Ⓐ Ⓑ Ⓒ Ⓓ Ⓔ
48. Ⓕ Ⓖ Ⓗ Ⓙ Ⓚ
49. Ⓐ Ⓑ Ⓒ Ⓓ Ⓔ
50. Ⓕ Ⓖ Ⓗ Ⓙ Ⓚ
51. Ⓐ Ⓑ Ⓒ Ⓓ Ⓔ
52. Ⓕ Ⓖ Ⓗ Ⓙ Ⓚ
53. Ⓐ Ⓑ Ⓒ Ⓓ Ⓔ
54. Ⓕ Ⓖ Ⓗ Ⓙ Ⓚ
55. Ⓐ Ⓑ Ⓒ Ⓓ Ⓔ
56. Ⓕ Ⓖ Ⓗ Ⓙ Ⓚ
57. Ⓐ Ⓑ Ⓒ Ⓓ Ⓔ
58. Ⓕ Ⓖ Ⓗ Ⓙ Ⓚ
59. Ⓐ Ⓑ Ⓒ Ⓓ Ⓔ
60. Ⓕ Ⓖ Ⓗ Ⓙ Ⓚ

ANSWER SHEET: *Practice Test C*

1. Ⓐ Ⓑ Ⓒ Ⓓ Ⓔ   21. Ⓐ Ⓑ Ⓒ Ⓓ Ⓔ   41. Ⓐ Ⓑ Ⓒ Ⓓ Ⓔ

2. Ⓕ Ⓖ Ⓗ Ⓙ Ⓚ   22. Ⓕ Ⓖ Ⓗ Ⓙ Ⓚ   42. Ⓕ Ⓖ Ⓗ Ⓙ Ⓚ

3. Ⓐ Ⓑ Ⓒ Ⓓ Ⓔ   23. Ⓐ Ⓑ Ⓒ Ⓓ Ⓔ   43. Ⓐ Ⓑ Ⓒ Ⓓ Ⓔ

4. Ⓕ Ⓖ Ⓗ Ⓙ Ⓚ   24. Ⓕ Ⓖ Ⓗ Ⓙ Ⓚ   44. Ⓕ Ⓖ Ⓗ Ⓙ Ⓚ

5. Ⓐ Ⓑ Ⓒ Ⓓ Ⓔ   25. Ⓐ Ⓑ Ⓒ Ⓓ Ⓔ   45. Ⓐ Ⓑ Ⓒ Ⓓ Ⓔ

6. Ⓕ Ⓖ Ⓗ Ⓙ Ⓚ   26. Ⓕ Ⓖ Ⓗ Ⓙ Ⓚ   46. Ⓕ Ⓖ Ⓗ Ⓙ Ⓚ

7. Ⓐ Ⓑ Ⓒ Ⓓ Ⓔ   27. Ⓐ Ⓑ Ⓒ Ⓓ Ⓔ   47. Ⓐ Ⓑ Ⓒ Ⓓ Ⓔ

8. Ⓕ Ⓖ Ⓗ Ⓙ Ⓚ   28. Ⓕ Ⓖ Ⓗ Ⓙ Ⓚ   48. Ⓕ Ⓖ Ⓗ Ⓙ Ⓚ

9. Ⓐ Ⓑ Ⓒ Ⓓ Ⓔ   29. Ⓐ Ⓑ Ⓒ Ⓓ Ⓔ   49. Ⓐ Ⓑ Ⓒ Ⓓ Ⓔ

10. Ⓕ Ⓖ Ⓗ Ⓙ Ⓚ   30. Ⓕ Ⓖ Ⓗ Ⓙ Ⓚ   50. Ⓕ Ⓖ Ⓗ Ⓙ Ⓚ

11. Ⓐ Ⓑ Ⓒ Ⓓ Ⓔ   31. Ⓐ Ⓑ Ⓒ Ⓓ Ⓔ   51. Ⓐ Ⓑ Ⓒ Ⓓ Ⓔ

12. Ⓕ Ⓖ Ⓗ Ⓙ Ⓚ   32. Ⓕ Ⓖ Ⓗ Ⓙ Ⓚ   52. Ⓕ Ⓖ Ⓗ Ⓙ Ⓚ

13. Ⓐ Ⓑ Ⓒ Ⓓ Ⓔ   33. Ⓐ Ⓑ Ⓒ Ⓓ Ⓔ   53. Ⓐ Ⓑ Ⓒ Ⓓ Ⓔ

14. Ⓕ Ⓖ Ⓗ Ⓙ Ⓚ   34. Ⓕ Ⓖ Ⓗ Ⓙ Ⓚ   54. Ⓕ Ⓖ Ⓗ Ⓙ Ⓚ

15. Ⓐ Ⓑ Ⓒ Ⓓ Ⓔ   35. Ⓐ Ⓑ Ⓒ Ⓓ Ⓔ   55. Ⓐ Ⓑ Ⓒ Ⓓ Ⓔ

16. Ⓕ Ⓖ Ⓗ Ⓙ Ⓚ   36. Ⓕ Ⓖ Ⓗ Ⓙ Ⓚ   56. Ⓕ Ⓖ Ⓗ Ⓙ Ⓚ

17. Ⓐ Ⓑ Ⓒ Ⓓ Ⓔ   37. Ⓐ Ⓑ Ⓒ Ⓓ Ⓔ   57. Ⓐ Ⓑ Ⓒ Ⓓ Ⓔ

18. Ⓕ Ⓖ Ⓗ Ⓙ Ⓚ   38. Ⓕ Ⓖ Ⓗ Ⓙ Ⓚ   58. Ⓕ Ⓖ Ⓗ Ⓙ Ⓚ

19. Ⓐ Ⓑ Ⓒ Ⓓ Ⓔ   39. Ⓐ Ⓑ Ⓒ Ⓓ Ⓔ   59. Ⓐ Ⓑ Ⓒ Ⓓ Ⓔ

20. Ⓕ Ⓖ Ⓗ Ⓙ Ⓚ   40. Ⓕ Ⓖ Ⓗ Ⓙ Ⓚ   60. Ⓕ Ⓖ Ⓗ Ⓙ Ⓚ

ANSWER SHEET: *Practice Test D*

1. Ⓐ Ⓑ Ⓒ Ⓓ Ⓔ
2. Ⓕ Ⓖ Ⓗ Ⓙ Ⓚ
3. Ⓐ Ⓑ Ⓒ Ⓓ Ⓔ
4. Ⓕ Ⓖ Ⓗ Ⓙ Ⓚ
5. Ⓐ Ⓑ Ⓒ Ⓓ Ⓔ
6. Ⓕ Ⓖ Ⓗ Ⓙ Ⓚ
7. Ⓐ Ⓑ Ⓒ Ⓓ Ⓔ
8. Ⓕ Ⓖ Ⓗ Ⓙ Ⓚ
9. Ⓐ Ⓑ Ⓒ Ⓓ Ⓔ
10. Ⓕ Ⓖ Ⓗ Ⓙ Ⓚ
11. Ⓐ Ⓑ Ⓒ Ⓓ Ⓔ
12. Ⓕ Ⓖ Ⓗ Ⓙ Ⓚ
13. Ⓐ Ⓑ Ⓒ Ⓓ Ⓔ
14. Ⓕ Ⓖ Ⓗ Ⓙ Ⓚ
15. Ⓐ Ⓑ Ⓒ Ⓓ Ⓔ
16. Ⓕ Ⓖ Ⓗ Ⓙ Ⓚ
17. Ⓐ Ⓑ Ⓒ Ⓓ Ⓔ
18. Ⓕ Ⓖ Ⓗ Ⓙ Ⓚ
19. Ⓐ Ⓑ Ⓒ Ⓓ Ⓔ
20. Ⓕ Ⓖ Ⓗ Ⓙ Ⓚ

21. Ⓐ Ⓑ Ⓒ Ⓓ Ⓔ
22. Ⓕ Ⓖ Ⓗ Ⓙ Ⓚ
23. Ⓐ Ⓑ Ⓒ Ⓓ Ⓔ
24. Ⓕ Ⓖ Ⓗ Ⓙ Ⓚ
25. Ⓐ Ⓑ Ⓒ Ⓓ Ⓔ
26. Ⓕ Ⓖ Ⓗ Ⓙ Ⓚ
27. Ⓐ Ⓑ Ⓒ Ⓓ Ⓔ
28. Ⓕ Ⓖ Ⓗ Ⓙ Ⓚ
29. Ⓐ Ⓑ Ⓒ Ⓓ Ⓔ
30. Ⓕ Ⓖ Ⓗ Ⓙ Ⓚ
31. Ⓐ Ⓑ Ⓒ Ⓓ Ⓔ
32. Ⓕ Ⓖ Ⓗ Ⓙ Ⓚ
33. Ⓐ Ⓑ Ⓒ Ⓓ Ⓔ
34. Ⓕ Ⓖ Ⓗ Ⓙ Ⓚ
35. Ⓐ Ⓑ Ⓒ Ⓓ Ⓔ
36. Ⓕ Ⓖ Ⓗ Ⓙ Ⓚ
37. Ⓐ Ⓑ Ⓒ Ⓓ Ⓔ
38. Ⓕ Ⓖ Ⓗ Ⓙ Ⓚ
39. Ⓐ Ⓑ Ⓒ Ⓓ Ⓔ
40. Ⓕ Ⓖ Ⓗ Ⓙ Ⓚ

41. Ⓐ Ⓑ Ⓒ Ⓓ Ⓔ
42. Ⓕ Ⓖ Ⓗ Ⓙ Ⓚ
43. Ⓐ Ⓑ Ⓒ Ⓓ Ⓔ
44. Ⓕ Ⓖ Ⓗ Ⓙ Ⓚ
45. Ⓐ Ⓑ Ⓒ Ⓓ Ⓔ
46. Ⓕ Ⓖ Ⓗ Ⓙ Ⓚ
47. Ⓐ Ⓑ Ⓒ Ⓓ Ⓔ
48. Ⓕ Ⓖ Ⓗ Ⓙ Ⓚ
49. Ⓐ Ⓑ Ⓒ Ⓓ Ⓔ
50. Ⓕ Ⓖ Ⓗ Ⓙ Ⓚ
51. Ⓐ Ⓑ Ⓒ Ⓓ Ⓔ
52. Ⓕ Ⓖ Ⓗ Ⓙ Ⓚ
53. Ⓐ Ⓑ Ⓒ Ⓓ Ⓔ
54. Ⓕ Ⓖ Ⓗ Ⓙ Ⓚ
55. Ⓐ Ⓑ Ⓒ Ⓓ Ⓔ
56. Ⓕ Ⓖ Ⓗ Ⓙ Ⓚ
57. Ⓐ Ⓑ Ⓒ Ⓓ Ⓔ
58. Ⓕ Ⓖ Ⓗ Ⓙ Ⓚ
59. Ⓐ Ⓑ Ⓒ Ⓓ Ⓔ
60. Ⓕ Ⓖ Ⓗ Ⓙ Ⓚ

ACT MATH GLOSSARY

abscissa: The x value of the point (x, y); aka 1st coordinate; the y value, the ordinate, aka 2nd coordinate; together x and y are the coordinates of the point (x, y).

absolute value:

1. If we are dealing with a real number, it is the positive value. $|5| = 5$; $|-3| = 3$; also $|0| = 0$

2. $|x| = \sqrt{x^2}$; $|5| = \sqrt{5^2} = \sqrt{25} = 5$; $|-3| = \sqrt{(-3)^2} = \sqrt{9} = 3$; $|0| = \sqrt{0^2} = \sqrt{0} = 0$.

3. $|x| = \begin{cases} x \text{ if } x > 0 \\ -x \text{ if } x < 0 \\ 0 \text{ if } x = 0 \end{cases}$; $|5| = 5$ since $5 > 0$; $|-3| = -(-3) = 3$ since $-3 < 0$; $|0| = 0$.

angle: Two rays with a common endpoint (called a vertex)

1. **acute angle:** A positive angle of less than 90°

2. **angle bisector:** A ray or line dividing an angle into two equal parts

3. **complementary angles:** Two angles adding to 90°

4. **exterior angle of a polygon:** An angle forms by extending the side of a polygon with the adjacent side of the polygon

5. **obtuse angle:** An angle of more than 90° but less than 180°

6. **reflex angle:** An angle of more than 180° but less than 360°

7. **right angle:** An angle of 90°

8. **straight angle:** An angle of 180°

9. **supplementary angles:** Two angles whose sum is 180°

10. **vertical angles:** Angles formed by two intersecting lines. They are opposite each other and are equal.

arithmetic progression: A sequence of numbers, either increasing or decreasing where the difference between any two consecutive numbers is the same; also an arithmetic sequence is possible where all the numbers are the same since the difference is the same, namely 0.

circle: The set of all points at a given distance from a fixed point; the fixed point is called the center; the given distance is called the radius.

1. **arc:** Part of the circumference of a circle

    A. **minor arc:** An arc of less than half a circle

    B. **major arc:** An arc of more than half a circle

    C. **semicircle:** An arc of half a circle

2. **chord:** A line segment drawn from one point of a circle to another point of the circle

3. **circumference:** The perimeter of a circle

4. **diameter:** A line segment drawn from one point of a circle through the center to another point of the circle; the largest chord of a circle

5. **radius:** A line segment drawn from the center of a circle to a point on the circle

6. **secant:** A line going through a circle in two points

7. **sector:** Part of the area of a circle formed by an arc and two radii drawn to the end of the arc

8. **tangent:** A line touching the circle in one point, called the point of tangency: This point is where a tangent touches an endpoint of the radius.

complex number: All numbers of the form $a + bi$, and b are real numbers and $i = \sqrt{-1}$

composite number: Any number with more than two distinct factors: 9 is composite since 1, 3, and 9 are factors of 9

difference: The answer is subtraction

distributive law: $a(b + c) = ab + ac$; $4(3x - 7) = 12x - 28$; $x(x^2 + 3x + 7) = x^3 + 3x^2 + 7x$

divisor: If $(a)(b) = c$, then a and b are factors (or divisors) of c; $(2)(3) = 6$; 2 and 3 are factors of 6; aka factor

equation: Two algebraic expressions with an equals sign between them: $2x + 5 = 7$; $x^2 = 25$

solution or root: A value that makes each side of the equation the same; in the equation $2x + 5 = 7$, the root is $x = 1$; in the equation $x^2 = 25$, the roots are $+5$ and -5

even integers: $\{0, 2, \pm 4, \pm 6, \ldots\}$

exponents: The number or letter which tells how many times you multiply that number or letter by itself

1. **positive exponents:**

    A. $A^3 = A(A)(A)$ [it is read A to the third power or A cubed], $5^3 = 5(5)(5) = 125$

    B. $B^2 = B(B)$ [it is read B squared or B to the second power]; $100^2 = 100(100)$ $= 10,000$

    C. $C = C^1$

2. $X^0 = 1$ if $X \neq 0$; 0^0 is undefined

3. **negative exponents:** Means reciprocal; $x^{-3} = \dfrac{1}{x^3}$; $2^{-3} = \dfrac{1}{2^3} = \dfrac{1}{8}$

4. **fractional exponents:** $x^{p/r}$; p is the power and r is the root; always do the root first; $8^{4/3} = \left(\sqrt[3]{8}\right)^4 = 2^4 = 16$

factor: If $(a)(b) = c$, a and b are factors of c; if $(2)(3) = 6$, 2 and 3 are factors of 6; aka: divisor

function: Given a set D (called the domain), to every element in D we assign (the assignment is called a map or a mapping) one and only one element (the set of numbers that is assigned is called the Range R) when we think of the domain we should think of the x values; when we think of the range, we should think of the y values

geometric progression: In a sequence of numbers, either increasing or decreasing, the ratio of any two consecutive numbers is the same; also a sequence of numbers that are all the same, except 0, is a geometric sequence since the ratio will be 1

integers: $\{0, \pm 1, \pm 2, \pm 3, \pm 4, \ldots\}$

irrational number: a real number with an infinite number of decimal places that does not repeat; examples: $\sqrt{2}$, e, π

like terms: terms with the same letter combination (or no letters); corresponding letters have the same exponents: 4 and -9, $3x$ and $-7x$, $8xy^2$ and $-2y^2x$

linear equation: An equation of the form $Ax + By = C$, where A, B are not both 0.

logarithm: An exponent: if $\log_b x = y$ then $b^y = x$, $b =$ base

matrix: An array of numbers and/or letters, with rows and columns; for example, a 3-by-2 matrix has 3 rows, 2 columns, and 6 elements in all

mean: Add up n numbers and divide by n

median: In a triangle it is a line segment drawn from a vertex to the middle of the opposite side; in a trapezoid it is a line segment connecting the midpoints of the non-parallel sides; in a group of numbers arranged from highest to lowest or lowest to highest, it is the middle value

midpoint: On a line segment it is the point halfway between the two endpoints.

mode: In a list of numbers, it is the most common number(s)

multiple: If $a(b) = c$, c is a multiple of both a and b; $2(3) = 6$, 6 is a multiple of both 2 and 3; also take a positive integer; multiply this positive integer by 1, 2, 3, 4, 5, and you get all positive multiples of that positive integer. Thus, 5, 10, 15, 20, 25, … are all positive multiples of 5

natural numbers: {1, 2, 3, 4, 5, …} aka positive integers

odd integers: {±1, ±3, ±5, …}

parabola:

1. A curve in the form $y = ax^2 + bx + c$, with $a \neq 0$, if $a > 0$, the parabola faces up; if $a < 0$, the parabola faces down

2. The set of all points equidistant from a point (focus) and a line (directrix)

parallelogram: A quadrilateral with opposite sides parallel

perfect number: A positive integer where all of the factors (divisors) of the number less than the number add up to the number; 28 is a perfect number since $1 + 2 + 4 + 7 + 14 = 28$

prime: Any positive integer or expression with exactly two distinct factors, itself and 1: 2, 3, 5, 7, 11, 13, 17, 19 are the first 8 primes; $x + 5$ is a prime since only 1 and $x + 5$ are factors of $x + 5$

product: The answer in multiplication

postulate: A law taken to be true without proof; aka axiom

quadrant: The result of dividing the coordinate plane into 4 parts using the x-axis and y-axis. Each part is a quadrant.

quadratic equation: An equation of the form $ax^2 + bx + c = 0$, $a \neq 0$. It always has at most two solutions, which can be always found using the quadratic formula $x = \dfrac{-b \pm \sqrt{b^2 - 4ac}}{2a}$

quadrilateral: A four-sided polygon

quotient: The answer in division

rational number:
1. Any number of the form $\dfrac{a}{b}$, where a and b are integers and $b \neq 0$
2. Any terminating or infinitely repeating decimal

rectangle: A parallelogram with right angles

range: In a set of numbers, it is the highest minus the lowest; in a function it is the y values

rhombus: An equilateral parallelogram

scientific notation: Any number written in the form $N = M \times 10^p$, where $1 \leq M < 10$ and p is an integer

slope: The slant m of a line which is given by the formula $m = \dfrac{(y_2 - y_1)}{(x_2 - x_1)}$ where (x_1, y_1) and (x_2, y_2) are two points on the line

square: A rectangle with equal sides

sum: The answer in addition

theorem: A proven law

trapezoid: A quadrilateral with exactly one pair of parallel sides (called bases)

trigonometry:

1. **cosine of an angle:** In a right triangle, it is the adjacent side over the hypotenuse; in general $\dfrac{x}{r}$

2. **degree:** one 360th of a circle

3. **identity:** An equation that is always true

4. **radian:** Alternate angle measurement; it equals $\dfrac{1}{2\pi}$ of a circle or about 57°. If you lay a radius on the circumference of a circle and join the two ends of the arc with two radii, it is the number of degrees in the central angle.

5. **sine of the angle:** In a right triangle, it is opposite side over the hypotenuse; in general $\dfrac{y}{r}$

6. **tangent of the angle:** In a right triangle, it is the opposite side over the adjacent side; in general $\dfrac{y}{x}$

whole numbers: {0, 1, 2, 3, 4, ...}

INDEX

NOTES

NOTES

NOTES

NOTES

NOTES

NOTES

NOTES

NOTES

NOTES

Also Available from REA

Visit www.rea.com for more information